New Jersey

Life, Accident, and Health Insurance

License Exam Manual

KAPLAN) FINANCIAL EDUCATION

At press time, this edition contains the most complete and accurate information currently available. Owing to the nature of license examinations, however, information may have been added recently to the actual test that does not appear in this edition. Please contact the publisher to verify that you have the most current edition.

This publication is designed to provide accurate and authoritative information in regard to the subject matter covered. It is sold with the understanding that the publisher is not engaged in rendering legal, accounting, or other professional services. If legal advice or other expert assistance is required, the services of a competent professional should be sought.

We value your input and suggestions. If you found imperfections in this product, please let us know by sending an email to **errata@kaplan.com**. Please include the title, edition, and PPN (reorder number) of the material.

NEW JERSEY LIFE, ACCIDENT, AND HEALTH INSURANCE LICENSE EXAM MANUAL, 3RD EDITION ©2007 DF Institute, Inc. All rights reserved.

Published by DF Institute, Inc.

Printed in the United States of America.

ISBN: 1-4277-5276-1

PPN: 5317-3103

09 10 10 9 8 7 6 5 4 3
J F M A M J J A S O N D

Contents

The topics addressed in this text are listed in this table of contents in their order of presentation by unit. Specific page references have been purposely omitted to discourage review of individual topics out of context. The state licensing examination requires candidates to obtain an in-depth understanding of the information presented in this text; this includes a recognition of the interrelationship of the topical information presented. If a topic warrants additional review, candidates are urged to cover the material immediately preceding and immediately following the topic targeted for additional study. This will enhance the individual's learning process and help retain the contextual integrity of the subject matter presented in each unit.

U N I T   1 0   **Other Health Insurance Concepts   151**

U N I T   1 1   **Accident and Health Insurance Practice
Final Examination   159**

Introduction

Welcome to the New Jersey Life, Accident, and Health Insurance License Exam Manual. This text applies adult learning principals to give you the tools you'll need to pass your exam on the first attempt.

Some of these special features include:

- exam-focused questions and content to maximize test preparation; and

- an interactive design that integrates content with notes and comments to increase retention.

IMPORTANT: CHECK FOR UPDATES

Exam publishers sometimes change topics on the exam unexpectedly or on short notice. To see if we have issued an update for this product to accommodate a change in the exam, please go to **www.kaplanfinancial.com**, where you will see a heading for *TestAlerts!* Click on *View Insurance TestAlerts!* to see a list of updates we have issued for our License Exam Manuals. Then, click on your state to see a link to a portable document file (PDF) that you can download to study with your License Exam Manual. (If you do not see a *TestAlert!* listed for your state, we have not issued one.) We suggest you check now, sometime during your study period, when you've completed your study, and one last time just before you take your exam.

PREPARING FOR THE EXAM

Are there any prerequisites to the licensing exam?

A number of states have prescribed specific prelicensing educational requirements that may require certification of completion before the candidate can take the licensing exam. These requirements typically involve attending an approved class or taking an approved self-study course on a correspondence basis. Some individuals may be exempt from the prelicensing requirement or even the licensing exam itself, usually on the basis of prior insurance education or experience. Contact your state's Department of Banking and Insurance to determine its specific licensing requirements and exemptions.

What topics will I see on the exam?

State insurance licensing exams cover a broad range of topics. Almost every state makes an outline of exam topics and content available through its test administrator. The licensing exam will include questions on the topics contained in the outline. These outlines also indicate the number of exam questions or the relative weight assigned to each main section of the exam. Contact your state's Department of Banking and Insurance to determine the test administrator in your state and obtain an exam outline from the administrator.

How is the License Exam Manual organized?

This manual is organized into specific Units that reflect the main topics of a state's insurance exam. These Units contain core content on basic insurance principles (life insurance/health insurance or property insurance/casualty insurance). Also included in this text is a unit covering the laws and regulations that apply to insurance in your state. At the end of each Unit is a short quiz that covers the subject matter presented in that Unit. Use these quizzes to gauge your understanding of the material presented in each Unit.

In addition, take the Practice Finals that cover the core content and state law. Grade your performance with the answer keys provided.

In addition to the regular text, each Unit also has some unique features designed to help with quick understanding of the material. When an additional point will be valuable to your comprehension, special notes are embedded in the text. Examples of these are included below.

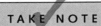

TAKE NOTE

These highlight special or unusual information and amplify important points.

TEST TOPIC ALERT

These highlight content that is likely to appear on the exam.

How will this manual prepare me for the exam?

State insurance licensing exams are designed to test a candidate's knowledge and understanding of the broad principles and concepts pertinent to the specific line of insurance he plans to represent. This manual focuses specifically on those principles and concepts. Designed by insurance instructors and subject matter experts who are experienced with insurance licensing exams, the text plainly presents and explains the topics that are testable. As noted, Practice Finals are included to help you gauge your understanding of the material.

SUCCESSFUL TEST-TAKING TIPS

Passing the exam depends not only on how well you learn the subject matter, but also on how well you take exams. You can develop your test-taking skills—and improve your score—by learning a few test-taking techniques:

- Read the full question
- Avoid jumping to conclusions—watch for hedge clauses
- Interpret the unfamiliar question
- Identify the intent of the question
- Memorize key points
- Beware of changing answers
- Pace yourself

Each of these pointers is explained below. Examples that show how to use them to improve your performance on the exam are also included.

Read the full question

You cannot expect to answer a question correctly if you do not know what it is asking. If you see a question that seems familiar and easy, you might anticipate the answer, mark it, and move on before you finish reading it. This is a serious mistake. Be sure to read the full question before answering it—questions are often written to trap people who assume too much. Here is an example of a question in which an assumption could produce a wrong answer.

1. Arthur incurs total hospital expenses of $8,300. His major medical policy includes a $500 deductible and an 80%/20% coinsurance feature. Assuming this is the first covered expense he incurs this year, how much will Arthur have to pay toward his hospital bill?
   A. $5,900
   B. $2,160
   C. $2,060
   D. $1,800

The answer is C. This is an easy question to answer only for someone who has read the full question, because this is the first application of the deductible. If you read the question too quickly, you might forget to account for the deductible.

Avoid jumping to conclusions

The questions on licensing exams are often embellished with deceptive distractors as choices. To avoid being misled by seemingly obvious answers, make it a practice to read each question and each answer twice before selecting your choice. Doing so will provide you with a much better chance of doing well on the test.

Watch out for qualifiers embedded in the question. (Examples of qualifiers include the words *if*, *not*, *all*, *none*, and *except*.) In the case of *if* statements, the question can be answered correctly only by taking into account the qualifier. If you ignore the qualifier, you will probably not answer correctly.

Qualifiers are sometimes combined in a question. Some that you will frequently see together are *all* with *except* and *none* with *except*. In general, when a question starts with *all* or *none* and ends with *except*, you are looking for an answer that is opposite to what the question appears to be asking. For example:

2. All of the following are excluded from the liability portion of commercial auto coverage EXCEPT
   A. expected or intended injury
   B. contractual injury
   C. insurer's cost of defense
   D. workers' compensation

If you neglect to read the except, you might select answer choices A, B, or D. The qualifier makes C the only correct option.

Interpret the unfamiliar question

Do not be surprised if some questions on the test seem unfamiliar at first. If you have studied your material, you will have the information to answer all the questions correctly. The challenge may be a matter of understanding what the question is asking.

Very often, questions present information indirectly. You may have to interpret the meaning of certain elements before you can answer the question.

3. Which type of authority does an insurer give to its agents by means of the agent's contract?
   A. Express
   B. Implied
   C. Fiduciary
   D. General

The correct answer is A. This question is asking you to apply knowledge of agency law in order to select the correct answer. It requires a knowledge of concepts such as express and implied agency.

This same content could have been tested in a different way, as illustrated by the next example.

4. An agent in XYZ Insurance Company, equipped with business cards, sample XYZ policies, and an XYZ rate book, informs a prospect that XYZ has given him unlimited binding authority. The prospect assumes this is true. Given the prospect's assumption, which of the following correctly defines the agent's authority in this case?
   A. Express
   B. Implied
   C. Apparent
   D. Binding

The correct answer is C. At first glance, the two questions appear very different, but in fact they test knowledge of the same principles of agency law. Be aware that the exam will approach a concept from different angles.

Identify the intent of the question

Many questions on licensing exams supply so much information that you lose track of what is being asked. This is often the case in story problems. Learn to separate the story from the question. For example:

5. Alan, age 39, is married and has one young son. He is employed as a sales manager by R.J. Links, a sole proprietorship that owes much of its success to Alan's efforts. He recently borrowed $50,000 from his brother-in-law, Pete, to finance a vacation home. Based on these facts, who of the following does NOT have an insurable interest in Alan's life?
   A. His spouse
   B. His employer
   C. His brother-in-law
   D. His customers

A clue to the answer is presented in the last sentence—who does not have an insurable interest?

Take the time to identify what the question is asking. Of course, your ability to do so assumes you have studied sufficiently. There is no method for correctly answering questions if you don't know the material.

Memorize key points

Reasoning and logic will help you answer many questions, but you will have to memorize a good deal of information. Key points at the beginning of each Unit indicate some of the most important points for memorization.

Mnemonic devices give you a shorthand way of remembering information with a single word or phrase. For example, the elements necessary for a risk to be insurable can be summarized as CANHAM:

C	Chance of loss must be **calculable**
A	Premiums must be **affordable**
N	Loss must be **noncatastrophic**
H	Large number of **homogenous** (similar) exposures must exist
A	Loss must be **accidental**
M	Loss must be **measurable**

Avoid changing answers

If you are unsure of an answer, your first hunch is the one most likely to be correct. Do not change answers on the exam without good reason. In general, change an answer only if you:

- discover that you did not read the question correctly; or

- find new or additional helpful information in another question.

Pace yourself

Some people will finish the exam early and some will not have time to finish all the questions. Watch the time carefully (your time remaining will be displayed on your computer screen) and pace yourself through the exam.

Do not waste time by dwelling on a question if you simply do not know the answer. Make the best guess you can, mark the question for review, and return to the question if time allows. Make sure that you have time to read all the questions so that you can record the answers you do know.

1

Introduction to Insurance Principles and Concepts

KEY TERMS

Pure Risk

Speculative Risk

Law of Large Numbers

Elements of Insurable Risk

Hazard

Peril

Risk Pooling

Methods of Handling Risk

Adverse Selection

I. THE ROLE OF INSURANCE

We all have a compelling need for security, peace of mind, and freedom from worry. Unfortunately, achieving complete financial security historically has been elusive, in part because of universal problems such as death, sickness, accidents, and disability. These problems can strike at any time. The emotional stress they bring is increased by the financial hardships that almost certainly follow.

A. THE NEED FOR ECONOMIC CERTAINTY AND SECURITY When death takes the life of a family provider prematurely, surviving family members suffer when they are left without adequate income or the means to provide basic necessities. On the other hand, some people face the unpleasant prospect of outliving their incomes—retirement may be forced on them before they have prepared adequately for a nonincome-earning existence. Sickness and disability also can leave economic scars, often more expensive than death. An accident or illness can easily result in catastrophic medical bills or the inability to work for months or years.

B. INSURANCE AS A PRACTICAL SOLUTION Insurance evolved to provide a practical solution to the problem of such economic uncertainties and losses. **Life insurance**, based on actuarial or mathematical principles, guarantees a specified sum of money on the death of the insured person. **Annuities** provide a stream of income by making a series of payments to the annuitant for a specific period of time or for a lifetime. Health insurance also evolved from scientific principles to provide funds for medical expenses due to sickness or injury and to cover loss of income during a period of disability. The true significance of insurance is its promise to substitute uncertainty with future economic certainty and to replace the unknown with a sense of security.

II. THE NATURE OF INSURANCE

We are exposed to many perils. The purpose of any insurance is to provide economic protection against losses that may incur due to a chance happening or event, such as death, illness, or accident. This protection is provided through an insurance policy, which simply is a device for accumulating funds to meet these uncertain losses. The policy is a legally binding contract that sets forth the company's promise and obligations as follows:

> *Whereby, for a set amount of money (the premium), one party (the insurer) agrees to pay the other party (the insured or his beneficiary) a set sum (the benefit) upon the occurrence of some event.*

In the case of life insurance, the benefit is paid when the insured dies. In the case of health or disability insurance, the benefit is paid if and when the insured incurs certain medical expenses or becomes disabled, as defined by the contract.

A. BASIC INSURANCE PRINCIPLES Insurance is based on two fundamental principles: the spreading or pooling of risks, also known as loss sharing, and the law of large numbers.

1. Risk Pooling To understand the concept of pooling risks and sharing losses, consider the following. Assume that 1,000 individuals in the same social club agree that if any member of their group dies, all of the members will pitch in to provide the deceased's family with $10,000. This $10,000, it was determined, would provide the family with enough funds to cover the immediate costs associated with death and to provide a

TAKE NOTE

The distinction between speculative and pure risks is important. Insurance does not protect individuals against losses arising out of speculative risks because these risks are undertaken voluntarily. However, not all pure risks are insurable.

cushion for at least a few months. Because it is not known when any one individual within the group will die, the decision is made to prefund the benefit by assessing each member $10, thus creating the $10,000 fund. Without the agreement to help provide for each other's potential loss, each group member (and family) would have to face the economic cost of death alone. But by sharing the burden and spreading the risk of death over all 1,000 group members, the most any one member pays is $10.

   a. **Transfer of risk from individual to group** By spreading a risk, or by sharing the possibility of a loss, a large group of people can substitute a small certain cost ($10 in our example) for a large unknown risk (the economic risk of dying). In other words, the risk is transferred from an individual to a group, each member of which shares the losses and has the promise of a future benefit. Insurance companies pool risks among thousands of insureds and apply mathematical principles to guarantee policyowners that the money will be there to pay a claim when it arises.

2. **Law of Large Numbers** In addition to spreading risks, insurance relies on the principle that the larger the number of individual risks (or exposures) in a group, the more certain the amount of loss incurred in any given period. In other words, given a large enough pool of risks, an insurer can predict with reasonable accuracy the number of claims it will face during any given time, or the aggregate risk. No one can predict when any one person will die or if any one person will become disabled. However, it is possible to predict the approximate number of deaths or the likelihood of disability among a certain group during a certain period. This principle, known as the **law of large numbers**, is based on the science of probability and the experience of mortality (death) and morbidity (sickness) statistics. The larger and more homogeneous the group, the more certain the mortality or morbidity predictions.

   a. **Example** Statistics may show that among a group of 100,000 40-year-old males, 300 will die within one year. While it is not possible to predict who the 300 will be, the number will prove quite accurate. Conversely, with a small group, an accurate prediction is not possible. Among a group of 100 40-year-old males, it is not statistically feasible to predict if any in the group will die within one year. Because insurers cover thousands and thousands of lives, it is possible to predict when and to what extent deaths and disabilities will occur and, consequently, when claims will arise.

   b. **The basis of insurance** All forms of insurance—life, health, accident, property, and casualty—rely on risk pooling and the law of large numbers. These principles form the foundation on which insurance is based and allow for its successful operation.

B. THE CONCEPT OF RISK Insurance replaces the uncertainty of risk with guarantees. But what exactly does the word *risk* mean? And how does insurance remove the uncertainty and minimize the adverse effects of risk?

1. **Risk Defined** Risk is defined as the uncertainty regarding loss. Property loss, such as the destruction of a home due to fire, is an example of risk. Negligence or carelessness can give rise to a liability risk if there is potential injury to an individual or damage to property. The inability to work and earn a living due to a disability is another example of risk, as is loss of a family's income due to the death of the breadwinner. The loss inherent in all of these risks is characterized by a lessening or disappearance of value.

   a. **Risk classification** A class of risks is a homogenous group of loss exposures. Risks can be divided into two classes: speculative and pure.

      1.) **Speculative risks** involve the chance of both loss and gain. Betting at the race track and investing in the stock market are examples of speculative risks.

      2.) **Pure risks** involve only the chance of loss; there is never a possibility of gain or profit. The risk associated with the chance of injury from an accident is an example of pure risk. There is no opportunity for gain if the event does not occur—only the opportunity for loss if it does occur. Only pure risks are insurable.

   b. **When and what insurance protects** With life insurance, the risk involved is when, not if, death will occur. It can be tomorrow, next week, next year, or well into the future, but loss can result if death is premature or comes too late. With health insurance, the risk is not when, but if, illness or disability will strike. Losses associated with health risks include medical costs and loss of income. With annuities, the risk is living too long and outlasting one's income. Annuities cover this risk by paying a guaranteed income to the annuitant for life.

2. **Perils and Hazards** Perils and hazards are factors that cause or give rise to risk.

   a. **Peril** A peril is the immediate specific event causing loss and giving rise to risk. It is the cause of a risk. When a building burns, fire is the peril. When a person dies, death is the peril. When an individual is injured in an accident, the accident is the peril. When a person becomes ill from a disease, the disease is the peril.

   b. **Hazard** A hazard is any factor that gives rise to a peril. For purposes of life and health insurance, there are three basic types of hazards: physical, moral, and morale.

1.) Physical hazards are individual characteristics that increase the chance of peril. They may exist because of a person's physical condition, past medical history, or condition at birth. Blindness and deafness are physical hazards.

2.) Moral hazards are tendencies that increase risk and the chance of loss. Alcoholism and drug addiction are considered moral hazards.

3.) Morale hazards are also individual tendencies, but they arise from an attitude or state of mind that causes indifference to loss. For instance, driving recklessly without fear of death or injury is a morale hazard.

3. **Treatment of Risk** How risks are treated varies greatly depending on the situation, the degree of potential loss, and the individual. Generally, there are four options: avoid, reduce, retain, or transfer the risk.

   a. **Risk Avoidance** One method of dealing with risk is **avoidance**—simply avoiding as many risks as possible. By choosing not to drive or own an automobile, one could avoid the risks associated with driving. By never flying, one could eliminate the risk of being in an airplane crash. By never investing in stocks, one could avoid the risk of a market crash.

   b. **Risk Reduction** Risk reduction is another means of dealing with risk. Because we cannot avoid risk entirely, we often attempt to lessen the possibility of loss by taking action to reduce the risk. Installing a smoke alarm in a home will not lessen the possibility of fire, but it may reduce the risk of loss from fire.

   c. **Risk Retention** Risk retention is another method of coping with risk. This means accepting the risk and confronting it if and when it occurs. One way to handle a retained risk is self-insurance, for instance, setting up a fund to offset the costs of a potential loss.

   d. **Risk Transference** The most effective way to handle risk is to transfer it so that the loss is borne by another party. Insurance is the most common method of transferring risk—from an individual or group to an insurance company. Though purchasing insurance will not eliminate the risk of death or illness, it relieves the insured individual or group of the losses these risks bring. Insurance satisfies both economic and emotional needs—it replaces the uncertainty surrounding risk with the assurance of guarantees, and it transfers the financial consequences of death, illness, or disability to the insurer.

C. ELEMENTS OF INSURABLE RISK Though insurance may be one of the most effective ways to handle risk, not all risks are insurable. As noted earlier, insurers will insure only pure risks or those that involve only the chance of loss. However, not all pure risks are insurable. Certain characteristics or elements must be evident before a pure risk can be insured.

1. **The loss must be due to chance.** To be insurable, a risk must involve a chance of loss that is fortuitous and outside the insured's control.

2. **The loss must be definite and measurable.** An insurable risk must involve a loss that is definite as to cause, time, place, and amount. An insurer must be able to determine how much the benefit will be and when it will become payable.

3. **The loss must be predictable.** An insurable risk must have occurrence that can be predicted statistically. This enables insurers to estimate the average frequency and severity of future losses and set appropriate premiums. Death, illness, and disability all are events whose rates of occurrence can be projected based on statistics.

4. **The loss cannot be catastrophic.** Insurers typically will not insure risks that will expose them to catastrophic losses. There must be limits that insurers can be reasonably certain their losses will not exceed. For instance, an insurer would not issue a policy for $1 trillion on a single life, because that one death would create a catastrophic loss to the company.

5. **The loss exposures to be insured must be large.** An insurer must be able to predict losses based on the law of large numbers. Consequently, there must be a sufficiently large pool to be insured and those in the pool (the exposures) must be grouped into classes with similar risks. Individuals, for example, are grouped according to age, health, sex, occupation, and other classifications.

6. **The loss exposures to be insured must be selected randomly.** Insurers must have a fair proportion of good risks and poor risks. A large proportion of poor risks would financially threaten the insurance company because there would be many claims without sufficient premiums to offset them. Keep in mind that there is a tendency, called **adverse selection**, for less favorable insurance risks (e.g., people in poor health) to seek or continue insurance to a greater extent than other risks.

TEST TOPIC ALERT

A typical question on the license exam may ask you to identify the ways that individuals treat risk.

III. THE ECONOMIC BASIS OF LIFE AND HEALTH INSURANCE

To fully appreciate the purpose and function of insurance, it is important to understand that its roots lie in economics and the concept of human life value.

It has long been recognized that individuals have an economic value that can be measured in part by their future earning potential. This earning potential is the sum of one's net future earnings or, more precisely, the dollar value of an individual's future earning capability. The true significance of this earning potential extends beyond the individual to those who depend on the individual for their financial security. Thus, by definition, human life value is the value today of an individual's future earnings that are devoted to dependents.

In the abstract, human life value is the means by which homes are purchased, college educations are provided, and monthly bills are paid. In short, it is the essence of an individual's or family's economic existence. Yet this value is subject to loss through death, retirement, disability, or poor health. Any one of these perils affects earning capacity in some degree and, consequently, diminishes human life value. It is to conserve and protect human life value that life and health insurance exist.

UNIT QUIZ

1. Which of the following insurance concepts is founded on the ability to predict the approximate number of deaths or frequency of disabilities within a certain group during a specific time?
   A. Principle of large loss
   B. Quantum insurance principle
   C. Indemnity law
   D. Law of large numbers

2. The owner of a camera store is worried that new employees may help themselves to items from inventory without paying for them. What kind of hazard is this?
   A. Physical
   B. Ethical
   C. Morale
   D. Moral

3. All of the following actions are examples of risk avoidance EXCEPT
   A. refusing to fly
   B. not investing in stocks
   C. paying an insurance premium
   D. refusing to drive

4. Which of the following statements is CORRECT?
   A. Only speculative risks are insurable.
   B. Only pure risks are insurable.
   C. Both pure risks and speculative risks are insurable.
   D. Neither pure risks nor speculative risks are insurable.

5. All of the following statements describe elements of an insurable risk EXCEPT
   A. the loss must not be due to chance
   B. the loss must be definite and measurable
   C. the loss cannot be catastrophic
   D. the loss exposures to be insured must be large

6. In the insurance business, risk can best be defined as
   A. sharing the possibility of a loss
   B. uncertainty regarding the future
   C. uncertainty regarding loss
   D. uncertainty regarding when death will occur

7. Buying insurance is a means of
   A. avoiding risk
   B. transferring risk
   C. reducing risk
   D. retaining risk

8. Which of the following best describes the function of insurance?
   A. It is a form of legalized gambling.
   B. It spreads financial risk over a large group to minimize the loss to any one individual.
   C. It protects against living too long.
   D. It creates and protects risks.

9. A tornado is an example of a
   A. physical hazard
   B. speculative risk
   C. peril
   D. moral hazard

10. An insured keeps a $50,000 diamond ring in a safe deposit box at a local bank. This is an example of risk
    A. avoidance
    B. reduction
    C. retention
    D. transference

ANSWERS

1. D	2. D	3. C	4. B	5. A
6. C	7. B	8. B	9. C	10. B

DISCUSSION QUESTIONS

1. How does life and health insurance protect policyowners from the uncertainty of economic loss?

2. Explain the concept of risk pooling.

3. Explain the principle of the law of large numbers and how it relates to insurance.

4. How does speculative risk differ from pure risk?

5. Distinguish between a hazard and a peril. Give examples of each.

6. What are the three types of hazards? Give examples of each.

7. What are the four ways in which one can treat risk?

8. What are the six elements of insurable risk?

2

Application, Underwriting, and Policy Delivery

KEY TERMS

Insurers

Producers

Application

Materiality

Insurable Interest

Legal Capacity

Legal Purpose

Consideration

Warranties

Representations

Binding and
  Conditional Receipts

Underwriting

I. HOW INSURANCE IS SOLD

Although there are many ways to classify organizations that provide insurance, in the broadest of terms, there are two classifications: private and government. Within these two classes are many categories of insurance providers, as well as insurance plans and insurance producers.

A. PRIVATE INSURERS Private insurers offer many lines of insurance. Some sell primarily life insurance and annuities, some sell accident and health insurance, and some sell property and casualty insurance. Companies that write more than one line of insurance are known as **multiline insurers.** Within this broad category of private insurers are specific types of insurance companies. A discussion of each type follows.

1. Stock insurance companies A **stock insurance company** is a publicly owned, private organization that is incorporated under state laws for the purpose of making a profit for its stockholders. It is structured the same as any corporation. Stockholders may or may not be policyholders. When declared, stock dividends are paid to stockholders. In a stock company, the directors and officers are responsible to the stockholders.

2. Mutual insurance companies **Mutual insurance companies** are also organized and incorporated under state laws, but they have no stockholders. Instead, the owners are the policyholders. Anyone purchasing insurance from a mutual insurer is both a customer and an owner and has the right to vote for members of the board of directors. By issuing participating policies that pay policy dividends, mutual insurers allow their policyowners to share in any company earnings.

3. Assessment mutual companies **Assessment mutual insurance companies** are typified by the way in which they charge premiums. A pure assessment mutual company operates on the basis of loss sharing by group members. No premium is payable in advance; instead, each member is assessed an individual portion of losses that actually occur. An advance premium assessment mutual company charges a premium in advance, at the beginning of the policy period. If the original premiums exceed the operating expenses and losses, the surplus is returned to the policyholders as dividends. If total premiums are not enough to meet losses, additional assessments are levied against the members. Normally, the amount of assessment that may be levied is limited, either by state law or as a provision in the insurer's bylaws.

4. Reciprocal insurance companies Similar to mutual insurers, **reciprocal insurers** are organized on the basis of ownership by their policyholders. However, with reciprocal insurers it is the policyholders themselves who insure the risks of the other policyholders. Each policyholder assumes a share of the risk brought to the company by others. The insurer is a risk-sharing mechanism. Reciprocals are managed by an attorney-in-fact.

5. Lloyd's of London Lloyd's of London is not an insurer, but rather an association of individuals and companies that individually underwrite insurance. Lloyd's gathers and disseminates underwriting information, helps its associates settle claims and disputes, and through its member underwriters, provides coverages that might otherwise be unavailable in certain areas.

6. **Reinsurers** Reinsurers make up a specialized branch of the insurance industry that insures insurers. Reinsurance is an arrangement by which an insurance company transfers a portion of a risk it has assumed to another insurer. Usually, reinsurance takes place to limit the loss any one insurer would face should a very large claim become payable. The company transferring the risk is called the ceding company; the company assuming the risk is the reinsurer.

7. **Risk retention group** A **risk retention group (RRG)** is a mutual insurance company formed to insure people in the same business, occupation, or profession, such as pharmacists, dentists, or engineers.

8. **Fraternal benefit societies** Insurance also is issued by **fraternal benefit societies,** which have existed in the United States for more than a century. Fraternal societies, noted primarily for their social, charitable, and benevolent activities, have memberships based on religious, national, or ethnic affiliations. Fraternals first began offering insurance to meet the needs of their poorer members, funding the benefits on a pure assessment basis. Today few fraternals rely on an assessment system, most having adopted the same advanced funding approach other insurers use.

   a. To be characterized as a fraternal benefit society, the organization must be nonprofit, have a lodge system that includes ritualistic work, and maintain a representative form of government with elected officers.

   b. Fraternal society insurance is typically sold only to members of the society. Most fraternals today issue insurance certificates and annuities with many of the same provisions found in policies issued by commercial insurers.

9. **Service insurers or providers** Service insurers, or **service providers,** offer health insurance and health care services. One of the most well known service providers is Blue Cross and Blue Shield. These two organizations are nonprofit and differ from other insurers in that they sell medical and hospital care services, not insurance. These services are packaged into various plans, and those who purchase these plans are known as subscribers. Blue Cross offers prepayment plans to cover hospital expenses such as room and board and miscellaneous expenses. Blue Shield covers surgical expenses and other medical services performed by physicians.

   a. Another type of service provider is the **health maintenance organization (HMO).** HMOs offer a wide range of health care services to member subscribers. For a fixed periodic premium paid in advance of any treatment, these subscribers are entitled to the services of certain physicians and hospitals contracted to work with the HMO.

   b. A third type of service provider is the **preferred provider organization (PPO).** Under the usual PPO arrangement, a group (employer or union, for instance) desiring health care services will obtain price discounts or special services from certain select health care providers in exchange for referring its employees or members to them. PPOs can be organized by employers or by the health care providers themselves. The contract between the employer and the health care professional, be it a physician or a hospital, spells out the kind of services to be provided. Insurance companies can also contract with PPOs to offer services to insureds.

10. **Home service insurers** Insurance is also sold through a special branch of the industry known as home service, or debit, insurers. These companies specialize in a particular type of insurance called industrial insurance, which is characterized by relatively small face amounts, usually $1,000 to $2,000, with premiums paid weekly.

B. **GOVERNMENT AS INSURER** Federal and state governments also are insurers, providing what are commonly called social insurance programs. The major difference between these government programs and private insurance programs is that the government programs are funded with taxes and serve national and state social purposes. Social insurance programs include:

■ Old Age, Survivors, and Disability Insurance (OASDI), commonly known as Social Security;

■ Social Security Hospital Insurance (HI) and Supplemental Medical Insurance (SMI), commonly known as Medicare;

■ Medicaid; and

■ workers' compensation.

1. The federal government has also established life insurance programs to benefit active members and veterans of the armed services. Three of the most notable programs are Servicemembers' Group Life, Veterans' Group Life, and National Service Life.

2. The government plays a vital role in providing social insurance programs. These programs pay billions of dollars in benefits every year and affect millions of people.

C. **SELF-INSURERS** Though self-insurance is not a method of transferring risk, a discussion is appropriate here. Rather than transfer risk to an insurance company, a self-insurer establishes its own reserves to cover potential losses. Self-insurance is risk retention that is often used by large companies for funding workers' compensation and pension plans. Many times a self-insurer will look to an insurance company to provide insurance above a certain maximum level of loss, but will bear the amount of loss below that amount.

D. **PRODUCERS** Insurance is sold by a variety of companies through a variety of methods. Most consumers purchase insurance through licensed producers who present insurers' products and services to the public via active sales and marketing methods. Insurance producers may be either agents who represent a particular company, or brokers who are not tied to any particular company and can represent many companies' products.

1. Agents also are classified as **captive** (or **career**) agents or **independent agents**. A captive agent works for one insurance company and sells only that company's insurance policies. An independent agent works for himself or for other agents and sells the insurance products of many companies.

2. There are also solicitors, consultants, and special agents. **Solicitors** act for agents by seeking prospects, receiving applications, or collecting premiums, but they usually do not have the authority to bind coverage. A **consultant** is an independent advisor specializing in the design, implementation, and administration of insurance sharing plans. Consultants are usually licensed agents. **Special agents**, who do not actually solicit insurance business, work as field representatives, helping a company's central office and the agency's force in their territory.

3. Distribution systems   There are a number of systems that support the sale of insurance. The **career agency system**, the **personal producing general agency system**, and the **independent agency system** sell insurance through agents and brokers. There are also direct writers and mass marketers.

    a. **Career agencies** are branches of major stock and mutual insurance companies that are contracted to represent the particular insurer in a specific area. In career agencies, insurance agents are recruited, trained, and supervised either by a manager-employee of the company or a **general agent (GA)** who has a vested right in any business written by agents. GAs may operate strictly as managers or they may devote a portion of their time to sales. The career agency system focuses on building sales staffs.

    b. The **personal producing general agency (PPGA)** system is similar to the career agency system. However, PPGAs do not recruit, train, or supervise career agents. They primarily sell insurance, although they may build a small sales force to assist them. PPGAs are generally responsible for maintaining their own offices and administrative staff. Agents hired by a PPGA are considered employees of the PPGA, not the insurance company, and are supervised by regional directors.

    c. The **independent agency system**, a creation of the property and casualty insurance industry, does not tie a sales staff or agency to any one particular insurance company; rather, independent brokers represent any number of insurance companies through contractual agreements. They are compensated on a commission or fee basis for the business they produce. This system also is known as the American agency system.

    d. With the **direct selling** method, the insurer deals directly with consumers—no agent or broker is involved—selling its policies through vending machines, advertisements, or salaried sales representatives. Insurers that operate using this method are known as **direct writers** or **direct response insurers**.

    e. A large volume of insurance is also sold through **mass marketing** techniques, such as direct mail or newspaper, magazine, radio, and television advertisements. Mass marketing methods provide exposure to large groups of consumers, often using direct selling methods with occasional follow-up by agents.

E. REGULATION OF INSURERS   All insurers doing business within a state must be licensed or certified by that state. Thus, insurance companies are referred to as licensed or nonlicensed, or admitted or nonadmitted. An insurer's license is called a certificate of authority.

1. In addition, the following terms are frequently used to describe insurance companies and their site of incorporation:

   a. **Domestic insurers** A company is a domestic insurer in the state in which it is incorporated.

   b. **Foreign insurers** A foreign insurer is licensed to conduct business in states other than the one in which it is incorporated.

   c. **Alien insurers** Alien insurers are companies incorporated in a country other than the United States, the District of Columbia, or any US territorial possession.

F. **REGULATION OF PRODUCERS** Every state requires that those who sell insurance have a license from the state. However, before an Insurance Department will issue such a license to a prospective producer, the candidate must pass a producer licensing exam administered by the Department. In some states, the producer's license is perpetual unless revoked; in other states, it must be renewed at stipulated intervals.

Individuals who sell variable contracts—variable annuities, variable life, and variable universal health—must also be licensed by the National Association of Securities Dealers (NASD) Automated Quotation System. This requires passing the Series 6 (Investment Company/Variable Contracts Limited Representative) or the Series 7 (General Securities Representative) exam. Variable products are considered both securities and life insurance.

II. THE INSURANCE APPLICATION

The primary source of underwriting information with regard to a life insurance risk is the information found in a completed **application**. It is extremely important for an agent to see that an applicant's answers to all questions on the application are recorded accurately and with as much detail as possible.

Actual life and health insurance applications will differ among companies but all will ask for the applicant's name, address, date of birth, sex, occupation, hobbies, the type and amount of insurance applied for, any current life insurance in existence, the name of the beneficiary, and so forth.

There are several factors that have a direct effect upon the premium charged for a life or health insurance policy including the age, sex, and occupation of the insured, his hobbies (avocations), and his health condition.

A. **APPLICATION INFORMATION** The life or health insurance application presents many questions which are critical to the process of underwriting the risk. The age of the applicant is important because the older the applicant, the higher the mortality risk and the higher the premium charged. The sex of the applicant is also important because women have a longer life expectancy and are charged lower rates than men. The medical sections of a life insurance application and the agent's report are also extremely important to the underwriting process. The medical questions provide information to the company's underwriters that will enable them to determine how much coverage the insurer may issue to a life insurance applicant based on his medical condition. Any existing life or health insurance policies owned by the applicant should also be listed on the application. When discussing disability income insurance, the applicant's occupation must be listed. The underwriting department also obtains information from the agent's report.

1. **Physical examination** When additional medical information is considered necessary, the underwriter may ask that the applicant submit to a physical examination or request an attending physician's statement that would provide specific information concerning prior treatment. Generally, the back page of the application provides a section for the agent's comments. Here the agent states how long he has known the applicant and if proposed insurance will replace existing coverage. A space is provided for the agent's signature.

2. **Required signatures** Several signatures are required to complete a life or health insurance application. If any of the required signatures are not included, there will be a delay in issuing the policy. Required signatures include the applicant, the proposed insured (if different from the applicant), and the agent soliciting the insurance. In situations where a corporation is the policyowner, one or more of the partners or officers must sign the application.

    a. If replacement of an existing life insurance policy is involved, the applicant must sign a completed replacement form stating that he realizes that a replacement is taking place. The agent must also sign the form.

    b. When consumer reports are required or additional medical information is needed, forms authorizing these actions must also be signed by the applicant and the agent. Any form requesting information from the applicant's personal physician (such as an attending physician's statement), hospital, or any investigative agencies must also include appropriate signatures.

    c. The agent's report must be completed and signed by the agent only.

    d. In addition, the Fair Credit Reporting Act Notice of Disclosure ("Notice to the Applicant") is also to be completed with the appropriate signatures.

3. **Changes in the application** Any changes made to an insurance application after it is completed must be initialed by the applicant. It is permissible to change information but the insurer requires verification that the applicant is aware of any change: thus, the requirement that the applicant initial the changes.

    a. Some insurers require that the agent also initial application changes.

    b. The reason an insurer would require initialing is to protect itself in the event a dispute arises and the applicant and the agent do not recall the changes that were made.

4. **Consequences of incomplete applications** Since the application is the critical tool used by the company in the underwriting process, the agent has the responsibility to see that an applicant's answers to the questions are recorded accurately and completely.

    a. Any incomplete applications sent to the underwriting department will be returned to the agent for completion.

    b. This means that a delay in the underwriting process will ensue, requiring that the applicant wait to have the proper protection issued.

    c. It is advantageous for an agent to ensure that applications are filled out completely to avoid embarrassment and unnecessary inconveniences. In some cases, if delays occur, the applicant may simply withdraw the application for coverage.

5. Warranties and representations Statements made by an applicant for life or health insurance are considered to be representations. These statements, whether made on the application, to a physician or other medical examiner, are not considered to be warranties. Nevertheless, the applicant must act in good faith, and if the information given is false or incomplete, the insurer may be in a position to rescind or cancel the contract if the misrepresentation is considered material. Obviously, if the applicant was involved in any concealment or provided false information, the insurer could rescind the contract due to a material misrepresentation. The difference between a warranty and a representation is as follows.

    a. Warranty Warranties are statements and descriptions on the application that are guaranteed to be true.

    b. Representation A representation is a statement made to the insurer for the purpose of giving information or as an inducement to accept the risk. Representations will be deemed misrepresentations if the information provided is incorrect. Misrepresentations will not have much of an affect on a life or health insurance contract unless they are of a material nature. A representation is substantially true to the best knowledge of the applicant making the statement.

    c. Test of materiality The determination of whether a statement or representation is true is simply stated: would the insurance company have taken a different course of action had the truth been known? If so, the statement is material. If not, the statement is not material.

6. Collecting the initial premium and issuing the receipt Generally, an insured is provided with a receipt at the time the application is completed and an initial premium is paid. A receipt is proof that coverage under the contract will go into effect following the completion of a medical examination if one is required.

    a. Binding receipt If an insurer issues a binding receipt, coverage becomes effective as of the date of the receipt and will continue until the insurer rejects the application. Coverage begins immediately when the premium is paid and the receipt provided to the applicant. However, if the application is underwritten and the company determines that coverage is not to be extended, the premium will be returned and the applicant will be notified that coverage will not be provided. A binding receipt provides for coverage until the application is rejected by the insurer. For example, if a binding receipt is provided to an applicant for life insurance and he is killed in an accident the next day, coverage is effective and the claim will be paid even if the application would later be denied after the underwriting process has been completed.

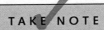

TAKE NOTE

Statements made by an applicant for insurance in the application are considered to be representations, not warranties.

b. Conditional receipt Under the terms of a conditional receipt, insurance coverage becomes effective as of the date of the receipt if the application is approved for the plan of insurance applied for, the coverage applied for, and the premium rate applied for. This receipt is normally provided to an applicant when the initial premium is paid at the time of application.

1.) Explanation of the conditional receipt The agent must explain how the receipt functions. The agent must inform the applicant that coverage is effective as of the date of the receipt if the insurer ultimately determines that the applicant qualifies for the policy as applied for. If the applicant qualifies, protection is in effect as of the date of the receipt. He does not have to wait for coverage until the policy is actually issued and delivered.

2.) Coverage and the receipt If the applicant completes an application for life or health insurance and pays the initial premium to the agent, he will be issued a conditional receipt. If the applicant is injured, suffers an illness, or dies after the date on the receipt and before the issuance of the policy, the applicant will still qualify for coverage if the policy would have been issued based on the company's underwriting criteria such as the applicant's health or the results of a physical exam (if one was required).

B. EXPLAINING SOURCES OF INSURABILITY INFORMATION It is the responsibility of a producer to explain to an applicant the various resources from which the insurer will obtain information regarding that applicant's insurability. Several resources are available to an insurer. The more common resources include the following.

1. The MIB report The Medical Information Bureau (MIB) is an intercompany data bank that allows member insurance companies to check applicants against the Bureau's record of medical impairments that were uncovered during the underwriting of life or health applications previously submitted (to any member company) by a prospective insured. The MIB serves as an aid to underwriting since it will attempt to guide an insurer toward other sources of information if some medical impairment is detected. The MIB also compiles confidential information regarding past applications for life or health insurance submitted by an applicant. This permits an insurer to compare information on a current application with that found on another application.

2. Consumer reports A consumer report may be oral or written and includes information concerning an individual's credit history, reputation, character, and habits. A consumer report is usually used to help determine an applicant's eligibility for insurance, employment, or credit. Every insurer has the option of verifying or acquiring additional information regarding an applicant for life or health insurance.

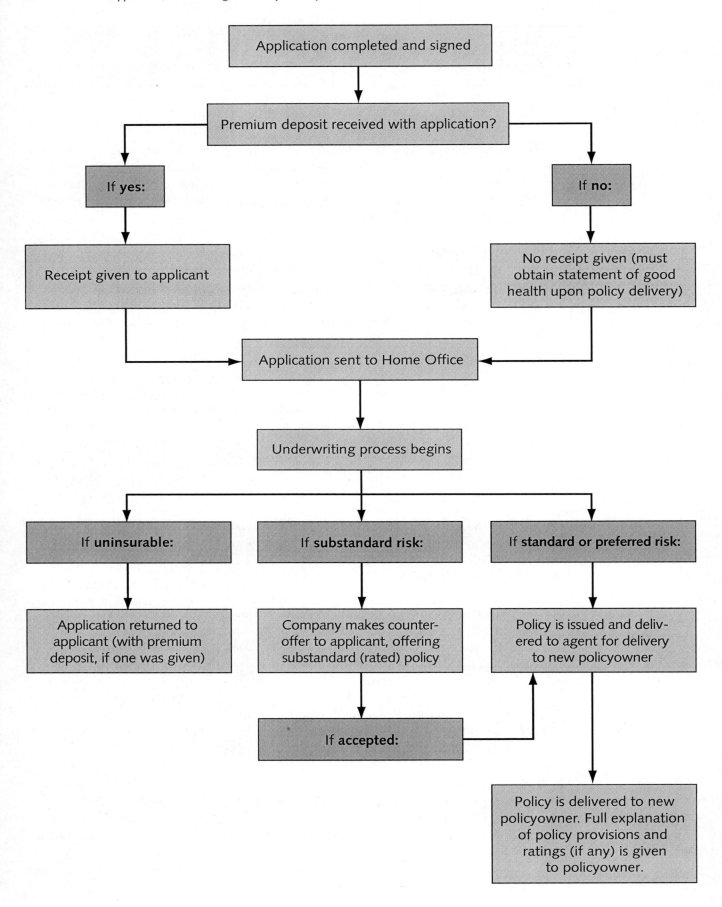

TAKE NOTE

Sources of insurability information: the application; MIB; consumer reports; and agent's report.

3. Fair Credit Reporting Act All insurers and their producers must comply with the federal Fair Credit Reporting Act regarding information obtained from a third party concerning the applicant.

   a. The Fair Credit Reporting Act states that when an applicant is denied coverage due to information obtained from a third-party source, the applicant will be informed of the source.

   b. The insurer must permit an applicant to refute any adverse information.

   c. Insurance companies may use consumer reports, or investigative consumer reports, to compile additional information regarding the applicant.

   d. If applicants feel that the information compiled by the consumer inspection service is inaccurate, they may send a brief statement to the reporting agency with the correct information.

   e. A Notice to the Applicant must be issued to all applicants for life or health insurance coverage. This notice informs the applicant that a report will be ordered concerning their past credit history and any other life or health insurance for which they have previously applied. The agent must leave this notice with the applicant along with the receipt.

C. SUBMITTING THE APPLICATION It is the responsibility of the agent to review the application before sending it to the home office underwriting department. This provides another opportunity to ensure that the application is filled out completely so that no delay in policy issuance will take place if the applicant qualifies for coverage. If an initial premium is paid by the applicant at the time of application, it must also accompany the application.

D. OBTAINING A SIGNED STATEMENT OF CONTINUED GOOD HEALTH In some cases, the initial premium is not paid until the policy is delivered. Most insurers require that when an agent collects the premium at policy delivery, they also obtain a statement signed by the insured attesting to his continued good health before leaving the policy with the insured.

   1. The agent then submits the premium, along with a signed statement of good health, to the insurer.

   2. The purpose of this requirement is to make sure the insured has remained in good health during the underwriting period (from the time the application was completed to when the policy was actually delivered).

Notice to the Applicant

Section 14: Authorization and Signatures

I hereby authorize any licensed physician, medical practitioner, hospital, clinic, or other medical or medically related facility, insurance company, the medical information bureau or other organization, institution, or person, that has any information (records or knowledge) of me or my health (all medical information, including psychiatric, drug, or alcohol use history), to give any such information to _____ Corporation and its reinsurers for use in the processing and evaluation of my application for insurance and claims for benefits thereunder.

I also authorize _____ Corporation and its reinsurers to release any such information to the medical information bureau and to other life insurance companies to which I may apply for life or health insurance or to which a claim for benefits may be submitted, for use in the processing and evaluation of such applications or claims.

This authorization also covers such information pertaining to my children proposed for insurance; their names are: (insert "none" if no minor children are proposed for insurance.)

I understand _____ Corporation will provide me with a copy of this authorization at my request. I agree that a photographic copy of this authorization will be as valid as the original, and that this authorization will be valid for a future period of 2½ years from the date shown below.

I (we) have paid $_____ (if none say none) to the agent in exchange for the conditional coverage receipt and I (we) acknowledge that (we) fully understand and accept its terms.

Dated at city_____state_____this_____ day of_____, 20_____.

III. UNDERWRITING

The process of **underwriting** life and health insurance policies includes reviewing the background information and medical history of the applicant. This information permits an insurance company to determine whether to accept or reject an applicant for coverage. In addition, this information also determines whether the insurer will charge standard or modified premium rates. There are several underwriting considerations involved in the issuance of insurance, including the following.

A. INSURABLE INTEREST Every life and health insurance contract is subject to the doctrine of **insurable interest.** This doctrine states that the individual purchasing insurance coverage must have a direct and identifiable interest in the individual to be insured. It must be clear that the party purchasing insurance coverage has an economic interest of some sort in the insured. The purpose of this doctrine is to prevent individuals from profiting from the purchase of life or health insurance on the lives or health of others.

1. When the applicant for life or health insurance coverage is also the insured, this doctrine does not apply. Individuals are assumed to have insurable interest in themselves.

2. Insurable interest in a life or health insurance contract must exist at the time of application; it need not remain for the duration of a life insurance policy. For example, a wife may buy coverage on her husband's life and maintain it after they divorce.

3. A beneficiary need not possess insurable interest in an insured except in a situation where the beneficiary is also the applicant for insurance coverage.

4. The doctrine of insurable interest is closely connected with the principle of indemnification.

5. The most common areas involving acceptable insurable interest include blood relationships such as fathers, mothers, sons, and daughters (but not nephews and nieces); marital relationships involving husbands and wives; and business relationships.

6. A company may refuse to honor a death claim if it proves that no insurable interest existed at the time of application.

B. **MEDICAL INFORMATION AND CONSUMER REPORTS** As noted before, life and health insurance companies may draw upon a number of sources to compile information on applicants for insurance coverage. The primary sources of information include the application, medical examinations, inspection reports, and the agent's report. One of the more comprehensive sources of information available to insurance companies is the **Medical Information Bureau (MIB)**.

C. **RISK CLASSIFICATION** The majority of life and health insurance companies have established certain basic underwriting requirements to obtain a desired level of business. Most insurance companies attempt to write a large percentage of standard risks. **Standard risks** are those insurable at standard premium rates. Almost all applicants for life or health insurance are in the standard risk category. **Preferred risk** is another form of risk classification used by insurers. It refers to the type of risk profile that offers the lowest chance of loss and, for obvious reasons, is preferred by insurers. For instance, life underwriters prefer nonsmokers because the potential for heart and lung diseases is less for these individuals than for a smoker. An additional risk classification includes substandard risks. **Substandard risks** present the insurance company with additional exposures to loss that may be due to adverse health conditions, moral hazards, or hazardous occupations or avocations. These risks are usually issued rated policies (policies that are issued with a higher than standard premium).

1. There are various methods insurers use to rate up a policy including assessing a flat rate charge which may vary depending upon the risk involved; applying a step-up in age, which means that the insurer may treat the applicant as a 40-year-old for rating purposes (even though the applicant is actually age 30) due to the substandard nature of the risk, or as a percentage of the normal rate.

2. There are numerous factors which influence the underwriting of a life insurance risk including age and sex, occupation and hobbies, family health history, physical condition, moral character, personal history and habits, the type of insurance applied for, financial condition, aviation or military involvement, and the amount of travel outside the country.

IV. DELIVERING THE POLICY

One of the most important services provided by an agent to a client who purchases a life insurance contract is policy delivery. When the agent delivers the policy, he should review the insured's original goals and needs associated with the purchase of the policy. The delivery process involves far more than just delivering the contract. The insured may have additional questions with regard to the policy. Some of the more important aspects of this process are as follows.

A. EXPLAIN WHEN COVERAGE BEGINS Once the initial premium is paid, the application has been approved by the underwriting department, and there are no other conditions to be satisfied, coverage begins as of the date of the receipt. If the premium is paid when the policy is delivered, coverage begins as of delivery.

B. OBTAIN A STATEMENT OF GOOD HEALTH As noted earlier, in many cases, the initial premium is not paid until the policy is delivered. In these instances, most insurers require that when the agent collects the premium, he must also obtain a statement signed by the insured attesting to the insured's continued good health before leaving the policy with the insured.

1. The agent submits the signed statement and the initial premium to the insurer.

2. The purpose of this requirement is to make sure that the insured has remained in good health during the underwriting period.

C. **EXPLAIN THE POLICY AND ITS PROVISIONS, RIDERS, EXCLUSIONS, AND ANY RATINGS TO THE CLIENT** The majority of insureds will not remember everything about the life or health insurance contract after the application has been submitted to the underwriting department for approval. This is the primary reason why an agent should deliver the contract in person. During policy delivery, the agent should again explain the policy, its provisions, and exclusions. In addition, the agent will also discuss any possible riders attached to the contract and any change in rating that may have occurred.

1. Explaining the policy, its provisions, and exclusions to the policyowner will help eliminate any future misunderstandings or policy lapses.

2. If the insured turns out to be a substandard risk, the agent will explain any change in the policy rating. The agent must also provide the reasons why the policy has been rated.

3. Any rider which has been attached to the contract for any adverse health conditions (or for any other reason) must also be explained to the insured. In many cases, an insured must sign and return to the insurer a statement verifying that he understands that a rider is being attached and what restrictions are involved.

4. Once the policy is delivered, the free look period begins and lasts for 10 or 20 days.

D. **NATIONAL DO NOT CALL REGISTRY** Many consumers have registered their private telephone numbers on the National Do Not Call Registry in an attempt to stop most telemarketing calls. However, calls from or on behalf of political organizations, charities, and telephone surveyors are still permitted, as well as calls from companies with which the consumer has an existing business relationship, or from those that have the express written permission of the consumer. Businesses that violate consumers' requests can be subject to severe monetary fines.

1. A consumer can establish a business relationship with an insurer by requesting information from it or submitting an application to it.

2. Even if a business relationship exists between a consumer and the insurer, the consumer may specifically request that the insurer not call.

V. CONTRACT LAW

A. **REQUIREMENTS OF A CONTRACT** An insurance policy is a contract between the insurer and the policyowner. For an insurance contract to be a valid or legal contract, it must satisfy four requirements.

1. **Agreement** An agreement must exist between the parties (insured and insurer) based on an offer made by one of the parties and an acceptance of that offer by the other party. Both parties must agree to the contract terms.

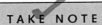

TAKE NOTE

In all jurisdictions, insurance contracts are considered to have a legal purpose.

2. **Consideration** For a contract to be valid, there must be an exchange of values. With an insurance contract, the insured's consideration is the premium paid; the insurer's consideration is its promise to pay covered claims.

3. **Legal capacity** The parties to a contract must be legally capable of entering into a contract. All individuals are considered to be legally capable except for (1) minors, (2) insane individuals, (3) persons who are intoxicated or under the influence of narcotics, and (4) enemy aliens (those who are citizens of a country with which Congress has declared war).

4. **Legal purpose** A valid contract must be for a lawful or legal purpose. In other words, the agreement cannot be against public policy or against the law. For example, a contract to commit a crime is not a contract with a legal purpose.

B. **CHARACTERISTICS OF THE LIFE AND HEALTH INSURANCE CONTRACT** Life and health insurance contracts share some characteristics, including the following.

1. **Conditional** A life or health insurance contract is conditional in that the obligation of the insurer to pay a claim depends upon the performance of certain acts by the insured (meeting conditions), such as the payment of premiums and the furnishing of proof of death, illness, or injury.

2. **Unilateral** Only one party, the insurance company, gives a legally enforceable promise in the establishment of the contract. The owner of the policy makes no promise to continue premium payments. However, if premiums are paid in a timely manner, the company is bound to accept them and meet its obligations under the contract. Conversely, if premiums are not paid, the insurer can cancel the policy.

3. **Contracts of adhesion** This is a contract where one party (the insurer) creates the contract terms and the other party (the insured) must accept the terms unconditionally. No bargaining or negotiating as to the contract terms or conditions takes place.

   a. A contract of adhesion is sometimes referred to as a one-sided contract.

   b. Insureds are protected by the courts with regard to insurance contracts when ambiguities arise. In these cases, courts will interpret the ambiguity in a way that is most favorable to the party that did not draft the contract.

4. **Insurable interest** As noted above, all life and health insurance contracts are subject to the doctrine of insurable interest. This doctrine states than an individual purchasing insurance coverage must have a direct and identifiable interest in the individual to be insured. It must also be clear that the party purchasing insurance coverage has an economic interest of some type in the insured. The purpose of this doctrine is to prevent individuals from profiting from the purchase of insurance on the lives of others.

5. **Warranties and representations** Statements made by an applicant on an application for health insurance are, for the most part, considered to be representations. To emphasize, representations are statements which are true to the best knowledge of the individual making the statement. Misrepresentations are statements made that are incorrect. Misrepresentations will not void an insurance contract unless they are of a material nature. (The test of materiality is to ask whether either party to the contract would have taken a different course of action had the truth been known.) Warranties are statements made which are guaranteed to be absolutely true. A breach of warranty will void the contract.

U N I T   Q U I Z

1. A man would be considered to have an automatic insurable interest in the lives of all of the following EXCEPT his
   A. wife
   B. son
   C. nephew
   D. daughter

2. Which of the following is provided by the Fair Credit Reporting Act?
   A. The availability of credit life insurance on an impartial basis
   B. Protection to debtors against credit collection agencies
   C. The requirement that an applicant for insurance be informed that a consumer report may be requested regarding his application
   D. Information concerning any previous applications for insurance by an applicant

3. Which of the following is CORRECT regarding the existence of insurable interest in a life or health insurance policy?
   A. Insurable interest must exist at the time of loss.
   B. Insurable interest must exist at the time of application.
   C. Insurable interest must exist throughout the duration of the policy.
   D. Insurable interest must exist at the time of the insured's death.

4. Which of the following statements concerning warranties is CORRECT?
   A. A warranty is guaranteed to be true.
   B. Most statements made by an insurance applicant are considered to be warranties.
   C. All statements made by an insurance applicant are considered to be warranties.
   D. A warranty is an enforceable representation.

5. All of the following statements are correct regarding the completion of a life or health insurance application EXCEPT
   A. any life insurance application submitted to the underwriting department must include the signatures of the policyowner, proposed insured, and agent
   B. any changes made to an application before its submission to the insurer must be initialed by the applicant
   C. the initial premium must be submitted to the insurer with the completed application
   D. incomplete applications may delay the underwriting process

6. Which of the following most accurately defines a representation?
   A. A statement guaranteed to be absolutely true
   B. A statement that is true to the best knowledge of the applicant
   C. A statement that is material to the risk involved
   D. A statement pertaining to the substandard nature of the risk to be insured

7. All of the following are risk classifications involved in a life or health insurance policy application EXCEPT
   A. substandard risks
   B. standard risks
   C. preferred risks
   D. adverse risks

8. A premium receipt that provides for coverage immediately once the premium is paid and the receipt given to an applicant best describes a(n)
   A. conditional receipt
   B. constructive receipt
   C. binding receipt
   D. insurability receipt

9. All of the following are factors that an underwriting department will consider in its decision to rate-up, accept, or reject a life or health insurance risk EXCEPT the
    A. health of the applicant
    B. applicant's hobbies
    C. beneficiary's age
    D. applicant's age and sex

10. All of the following are primary sources of information available to a life or health insurance company's underwriting department concerning insurance applicants EXCEPT
    A. medical examination
    B. application
    C. agent's report
    D. statement of good health

11. Which of the following best describes the Medical Information Bureau?
    A. An industry agency that provides computation of premium payments for medical impairments
    B. An industry agency that offers health underwriting services to insurance companies
    C. An industry agency that provides background checks on physicians who perform medical exams on insurance applicants
    D. An industry agency that provides medical information on life and health insurance applicants

12. With regard to insurance applications, the Fair Credit Reporting Act requires that
    A. the applicant be advised that the application may be rejected
    B. the applicant be advised that a consumer report may be requested
    C. the insurer advise the applicant whether coverage is accepted or denied
    D. the applicant be advised of the maximum limit of coverage available

13. An insurance policy's free look period begins
    A. upon the payment of the initial premium
    B. upon receipt of the attending physician's statement
    C. when the insurer receives the application
    D. when the policy is delivered

14. All of the following are required to form a valid contract EXCEPT
    A. an agreement
    B. enforceable promises on the part of both parties
    C. consideration
    D. legal capacity

15. A statement guaranteed to be absolutely true best describes a(n)
    A. representation
    B. condition
    C. warranty
    D. aleation

16. An insurance company organized and headquartered in Indiana can be described as what type of company when doing business in Indiana?
    A. Alien
    B. Home-based
    C. Foreign
    D. Domestic

17. In an insurance transaction, licensed agents legally represent which of the following?
    A. The insurer
    B. The applicant and insured
    C. The state Insurance Department
    D. Themselves

18. An insurance company organized in Illinois, with its home office in Philadelphia, is licensed to conduct business in Wisconsin. In Wisconsin, this company would be described as which of the following types of insurers?
    A. Domestic
    B. Alien
    C. Foreign
    D. Regional

19. Which of the following is NOT considered a service insurer?

    A. HMO
    B. Blue Cross
    C. Lloyd's of London
    D. PPO

DISCUSSION QUESTIONS

1. Why should an application for life or health insurance be filled out completely and accurately?

2. Whose signatures are required on a life or health insurance application?

3. Compare and contrast a warranty and a representation.

4. Contrast a binding and conditional receipt.

5. Discuss the concept or insurable interest. What other principle does this doctrine follow closely?

6. What is the primary purpose of the Fair Credit Reporting Act?

7. What effects will standard or substandard risks have on the rating of an applicant for life or health insurance?

8. Why may a statement of good health be required from an applicant during the process of delivering a policy?

9. What type of information is provided to an insurer by the MIB?

10. Why is it important that the agent explain the contract provisions and any riders to the newly insured individual?

11. What can an applicant do if he finds that incorrect information is included on his consumer report?

12. What type of information is provided to an applicant in the notice left with him by the agent?

13. When does the free look period begin?

14. Identify the four elements of a valid contract.

15. Who is considered a person with legal capacity?

3

Introduction to Life Insurance and Types of Policies

KEY TERMS

Policyowner	Joint Life	Limited-Pay
Single Premium	Ordinary Life	Variable
Adjustable	Modified	Level
Variable/Universal	Universal	Renewable
Decreasing	CAWL	Immediate
Convertible	Increasing	Variable
Deferred	Annuitant	Family Maintenance
Endowments	Fixed	Annuities

I. DEFINITION OF LIFE INSURANCE AND TYPES OF POLICIES

Life insurance is a contract under which one party (the insurer) in consideration of the premium payment, agrees to pay an amount stipulated in the contract to a designated person (the beneficiary) upon the occurrence of a contingency defined in the contract (usually that of death).

A. **PURPOSE OF LIFE INSURANCE** One of the most important factors associated with life insurance is that it involves the immediate creation of an estate. The full amount of the estate is always created immediately and this occurs at the precise moment when it is most needed: at the death of the insured. There are two parties involved in the contract: the policyowner and the insurer. A beneficiary is not a party to the contract.

   1. **Policyowner** The **policyowner** is the individual who pays the premiums and has other rights under the contract such as naming the beneficiary, receiving dividends, and borrowing from the cash value. The owner of a life insurance policy may also be the insured, the beneficiary, or another third party, such as a creditor or business partner.

   2. **Insured** The **insured** is the individual whose death causes the policy benefits (face amount) to be paid. The insured in a life insurance contract can also be the owner of the policy.

   3. **Beneficiary** The **beneficiary** is the person, organization, or trust that will receive the benefits (face amount) payable upon the death of the insured. A beneficiary may also be the owner of the policy. A beneficiary is not a party to the contract (unless she is also the owner).

B. **TYPES OF POLICIES** Several types of life insurance policies are available to today's insurance consumers including term insurance, whole life, and endowments.

   1. **Term life insurance** A **term life insurance policy** may be defined as a contract that provides protection for a limited number of years, the face amount being payable only if death occurs during the stipulated term and nothing being paid if the insured survives the stipulated period. Term insurance has no cash savings value and has also been defined as temporary or pure protection. Since it only provides pure protection, it furnishes the maximum amount of death benefit for the lowest annual price.

      a. **Types of term policies** There are several types of term insurance policies available. The more common types include the following:

         1.) **Level term** A **level term** policy provides term insurance protection for a specified amount of insurance for the length or period of the contract. The premium for such a contract will increase according to the age of the insured.

            a.) For example, a one-year $100,000 level term policy may cost $200 for a 32-year-old male. Following that one-year period, if the insured wishes to continue such protection, his premium may increase to $215 and so on. For policies that are written for five-year periods, the premium will remain constant for those five years but will increase for a subsequent five-year policy period based on the age of the insured at renewal.

TAKE NOTE

Level term insurance   Provides a level amount of protection for a specified period, after which the policy terminates.

Decreasing term insurance   Provides protection that gradually declines over the policy's term.

2.) Decreasing term This type of contract may be utilized as a rider for a whole life contract or written as a separate contract. It is characterized by a decreasing or declining face amount of protection from year to year. Because the face amount decreases, the premium remains constant throughout the life of the contract. At the end of the contract period, the policy face amount will be zero. This type of policy is best utilized to cover a decreasing obligation such as a home mortgage or an auto loan. The premium is very low due to the fact that the face amount decreases as the rate per unit of insurance increases.

a.) The most common use for this type of contract is in connection with a mortgage. For this reason, a decreasing term policy is known as a **mortgage protection** or **redemption plan**.

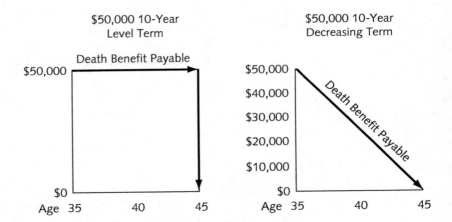

A level term policy provides a straight, level benefit amount over the entire term of the policy. A decreasing term policy pays a gradually decreasing benefit over the term of the policy.

3.) Increasing term This type of coverage is usually written as a rider but rarely as a separate contract. This coverage is characterized by an increasing face value with each succeeding payment of premium. In the majority of cases, it is primarily used in connection with a combination policy where increasing life insurance is added to an underlying contract.

a.) For example, a return of premium policy illustrates this concept where increasing term insurance is used to offset the payback of premiums at the time of the insured's death. As a result, the insurance company will repay all premiums paid while paying to the beneficiary the face amount of the policy upon the death of the insured.

TAKE NOTE

Attained age   Jonas takes out a five-year term policy at age 30 and converts it to whole life at age 35. Going forward, Jonas pays the premium rate assigned to a 35-year-old male.

Original age   Shirley takes out a five-year term policy at age 30 and converts it at age 35. She pays all of the premiums that would have required had she been issued a whole life policy at 30 and, going forward, continues to pay the premium for a 30-year-old female.

4.) A jumping juvenile or junior estate builder is a type of policy that provides term insurance for juveniles. It is usually issued in $1,000 units for juveniles who are one to 15 years old. When the child reaches 21 years of age, the face amount increases to five times the original amount with no increase in the premium.

b. Features of term insurance Most term life insurance policies have two major features that provide additional flexibility for an insured/policyowner.

1.) Renewable feature Several forms of term protection provide renewal at the end of the term without requiring proof or evidence of insurability. In effect, the renewal of the policy is accomplished at attained age. If an insured purchased term insurance without such a feature, he may be at a disadvantage once the policy period ends and may have developed a physical condition that might make it difficult to obtain insurance protection.

a.) The cost of a term policy with this feature is higher due to the chance of adverse selection.

b.) Most renewable features are available to policies with one-, five-, and 10-year policy periods.

c.) Renewal premiums are based on attained age.

d.) Renewable term insurance protects the insurability of an insured.

e.) An age limitation is usually included in these contracts, such as "Renewable to Age 65."

2.) Convertible feature This feature permits a policyowner/insured to exchange a term policy for a whole life contract without evidence of insurability. This exchange is allowed at any time during the policy period and may be effected in one of two ways.

a.) Attained age method This involves the issuance of a whole life policy at the conversion date with premiums based on the current or attained age of the insured.

b.) Original age method This involves a retroactive conversion where the whole life policy being purchased bears the date and premium rate that would have been charged had it originally been purchased instead of the term protection. Many companies require that this option be activated within the first five years of the term policy or it will be lost.

c. Term insurance evaluation There are many uses, advantages, and disadvantages of term insurance.

1.) Uses and advantages Term policies are designed to provide protection against contingencies that require only temporary protection and necessitate large amounts of coverage for the smallest outlay of funds. Term insurance may be used:

- for families with lower incomes where some sort of protection is needed;
- to protect an individual's insurability;
- for protection on borrowed funds (mortgages, auto loans, education loans);
- as a supplement to cash value insurance where term is purchased as a rider to a whole life contract; and
- as a way of hedging against known contingencies (for example, purchasing term coverage until the insured reaches age 65 when a pension plan begins to pay monthly amounts).

2.) Disadvantages There are also disadvantages present that must be conveyed to the purchaser of term life insurance.

a.) Although the outlay of funds is low in the early years, premiums increase dramatically in the insured's later years.

b.) There may come a time when an insured has no protection after term insurance ends.

c.) Term insurance is actually more expensive (with no cash value return) than whole life if the insured survives a reasonable number of years (such as living to the end of the policy term).

2. Traditional whole life products In contrast to term insurance, whole life insurance provides protection for an individual's life; it is not limited in its duration. There are a number of variations of whole life insurance, including ordinary (straight) whole life and limited payment whole life.

a. Ordinary (straight) whole life An ordinary, or straight, life insurance contract is one of the major types of life insurance policies. These contracts are based on the assumption that the premiums will be paid by the policyowner throughout the insured's lifetime. In many instances, an individual purchases a life insurance contract with no intention of paying premiums for his entire lifetime. His intention is to use dividends to pay up the policy in a shorter period of time, surrender the policy for a paid-up policy with a lower death benefit, or surrender the policy

---

TAKE ✓ NOTE

The names of limited pay policies denote how long premiums are payable: for example, 20-pay life (premiums are payable for 20 years); paid-up at 65 (premiums are payable until the insured reaches age 65).

---

upon retirement in exchange for an annuity. Therefore, an ordinary or straight life insurance contract is flexible and does not legally commit an owner to make premium payments for the rest of his life.

1.) Permanent protection combined with savings feature An ordinary or straight life policy provides permanent protection because it never has to be renewed or converted. This type of contract provides the insured protection at a level premium rate throughout the life of the policy. These policies are characterized by **cash value** build-up during the life of the contract.

2.) Maturity at age 100 A straight whole life policy is designed so that its cash value accumulation reaches the policy's face value amount at the insured's age 100.

Ordinary or straight life policies continue to be the most common type of protection sold, although interest in term insurance and universal life products have increased dramatically during the past several years. The cash surrender value in a straight life policy represents the savings element of this life insurance policy.

$50,000 Policy Face Amount

When the insured reaches age 100, the cash value of a whole life policy will equal the face amount and will be paid to the insured as a living benefit, if he is still living.

b. Limited-pay and single-premium life policies

1.) Limited-pay policy Limited-payment life insurance policies emphasize savings more than straight life policies. These policies also make it possible for an insured to stop premium payments at the expiration of a specified period of time without any reduction in the amount of the insurance for as long as the insured survives. In other words, the policy is fully paid at the time of the last payment. The most common types of limited-pay policies are 10-payment life, 20-payment life, or life paid-up at age 65.

a.) For example, a life paid-up at age 65 policy would be useful to an insured who desires permanent protection but does not want the premiums to continue beyond the end of his normal earning period (at retirement age). This type of policy also provides a larger savings element than a straight life insurance policy. If an insured purchases an adequate amount of protection under a policy with the premium payments limited to a short period of time, he has the advantage of knowing that his insurance program will be completed at the end of that time and that a sizeable savings fund is accumulating.

2.) Single premium life policies A contract for which a single premium is paid at the inception of the policy and becomes fully paid is called **single payment** or **single premium life insurance**. Advantages of such a plan include:

- tax-free buildup of cash value at desirable rates;
- minimal sales commissions;
- below-market interest rates on borrowing;
- use of cash build-up; and
- gifting opportunities.

c. Adjustable life insurance At any particular point, this policy is a level-premium, level-death benefit policy. It may be limited-payment or term insurance but it is actually a combination of both.

1.) This contract has all the usual features of level-premium cash-value life insurance. It possesses cash and other nonforfeiture values, dividend options, and policy loan provisions.

2.) This policy contains adjustment provisions that allow premiums to be increased or decreased, the face amount to be increased or decreased, and additional extra premiums to be paid. Whenever these adjustments occur, the plan of insurance may also change, but with respect to the future only.

3.) An increase in premium increases future cash values and a decrease in premium reduces cash values.

3. Endowments An endowment policy provides for the payment (to the beneficiary) of the face amount upon the death of an insured during a specified period or the payment of the face amount at the end of the specified period if the insured is still alive, whichever comes first. Endowments are not as popular today as they once were. These contracts were originally designed to combine life insurance and savings elements.

a. Endowment policies may be issued for specified periods such as 5, 10, 20, 25, or 30 years, or up to a specified age such as age 65.

b. Once the specified period has passed and the insured is living, the face amount would be paid to that insured in a lump sum or in installments.

> **TAKE NOTE**
>
> **LIFO** Last-in first-out means that monies invested last (interest earnings) are considered to be the first monies withdrawn and are therefore subject to income tax.

   c. The premium payments for an endowment policy are greater than the traditional whole life contracts because their savings features and premium levels depend upon the endowment period selected.

      1.) For example, if a 35-year-old male purchases a $50,000 20-year endowment, his annual premium may be $2,200. A $50,000 whole life contract may cost $950. If the insured survives the 20-year period, he then is paid the $50,000 face amount since his contract has matured. If he does not survive the 20-year period, his beneficiary receives the $50,000 death benefit.

4. Modified endowment contracts (MECs) To discourage the use of life insurance contracts with high premiums as investments, federal law subjects all permanent policies to a test. A life insurance policy that fails the test will be considered a **modified endowment contract** which makes the policy subject to less favorable tax treatment. Before this test, single premium life policies (and other types of limited-pay contracts) were taxed the same as other life insurance policies. A policyowner was able to borrow (make withdrawals, etc.) from the policy's cash value without paying tax. A modified endowment contract is a life insurance policy whose premiums exceed what would have been paid to fund a similar type of life insurance policy with seven annual premiums (the seven-pay test).

   a. For example, if the total aggregate premiums paid at any time during the policy's initial seven years exceed the total premium that would have been paid on a seven-year level annual premium basis for the same period, the contract will not meet the required seven-pay test and will be considered a modified endowment contract.

   b. Modified endowment contract tax treatment makes the utilization of a high premium life policy as a short term investment less attractive since it will be more costly. Funds withdrawn are subject to last-in first-out (LIFO) treatment which assumes that the investment or earnings portion of the contract's values is withdrawn first (making these funds fully taxable as ordinary income) before the insured's basis (the total amount of premiums paid; the insured's basis in the contract is always returned without being subject to income taxation).

      1.) In addition to paying income tax on withdrawn amounts, a penalty of 10% is imposed on withdrawals made prior to age 59½. Since it is more costly, the return on investment experienced by an MEC policyowner will be less. Like an annuity, the cash value buildup accumulates tax free unless it is withdrawn.

   c. Once a policy is classified as a modified endowment contract, it will also automatically make any policy subsequently received in exchange for it a modified endowment contract even if the new policy would otherwise pass the seven-pay test.

5. Other types of permanent life products

a. Universal life insurance Universal life insurance, also called flexible premium adjustable life insurance, is a variation of whole life insurance, characterized by considerable flexibility. Unlike whole life, with its fixed premiums, fixed face amounts, and fixed cash value accumulations, universal life allows it policyowners to determine the amount and frequency of premium payments and to adjust the policy face amount up or down to reflect changes in needs. Consequently, no new policy need be issued when changes are desired.

1.) Universal life provides this flexibility by unbundling, or separating, the basic components of a life insurance policy—the insurance (protection) element, the savings (accumulation) element, and the expense (loading) element. As with any other life policy, the policyowner pays a premium. Each month, a mortality charge is deducted from the policy's cash value account for the cost of the insurance protection. This mortality charge also may include an expense, or loading, charge.

2.) Like term insurance premiums, the universal life mortality charge increases steadily with age. Actually, universal life technically is defined as term insurance with a policy fund value. Even though the policyowner may pay a level premium, an increasing share of that premium goes to pay the mortality charge as the insured ages.

3.) As premiums are paid and cash value accumulates, interest is credited to the policy's cash value. This interest may be either the current interest rate declared by the company (and dependent on current market conditions) or the guaranteed minimum rate specified in the contract. As long as the cash value account is sufficient to pay the monthly mortality and expense costs, the policy will continue in force whether or not the policyowner pays the premium.

4.) At stated intervals (and usually on providing evidence of insurability), the policyowner can increase or decrease the face amount of the policy. A corresponding increase (or decrease) in premium payments is not required, as long as the cash values can cover the mortality and expense costs. By the same token, the policyowner can elect to pay more into the policy, thus adding to the cash value account, subject to certain guidelines that control the relationship between the cash values and the policy's face amount.

5.) Another factor the distinguishes universal life from whole life insurance is the fact that partial withdrawals can be made from the policy's cash value account. (Whole life insurance allows a policyowner to tap cash values only through a policy loan or a complete cash surrender of the policy's cash values, in which case the policy terminates.) Also, the policyowner may surrender the universal life policy for its entire cash value at any time. However, the company will probably assess a surrender charge unless the policy has been in force for a certain number of years.

6.) Universal life insurance offers two death benefit options, level or increasing.

a.) Under the level death benefit option, the policyowner may specify the amount of insurance. The death benefit equals the cash values plus the remaining pure insurance (decreasing term plus increasing cash values). This keeps the death benefit level. If the cash values approach the face amount before the policy matures, an additional amount of insurance, called the corridor, is maintained in addition to the cash values. This corridor must exist for the policy to continue to qualify as life insurance and retain its tax-sheltered cash value accumulation status.

b.) Under the increasing death benefit option, the death benefit equals the face amount (pure insurance) plus the cash values (level term plus increasing cash values). To comply with the Internal Revenue Code's definition of life insurance, the cash values cannot be disproportionately larger than the term insurance protection.

Level Death Benefit Option

Minimum Amount of Pure Protection

Death Benefit

Corridor

Pure Insurance

Cash Values

Increasing Death Benefit Option

Death Benefit

Pure Insurance

Cash Values

b. Variable life Variable life insurance (VLI) was designed to combine the protection and savings features of life insurance with the growth potential of common stocks. Variable life insurance is a contract under which the benefits, payable upon death or surrender, vary with the investment performance of an underlying portfolio of securities.

1.) These contracts provide a guaranteed minimum death benefit. Benefits paid may actually be higher but this depends upon the fluctuating market value of investments behind the contract at the time of the insured's death. The cash surrender value also fluctuates with the market value of the investment portfolio.

2.) VLI has cash values that increase or decrease daily depending upon investment results, with no guarantee as to the amount of cash value.

3.) Benefits will also vary in relationship to the investment experience.

4.) Loan provisions are included so that the policyowner may borrow from the cash value if necessary.

5.) Nonforfeiture and reinstatement provisions are similar to those found in traditional life insurance policies. Premiums paid on VLI are fixed.

c. Variable universal life insurance Variable universal life (VUL), or flexible premium variable life, blends many features of universal life and variable life. Premium flexibility, cash value investment control, and death benefit flexibility are key among these features. These features give VUL its unique characteristics and make it responsive to policyowners' needs.

1.) Every variable universal life insurance policy is issued with a minimum scheduled premium based on an initial specified death benefit. This initial premium establishes the plan, meets first-year expenses, and provides funding to cover the cost of insurance protection. Once they pay this initial premium, policyowners can pay whatever premium amount they wish, with certain limitations. Provided adequate cash value is available to cover periodic charges and the cost of insurance, they can suspend or reduce premium payments. Policyowners may even be able to avoid paying premiums indefinitely if their cash values realize consistently strong investment returns.

2.) Conversely, policyowners wishing to increase death benefits or take advantage of tax-favored accumulation of cash values can pay additional premiums into their plans. However, most policies contain maximum limits, and if the increase is above a certain amount, proof of insurability may be required.

3.) Cash value in a VUL plan is maintained separately from the rest of the plan. At the time of application, the policyowner elects to have the net premiums and cash values allocated to one or more separate account investment options. These accounts are usually mutual funds created and maintained by the insurance company and other investment companies. These funds are kept in separate accounts and function independently of the insurance company's assets. Earnings or losses accrue directly to the policyowner's cash value, subject to stated charges and management fees. Policyowners can redirect future premiums and switch accounts periodically, generally once a year, without charge. The result is a life insurance policy that provides policyowners with self-directed investment options.

4.) VUL policies offer both a level death benefit, which provides for a fixed death benefit (until the policy values reach the corridor level) and potential higher cash value accumulation, or a variable death benefit, which provides a death benefit that fluctuates in response to the performance of investments.

5.) Under the level death benefit, the policyowner specifies the total death benefit in the policy. This amount remains constant and does not fluctuate as cash values increase or decrease. Instead, cash values build up within the policy until they reach the corridor, at which time the death benefit will increase to corresponding increases in the cash value. Until that point the cash value simply accumulates, with each increase replacing a corresponding amount of pure insurance needed to keep the death benefit at the specified amount.

6.) Under the variable death benefit, the policyowner selects a specified amount of pure insurance coverage which remains constant. The death benefit payable at any time is a combination of the specified, or face, amount and the cash value within the policy. Essentially, the cash value is added to the specified amount to create the total death benefit. Under this option, the emphasis is on the potential for both cash value and death benefit growth. This option is recommended for policyowners who want favorable investment results and additional premiums reflected directly in increased benefits.

7.) Like universal life, VUL policies permit partial withdrawals, allowing the owner to tap the cash value without incurring any indebtedness. Policyowners need not repay those funds and no interest is incurred on the amount withdrawn. Withdrawals affect the policy's future earnings, and their effect on the death benefit depends on the death benefit option in force. Partial withdrawals taken in a policy's early years may be subject to surrender charges (when the insurer is trying to recover the costs of issuing the policy.)

d. Current assumption whole life (CAWL) Considered a form of interest-sensitive whole life, current assumption whole life (CAWL) products use:

- ■ an accumulation account (composed of the premium), less expense and mortality charges, and credited with interest based on current rates;
- ■ a surrender charge, fixed at issue, which is deducted from the accumulation account to derive the policy's net surrender value; and
- ■ a fixed death benefit and a maximum premium level set at time of issue.

1.) CAWL products may be classified into a low premium or high premium category. The low premium version includes a **redetermination provision** which states that after the initial guarantee period, the insurer can redetermine the premium using the same or new assumptions as to future interest.

2.) The high premium version possesses an **optional pay-up** which states that the policyholder may choose to cease paying premiums at a given point in time and actually have a paid-up policy. Incentive is provided to the policyowner to continue paying premiums because, unlike universal life, CAWL will lapse if the premium is not paid.

6. **Combination policies** Life insurance companies also make available special types of policies or combination contracts that may be purchased separately or added as a rider to whole life plans.

   a. **Family maintenance policy/rider (FMP/R)** This type of contract is most commonly used as a rider to a whole life plan. Family maintenance policies (FMP) are also designed to provide additional income to the survivors of the primary wage earner.

      1.) FMPs include a combination of level term insurance and whole life.

      2.) The FMP pays a monthly benefit amount to the insured's survivors for a specified payment period beginning with the date of the insured's death and continuing for the full (original) monthly benefit period.

         a.) For example, Mr. Smith purchases a $50,000 whole life policy and adds a family maintenance rider paying $500 per month for 10 years. Three years into the contract, Mr. Smith dies; the actual monthly benefit payment period begins at Mr. Smith's death. His survivors will receive $500 for the next 10 years. His beneficiary will also receive the face amount of $50,000, either at his death or when the monthly payments end.

   b. **Multiple or double protection policies** Many companies issue plans which pay a multiple of the face amount if the insured dies within a specified period and only the face amount if he dies following the expiration of that specified period.

   c. **Joint life insurance** This is a contract written on two or more lives. This type of contract promises to pay the face amount in the event of the first death with regard to all the lives covered. Therefore, there is no coverage provided after the first person dies.

      1.) If the policy is payable upon the death of the last of the two lives, it is referred to as a **survivorship-life** (last-survivor) **policy**.

      2.) Joint life policies may be written utilizing any type of whole life or term insurance plan.

II. ANNUITIES

An annuity is different from life insurance since it provides income to a person (the **annuitant**) while he is alive whereas life insurance provides income to survivors upon the death of an insured. An annuity may be defined as periodic payments made over a fixed period for the duration of a person's life. It may also be referred to as the systematic liquidation of an estate. An annuity may be classified according to how premiums are paid, when benefits are received, the amount of the monthly benefit, and more. Some of these classifications are as follows.

A. ACCORDING TO PREMIUM PAYMENTS

1. **Single premium plans** A **single premium annuity** is funded with a single, lump-sum amount, which creates the annuity principal. The insurer agrees to pay the annuitant (the person receiving the benefits) benefits in installments soon after it receives the premium or in the future. Payouts may be made monthly, semiannually, or annually.

2. **Periodic premium plans** These plans may be either level (scheduled) or flexible premiums.

    a. **Level premium** The insured agrees to pay the same premium per year to the insurer to a specified age. The purpose of level (scheduled) premium annuities is to create a specified amount of annuity funds. At the designated age, the annuity fund is annuitized and converted into a stream of payments to the annuitant.

    b. **Flexible premium** Under this plan, the annuitant/insured will pay a periodic flexible premium from the date of purchase until the plan matures. The premiums paid may vary from year to year. In other words, the insured may pay whatever he wishes each year. Most of these plans have a minimum premium requirement (such as $100) and the amount of the annuity benefit will depend upon the size of the accumulated funds when payouts begin.

B. ACCORDING TO THE TIME WHEN BENEFITS COMMENCE There are two basic classifications as to when annuity benefits begin.

1. **Immediate annuity** An **immediate annuity** is an annuity under which the first benefit payment is due one payment interval from the date of purchase. In other words, the first benefit payment to an annuitant would be made at the end of the initial income period (whether that is monthly, quarterly, or annually) following the purchase of an annuity. These annuities must always be purchased with a single premium. Therefore, no benefit payments are ever made until the entire purchase price of the annuity has been made to the insurer.

2. **Deferred annuity** A **deferred annuity** may be purchased with either a single or periodic premium. Under this type of annuity, there must be a period longer than one benefit payment interval before payments begin. The longer the deferred period, the more flexibility may be allowed in premium payments. In most cases, several years must elapse before benefit payments begin.

C. ACCORDING TO THE SOURCE (UNITS) OF ANNUITY INCOME Some annuities may also be classified by the source of the income payments made. In other words, annuities are designed according to the units in which the payout benefits are expressed or the amount of the monthly benefit.

1. Fixed annuity A fixed annuity guarantees a specified (fixed) number of dollars which will be paid each month once the payment period commences. With a fixed annuity, the annuitant knows the exact (fixed) amount that will be received each month. Most premiums paid for these annuities are invested in fixed-dollar investments such as bonds, which help guarantee the fixed benefit.

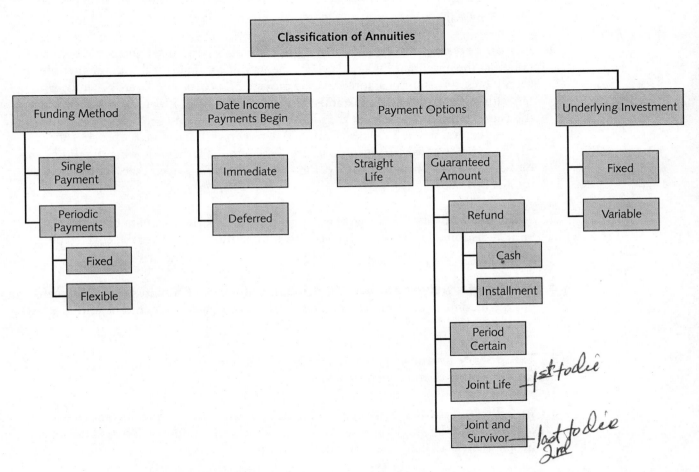

2. Variable annuity A variable annuity provides monthly benefits based upon a fixed amount of annuity units, rather than specific, fixed-dollar amounts which characterize fixed annuities. The exact value of a unit is determined each time the benefit is to be paid. Because premium payments are invested in common stocks and other equity investments, the value of the units generally varies each month and cannot be guaranteed.

3. Equity indexed annuities These annuities have most of the features of fixed annuity contracts, except that the interest credited to the annuity owner's account is tied to a stock market-related (equity) index, such as the Standard & Poor's 500 Index. Unlike variable annuities, an equity indexed annuity cannot decrease in value. Besides having a fixed minimum guarantee (somewhat similar to a fixed annuity), the value of an annuity owner's account can increase only because of stock market appreciation. If the market is flat or declining, the account value will not decrease in value.

D.   FORMS OF ANNUITY INCOME (SETTLEMENT OPTIONS)   The manner in which annuity payments are made can be matched to meet specific needs.

1.   **Life annuity (no refund)**   This form of annuity provides payments to an annuitant from a specified date and for the rest of the annuitant's life. Payments cease upon the annuitant's death with no refund to survivors. A pure life annuity has the potential for providing the maximum income per dollar of premium (if the annuitant lives beyond life expectancy).

2.   **Period certain annuity**   These annuities provide a guaranteed number of payments (whether the annuitant lives or dies). Payments will continue for the annuitant's life even if he survives the guaranteed period provided. These annuities are generally written with monthly payments guaranteed for a period of 5, 10, 15, or 20 years. The longer the period selected, the smaller the monthly income payment (i.e., $1,000 per month, 10 years certain versus $500 per month, 20 years certain). If a contract provides for $1,000 per month with 10 years certain and the annuitant dies following the third year, his beneficiary will receive $1,000 per month for remaining seven years (or an aggregate total of $84,000).

3.   **Joint life annuity**   This type of annuity provides a specified amount of income for two or more persons. The income received ceases upon the first death of the covered persons (annuitants).

4.   **Joint and survivor annuity**   Benefits under this type of annuity are paid throughout the lifetime of one or more annuitants. Therefore, payments continue until the last annuitant dies.

5.   **Temporary annuity**   This annuity pays benefits for a specific number of years or until the annuitant's death, whichever comes first.

6.   **Installment refund annuity**   This annuity guarantees to pay an income to the annuitant each year as long as he lives. Upon death, the annuity will refund the remaining payments to a beneficiary in installments.

7.   **Cash refund annuity**   This annuity pays, in a lump sum, the difference between the amount deposited into the annuity and the benefits received before the annuitant's death. The lump-sum payment will be made to the annuitant's beneficiary or estate.

E.   INCOME TAXATION OF ANNUITY BENEFITS   Annuity benefit payments are a combination of principal and interest. Accordingly, they are taxed in a manner consistent with other types of income. The portion of the benefit payments that represents a return of principal (i.e., the contributions made by the annuitant) are not taxed. However, the portion representing interest earned on the declining principal is taxed. The result, over the benefit payment period, is a tax-free return of the annuitant's investment and taxes on the balance (interest earned).

TEST TOPIC ALERT

For a given annuity sum, the life annuity provides the largest periodic benefit payment, compared to other forms of annuity payouts that are based on a lifespan.

TAKE NOTE

A 10% penalty tax is imposed on withdrawals from a deferred annuity before age 59½ . Withdrawals after age 59½ are not subject to the 10% penalty, but are still taxable as ordinary income.

1. **Exclusion ratio** An exclusion ratio is applied to each benefit payment the annuitant receives:

$$\frac{\text{Investment in the Contract}}{\text{Expected Return}} = \text{Exclusion Ratio}$$

The investment in the contract is the amount of money paid into the annuity. The expected return is the annual guaranteed benefit the annuitant receives, multiplied by the number of years of his life expectancy. The resulting ratio is applied to the benefit payments, allowing the annuitant to exclude a like percentage from income.

   a. **Example:** Joan purchased an annuity for $10,800. Under its terms, the annuity will pay her $100 a month for life. If Joan is 65 years old, her life expectancy, as taken from IRS life expectancy tables, is 20 years. Her expected return is $24,000 ([20 × 12] × $100). Her cost ($10,800) divided by her expected return of $24,000 equals 45%. This is the percentage of each annuity payment that she can exclude from her taxable income. Each year until Joan's net cost is recovered, she will receive $540 (45% of $1,200) tax free. She must include $660 ($1,200 – $540) in her taxable income.

2. **Deferred annuities** Deferred annuities accumulate interest earnings on a tax-deferred basis. While no taxes are imposed on the annuity during the accumulation phase, taxes are imposed when the contract begins to pay its benefits (in accordance with the exclusion ratio just described). To discourage the use of deferred annuities as 10% short-term investments, the Internal Revenue Code imposes a penalty (as well as taxes) on early withdrawals and loans from annuities. Partial withdrawals are treated first as earnings income and are thus taxable as ordinary income. Only after all earnings have been taxed are withdrawals considered a return of principal.

U N I T   Q U I Z

1. Which of the following types of annuities provides guaranteed unit amounts rather than guaranteed dollar amounts?
   A. Fixed
   B. Single premium
   C. Variable
   D. Flexible

2. A policy that provides life insurance protection during a specific period of time or the payment of the face amount if the insured lives beyond the specified period best describes
   A. a family income policy
   B. universal life
   C. adjustable life
   D. an endowment

3. Mr. James borrows funds from a bank to make improvements to his home. The bank suggests that he purchase life insurance that will pay off his loan amount in the event of his premature death. Which of the following would best help him achieve this objective?
   A. Level term
   B. Decreasing term
   C. Increasing term
   D. Convertible term

4. Which of the following statements regarding variable universal life insurance is CORRECT?
   A. It offers a combination of investment options and a guaranteed death benefit.
   B. The premiums paid are fixed at a level amount.
   C. This policy combines whole life and decreasing term coverage.
   D. Lower premiums are charged in the early years of the policy.

5. The contract which at issue provides the maximum amount of insurance protection at the lowest outlay of funds best describes
   A. term insurance
   B. whole life insurance
   C. universal life insurance
   D. endowments

6. A contract that is characterized by an increasing death benefit with each succeeding payment is known as
   A. level term
   B. decreasing term
   C. convertible term
   D. increasing term

7. When an insured purchases a decreasing term life insurance contract, which of the following elements decrease each year?
   A. Cash savings value
   B. Loan value
   C. Premium payment
   D. Face amount of coverage

8. Assume Amos, age 65, wants to ensure that he receives the largest possible monthly benefit from his fixed annuity contract. Which settlement option should he select?
   A. Life annuity
   B. Life and 10-year certain
   C. Life and 20-year certain
   D. Joint life

9. All of the following types of life insurance policies are characterized by having a cash value accumulation element EXCEPT
   A. Universal life
   B. Whole life
   C. Term life
   D. Variable life

10. A life insurance contract that combines level term insurance with a whole life policy describes a
    A. current assumption policy
    B. family maintenance policy
    C. family income policy
    D. double protection policy

ANSWERS

1. C	2. D	3. B	4. A	5. A
6. D	7. D	8. A	9. C	10. B

DISCUSSION QUESTIONS

1. Define life insurance.

2. Briefly describe some of the characteristics of an ordinary life contract.

3. List some advantages of a single premium life policy.

4. Discuss the advantages of a universal life policy.

5. Discuss the basic characteristics of a variable universal life policy.

6. Contrast level and decreasing term insurance.

7. Compare and contrast a term contract's renewable and convertible features.

8. Describe how an immediate annuity works.

9. Compare the characteristics of a fixed and variable annuity.

10. Briefly describe the following:
    A. Cash refund annuity
    B. Installment refund annuity
    C. Endowment
    D. Family maintenance policy

4

Life Insurance Policy Provisions, Riders, Options, and Exclusions

KEY TERMS

Waiver	Spendthrift Clause	Dividend Options
Insurability	Common Disaster	Incontestability
Payor	Revocable	Assignment
Living Benefits	Irrevocable	Settlement Options
Free Look	Grace Period	Conversion
Consideration	Mortality	Exclusions
Primary	Reinstatement	
Contingent	Nonforfeiture	

I. POLICY RIDERS

Supplemental additions called **riders** are frequently included or made a part of a life insurance policy. A rider may be used to add more life insurance or add a different type of insurance, such as disability or long-term care coverage to the base policy. A rider may also specify conditions that could affect the coverage.

A. WAIVER OF PREMIUM The waiver of premium rider found in a life insurance contract states that if an insured becomes totally disabled during the term of the policy, premium payments will be waived during the period of disability. The contract will remain in force just as if the insured continued to pay the premium. An additional premium is charged for this benefit and it is subject to a waiting period (typically, 90 days). If the insured is still disabled after this period, premiums are waived retroactively from the date of disability.

   1. Some life insurance contracts stipulate that disability must occur prior to a specified age, such as 60 or 65.

   2. The additional premium paid for this benefit does not increase the face amount of the policy nor the policy's cash value.

B. GUARANTEED INSURABILITY Many insurance companies now offer a **guaranteed-insurability option (GIO)**, also known as a **guaranteed-insurability benefit (GIB)**, which allows a policyholder to purchase specified amounts of additional insurance without evidence of insurability.

   1. The new insurance is issued at standard rates on the basis of the insured's attained age when the option is exercised.

   2. In most cases, this benefit allows an insured to purchase additional insurance coverage at three-year intervals beginning with the policy anniversary nearest his 25th birthday and terminating with the anniversary nearest his 40th birthday.

   3. The amount of additional insurance that may be purchased on each of the specified dates is equal to the face of the original policy or $10,000, whichever is less.

   4. Some insurers provide additional option dates at other important periods in the insured's life such as marriage or the birth of a child.

   5. This benefit is available for an additional premium.

C. PAYOR BENEFIT This rider or provision may be added to a life insurance contract which provides for the continuance of insurance coverage on the life of a juvenile in the event of the death or total disability of the individual responsible for the payment of the premiums (a parent or guardian). This benefit may be added for an additional premium and is also referred to as the **payor clause**.

   1. This benefit provides that premiums will be waived until the insured attains a specified age or the maturity date of the contract, whichever is earlier, in the event that the payor dies or becomes disabled.

2. A **jumping juvenile** or **junior estate builder** are types of policies that provide juvenile insurance. They are usually issued in $1,000 units for juveniles ages 1 to 15. When the child reaches age 21, the face amount increases to five times its original amount with no premium increases.

D. ACCIDENTAL DEATH An accidental death benefit clause or rider may also be added to a life insurance policy. This benefit is sometimes referred to as **double indemnity** because it provides double the face amount of the policy if the insured dies due to an accident.

   1. An additional premium will be charged for this benefit.

   2. To be covered, death must occur within 90 days of an accident. The basic purpose of this restriction is to make sure that the accident is the only cause of death.

   3. Payment will not be made by an insurer if death results from certain causes, including illegal activities; war; aviation activities (except passenger travel on scheduled or commercial airlines); or where an accident was involved in conjunction with illness, disease, or mental infirmity.

   4. Accidental death or double indemnity coverage is usually limited to age 60, 65, or, in few cases, age 70.

   5. Accidental death and dismemberment insurance (AD&D) This also provides benefits for death due to an accident (the death benefit is called the **principal sum**), or for the loss of one or more hands, feet, arms, legs, or loss of sight (this benefit is called the **capital sum** and is a percentage of the principal sum based on the extent of the dismemberment).

E. TERM RIDERS Term riders may be attached to amounts of whole life insurance to provide greater amounts of protection while reducing costs. For example, it is less expensive to purchase a $50,000 whole life policy with a $100,000 term rider than to purchase $150,000 of whole life.

F. OTHER INSUREDS Coverage for a spouse may be obtained to cover the extra expenses of child care and home-related costs by purchasing some sort of family term insurance. This insurance may also be used to protect dependent parents.

G. ACCELERATED (LIVING) BENEFITS This rider allows an insured to utilize a portion of the policy's death benefit while he is still alive. For example, if the insured is suffering from a terminal illness and his $100,000 policy includes a 50% accelerated benefit, he may withdraw up to $50,000 to pay for medical expenses. Whatever amount is withdrawn will be deducted from the face amount when death occurs. Accelerated benefits are paid free from federal income taxation if the insured person is terminally ill.

H. COST OF LIVING RIDER Some companies offer their applicants the ability to guard against the eroding effects of inflation. A cost of living (COL) or cost of living adjustment (COLA) rider can provide increases in the amount of insurance protection without requiring the insured to provide evidence of insurability. The amount of increase is tied to an increase in an inflation index, most commonly the Consumer Price Index (CPI). Depending on the type of base policy, these riders can take several different forms.

1. For standard whole life policies, a COL rider is usually offered as an increasing term insurance rider that is attached to the base policy. The COL rider provides for automatic increases in the policy death benefit in proportion to increases in the CPI. Generally, there is a maximum percentage increase, such as 5%, allowed in any one year. When the increase becomes effective, the policyowner is billed for the additional coverage.

2. Adjustable life insurance frequently includes a COL agreement. The COL agreement waives the requirement for evidence of insurability for limited face amount increases that are intended to match increases in the CPI. The face amount increase is accompanied by an increase in premium, although the agreement itself is usually offered at no charge to the policyowner.

3. The COL agreement can also be used, with certain restrictions, with term and whole life policies. They are not practical with universal life (UL) policies, however, because of the high degree of flexibility already present in UL policies.

II. COMMON POLICY PROVISIONS AND OPTIONS

From insurer to insurer and contract to contract, there are certain provisions that are included in virtually every life insurance policy. Specific wording will vary, but the content and effect of these provisions are fairly constant across the industry.

A. ENTIRE CONTRACT The entire contract provision is also referred to as the **entire contract clause**. This provision states that the policy and a copy of the application constitutes the entire contract between the insurer and the insured. A copy of the life insurance application is attached to the policy.

1. The life insurance contract provides that all statements made by the insured in the application will be considered as representations and not warranties.

2. The basic purpose of the clause is to provide assurance to the policyowner that he has in his possession all necessary documents with regard to his life insurance coverage.

3. The clause also prevents the policyowner and the producer from unilaterally amending the policy.

B. INSURING CLAUSE The insuring agreement or insuring clause states that the insurer agrees to provide life insurance protection for the named insured which will be paid to a designated beneficiary when proof of death is received by the insurer.

1. The insuring clause states the party to be covered by the life contract and names the beneficiary who will receive the policy proceeds in the event of the insured's death. If no beneficiary is named in the contract, the policy proceeds will be paid to the insured's estate.

2. The face page of the life insurance contract expresses the promise of the insurer and lists the name of the company, insured, amount of insurance carried, the mode and amount of premium, and when coverage is effective.

C. **FREE LOOK** This policy provision permits the policyowner to take a specified number of days to examine the life insurance contract. If the new policyowner decides that the purchase was unnecessary or unwise, the contract may be cancelled with the entire premium refunded by the insurer.

   1. The free look laws vary in each state and range from 10- to 20-day periods.

   2. The free look period begins when the policyowner receives the policy.

   3. For the applicant to receive a premium refund, the policy must be returned within 10 or 20 days from the date the policy is delivered.

D. **CONSIDERATION CLAUSE** This provision or clause in a life insurance policy provides that the insurance coverage is granted in consideration of the application and the payment of the initial premium. The payment of the initial premium is required to place the insurance coverage in effect.

   1. The insured's consideration is the premium paid and the representations made in the application.

   2. The insurer's consideration is the promise to pay the face amount of the contract to the named beneficiary upon the death of the insured.

E. **OWNER'S RIGHTS** The owner of a life insurance contract is usually the applicant, the insured, or the premium payer. The owner of a policy has several stipulated rights in the contract. Some of these rights include:
   - changing the beneficiary;
   - receiving dividends if any are paid;
   - borrowing funds from the cash value if they exist; and
   - assignment of some or all the rights of the contract to another party.

F. **THIRD-PARTY OWNERSHIP** Third-party ownership exists when a party other than the insured is the owner of the policy. For example, third-party owners could include a wife who is the owner of a husband's policy, a parent who is the owner of a child's policy, or a corporation that is the owner of a director or officer's policy.

G. **ELIGIBLE BENEFICIARIES** Life insurance companies place few restrictions on who may be named the beneficiary of a life insurance policy. The decision rests solely with the owner of the policy. However, in some cases, the insurer must consider the issue of insurable interest. Insurable interest is not a concern when the applicant for a policy is also the insured. By law, individuals are presumed to have an unlimited insurable interest in their own lives. The situation differs when the applicant is not the insured (a third-party applicant). When a third-party applicant names himself as beneficiary, insurable interest must exist between the applicant and insured. When a third-party applicant names yet another as beneficiary, most states require that insurable interest exist between that beneficiary and the insured.

1. **Individuals as beneficiaries** In most cases, an individual is selected to be the sole or proportional beneficiary of a life insurance policy. There may be one named individual or more than one.

2. **Businesses as beneficiaries** There is no question that insurable interest exists in business relationships. Professional sports clubs have an insurable interest in the lives of their best players. Partnerships have an insurable interest in the lives of their partners. Small corporations have an insurable interest in the lives of their key employees. Creditors have an insurable interest in the lives of their debtors. Life insurance policies may designate businesses as beneficiaries.

3. **Trusts as beneficiaries** A trust is a legal arrangement for the ownership of property by one party for the benefit of another. Designating a trust as the beneficiary of a life insurance policy means that the proceeds will be paid to the trust for the ultimate benefit and use by another. Trusts are managed by trustees who have the fiduciary responsibility to oversee and handle the trust and its funds for its beneficiaries.

4. **Estates as beneficiaries** Policyowners may designate their estates as beneficiaries so that, upon death, the proceeds can be used to meet federal estate taxes, debts, and other administrative costs, leaving other assets intact to pass on to heirs.

5. **Charities as beneficiaries** Life insurance is one of the most attractive and flexible ways to make a contribution to a church, educational institution, hospital, public welfare agency, or similar nonprofit organization. One of the benefits of making a contribution of life insurance proceeds—in contrast to leaving a bequest in a will—is that the gift cannot be contested by disgruntled heirs. This is because life insurance proceeds are not part of the insured donor's probate estate.

6. **Minors as beneficiaries** Naming minors as life insurance beneficiaries can present some legal and logistical complications. For instance, the minor may not have the legal capacity to give the insurance company a signed release for receipt of the policy pro-

ceeds. (Some states have adopted special laws that allow only minors of specified ages, such as age 15, to sign a valid receipt.) If an insurer were to pay the proceeds and not receive a receipt, the minor could legally demand payment a second time upon reaching the age of majority. Furthermore, the minor may lack the judgment or expertise to manage the proceeds properly. Nonetheless, insurers recognize that policyowners may want minors to benefit from an insurance policy. In those cases, and in accordance with the laws of the state, insurers may:

   a. make limited payments to an adult guardian for the benefit of the minor beneficiary;

   b. retain the policy proceeds at interest and pay them out when the child reaches majority or when an adult guardian is appointed; or

   c. place the proceeds in a trust for the present or future benefit of the minor, as determined by the trustee.

7. Classes as beneficiaries Rather than specifying one or more beneficiaries by name, the policyowner can designate a class or group of beneficiaries. For example, **children of the insured** and **my children** are class designations.

H.   PRIMARY AND CONTINGENT BENEFICIARIES

1. Primary beneficiary The **primary beneficiary** is the person designated by the applicant to receive the face amount of the proceeds upon the insured's death.

   a. The primary beneficiary may also be referred to as the **designated recipient**.

   b. In most cases, a husband stipulates that his wife will be the primary beneficiary and a wife usually designates her husband as her primary beneficiary.

2. Contingent beneficiary The **contingent beneficiary** is the individual who will be paid the policy proceeds if the primary beneficiary predeceases the insured. In other words, this **secondary beneficiary** will receive the face amount of the contract if the primary beneficiary is not living at the time the insured dies.

   a. Contingent beneficiaries may also receive installment payments that were being paid to the primary beneficiary if that person dies.

   b. The most common type of contingent beneficiary designation includes children of the insured.

   c. A **tertiary beneficiary** is the third party in line to receive policy proceeds if the primary and contingent beneficiaries predecease the insured.

   d. If no contingent beneficiary is present, proceeds are left to the insured's estate.

3. Beneficiary clauses

a. Common disaster clause This clause states that in case of death in a common accident (disaster), the insured will be presumed to have survived the beneficiary. This prevents the payment of the insurance proceeds to the estate of the beneficiary and thus permits the proceeds to be distributed to any contingent beneficiaries or wherever else provided for by the policy. This clause helps to reduce estate taxes since the proceeds will not be taxed in both estates.

1.) Uniform Simultaneous Death Act Enacted in most states, this law stipulates that if the insured and the primary beneficiary are killed in the same accident and there is insufficient evidence to show who died first, the policy proceeds are to be distributed as if the insured died last. This law allows the insurance company to pay the proceeds to a secondary or other contingent beneficiary. If no contingent beneficiary has been named, the insured's estate will receive the proceeds.

b. Spendthrift clause This is a clause that may be included in a life insurance contract, the purpose of which is to protect the policy proceeds from the claims of the beneficiary's creditors.

1.) This clause takes away all rights of the beneficiary to change the time of payment or the amount of installments. The beneficiary is unable to borrow or assign any of the proceeds as well, which protects the beneficiary from any detrimental spending habits.

2.) This clause may be attached to the contract as a rider or in the form of an endorsement.

3.) It prevents proceeds from being attached by creditors.

I. DISTRIBUTION BY DESCENT When life insurance proceeds are to be distributed to a person's descendants, a *per stirpes* or a *per capita* approach generally is used.

1. The term *per stirpes* means by the root or by way of branches. A per stirpes distribution means that a beneficiary's share of a policy's proceeds will be passed down to their living child or children in equal shares should they (the named beneficiary) predecease the insured.

2. The term *per capita* means per person or by the head. A per capita distribution means that a policy's proceeds are paid only to the beneficiaries who are living and have been named in the policy.

3. Example: Arthur makes the following designation with respect to the proceeds of his life insurance policy: To his four children—Amy, Brian, Charlie, and Denise—as co-beneficiaries to share equally in the proceeds, and to the surviving children of any deceased children of Arthur, per stirpes. Brian predeceases Arthur, leaving two children, Xavier and Yolanda.

a. The per stirpes distribution means that the surviving co-beneficiaries—Amy, Charlie, and Denise—will each receive a quarter share of the proceeds. Brian's quarter will be shared between Xavier and Yolanda, who will take their share by their father's representation.

b. On the other hand, Arthur could have made the following designation: to Amy, Brian, Charlie, and Denise in equal shares if they survive him, and to the surviving children of his children who predecease him, per capita. When Brian predeceases Arthur, Brian's children—Xavier and Yolanda—would be counted among the surviving beneficiaries to take an equal share. Consequently, the proceeds would be divided among Amy, Charlie, Denise, Xavier, and Yolanda, with each beneficiary taking a one-fifth share.

4. In short, the per capita beneficiary claims the policy's proceeds in his own right, while the per stirpes beneficiary receives the proceeds through the rights of another. Today, the per stirpes method of distribution is by far the more common approach.

J. REVOCABLE AND IRREVOCABLE BENEFICIARIES

1. Revocable beneficiary A revocable beneficiary is one that may be changed by the policyowner. The policyowner may change revocable beneficiaries without their knowledge or consent.

2. Irrevocable beneficiary The policyowner may also designate an individual to be an **irrevocable beneficiary**. In this case, the beneficiary designation cannot be changed without the consent of that named beneficiary. The policyowner retains all other ownership rights even though he selects an irrevocable beneficiary.

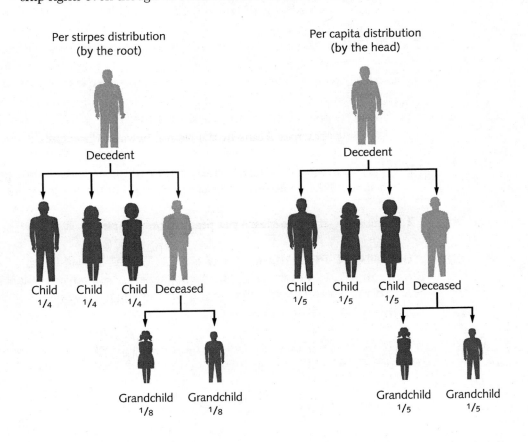

Per stirpes distribution (by the root)

Per capita distribution (by the head)

K. CHANGE OF BENEFICIARY Changing a designated beneficiary is an ownership right of the policyowner. If the policyowner desires to change the beneficiary, he must fill out an appropriate change of beneficiary form and return it to the insurer. The change of beneficiary form will stipulate the party (or parties) to be named as the new beneficiary. As mentioned previously, if a beneficiary has been named irrevocably, his permission must be secured before the policyowner can make any beneficiary change.

L. MODES OF PREMIUM PAYMENT The premium paying provision in a life insurance contract provides that all premiums (after the initial premium) must be payable in advance to the home office of the insurance company or to an agent designated by the company to collect premiums. Life insurance premiums may be paid annually, semiannually, quarterly, or monthly. If a policyowner pays the premium in any other mode but annually, an extra charge will be assessed.

1. Annual premiums are the least expensive of any mode, while monthly payments are the most expensive.

2. Monthly premiums may be paid to the company or withdrawn from the policyowner's checking account (check-o-matic or pre-authorized checking plans).

3. Life insurance premiums are based upon **mortality (mortality table statistics)**, interest, and expenses. The 1958 (or 1980) **commissioner's standard ordinary (CSO)** mortality tables are used to determine mortality costs, nonforfeiture values, and reserve calculations. Mortality tables are not used for rate-making.

4. The premiums for most whole life insurance policies remain level throughout the premium payment period. Flexible premium policies, such as universal life, permit the policyowner to decide the premium amount to be paid (within limits).

M. GRACE PERIOD Every life insurance contract contains a **grace period**. This is the period of time following the date that each premium is due during which the insurance policy remains in force and coverage is provided, even though the premium has not yet been paid.

1. Since the policy remains in force during the grace period, the face amount of the contract will be paid to a named beneficiary should the insured die during the grace period.

2. If proceeds are paid out during the grace period, any outstanding premium owed to the insurer will be deducted from the face amount of the contract.

3. Generally, the grace period in life insurance contracts is 31 days.

N. AUTOMATIC PREMIUM LOAN (APL) The APL provision may be added to a life insurance contract and protects the policyowner against the inadvertent lapsing of the contract. If the cash value is sufficient, a loan in the amount equal to the premium due is subtracted from the cash value to pay the premium.

1. In most instances, this provision must be requested by the policyowner at the time of application. Many companies do not allow it to be added once the policy is issued.

O. REINSTATEMENT If a life insurance contract was not surrendered for the cash savings value, many contracts permit reinstatement of the policy if it is effected within three years of the policy lapse.

   1. Proof of insurability may be requested by the insurer. In addition, all owed premiums (back premiums) must be paid.

   2. Many insurers request that a reinstatement application be completed. This means that statements made by the policyowner/applicant are again contestable for two years.

P. POLICY LOAN A policyowner has the right to borrow from the cash value and there is no legal obligation to repay the loan. Interest is assessed by the insurer for these borrowed funds and the interest rates are determined by each state. Currently, most life insurance contracts charge approximately 8% on some contracts and a variable interest rate on others.

   1. Any outstanding policy loans that are in existence at the time of the insured's death would reduce the policy proceeds. The outstanding loan would be subtracted from the face amount of the contract and the remainder paid to the named beneficiary.

   2. Interest on policy loans is payable annually at the rate specified. However, interest that is not paid when due will be added to the loan and bear interest at the same rate. If the total indebtedness equals or exceeds the cash value of the contract, the policy will terminate (subject to 31 days' notice to the insured or other policyowner).

Q. NONFORFEITURE OPTIONS These options or provisions provided by a life insurance contract are available to a policyowner who wishes to cease paying policy premiums. In situations where the policy premium is not paid, the nonforfeiture options prevent the loss of the investment in the life insurance policy since the cash value is not forfeited if the premium is not paid. Nonforfeiture options may go into effect automatically or, as stated, if desired by the insured. There are three nonforfeiture options: cash surrender, extended term insurance, and reduced paid-up insurance.

   1. Cash surrender value The first option available to the policyowner is to surrender the policy for its cash value. All types of permanent life insurance contracts may be surrendered to the company for the amount of cash which has accumulated. The cash surrender value increases each year that the policy remains in force. Therefore, the cash surrender value forms the basis of all the other surrender or nonforfeiture values.

      a. When an insured exercises the cash surrender value option, the policy is returned to the insurer and company has up to six months to pay the cash surrender value to the insured.

      b. In the majority of instances the insurer will send the cash surrender value payment to the insured within 30 days.

   2. Extended term insurance The second nonforfeiture option available to the policyowner provides extended term insurance. Under this option, the policyowner may request that the insurance company use the existing cash value to purchase term insurance equal to the face amount of the original policy with a single net premium. This term insurance will remain in effect for as long a period of time that can be purchased with the cash value available.

    a. Permanent insurance contracts include a table that illustrates to a policyowner the duration of the term period if this option is exercised.

    b. If a policyowner fails to select one of the nonforfeiture options when premium payments cease, this option generally goes into effect automatically.

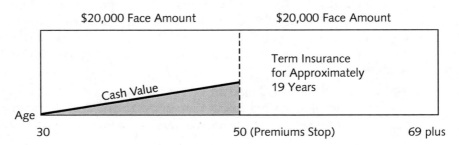

Extended Term Option

3. Reduced paid-up insurance With this option, the insurance company uses the cash value of the contract to purchase a single premium insurance contract of the same form (e.g., 20-pay life, ordinary life, and modified life) as the original policy. The amount of coverage will be much less than the original policy, but no more premium payments will be required. Thus, the policyowner/insured will receive a policy that is paid in full for life.

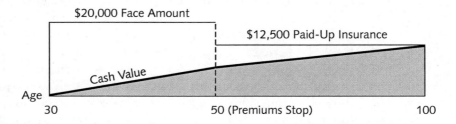

Reduced Paid-Up Term Option

R. DIVIDENDS AND DIVIDEND OPTIONS Life insurance policies that pay dividends are referred to as **participating policies**. Life contracts that do not pay dividends are referred to as **nonparticipating policies**. A participating policy refunds a portion of the premium to the insured in the form of an annual dividend. Dividends cannot be guaranteed by the insurer but, when paid, are based on the difference between the gross premium charged and the actual experience of the insurer.

    The experience of an insurer is determined by its ability to meet current obligations such as paying policy proceeds to a named beneficiary maintaining sound insurance company operations on a solvent financial basis, and other management and administrative expenses. There are several types of dividend options available to policyowners/insureds including the following.

1. **Cash payments** Dividends credited to a policyowner may be paid in cash to that individual and the insurer simply sends a check to the policyowner. Dividends paid in cash are not considered taxable income.

2. **Accumulation at interest** The policyowner may leave dividends with the insurer to accumulate at interest in much the same fashion as a savings account. The interest earned will be at a rate no less than the minimum rate specified in the contract. Dividends left with an insurer may be withdrawn at any time.

   a. If the insured dies, the insurer will add the dividends that have accumulated at interest to the face amount of the contract (which is paid to the named beneficiary).

   b. The interest earnings on dividends is considered taxable income when paid, even though the dividends themselves are not.

3. **Paid-up additions** Dividends may be used to purchase additional amounts of insurance which are added to the face amount of the contract. Paid-up additions are actually single premium purchases of as much life insurance as the amount of the dividend will purchase at the insured's attained age.

   a. The insurance additions will be paid-up or paid in full for life and actually increase the insured's death benefit.

4. **Reduced premium payments** A policyowner may apply dividends to reduce future premium payments. In this manner, the policyowner will pay the difference between the premium due and the dividend amount.

5. **One-year term insurance option** With this option, the policyowner may use dividends to purchase additional one-year term insurance up to the amount of the cash value of the policy. The cost is based on the attained age of the insured. This particular option may be advantageous to a policyowner/insured whose life insurance needs fluctuate from year to year.

S. INCONTESTABILITY The incontestable clause of a life insurance policy states that after a specified period of time, the insurer may not dispute or contest the validity of the contract or the statements. After the contract has been in effect for a specific length of time, the insurance company agrees not to challenge any statements made by the applicant on the application.

1. The existence of this clause is unique to insurance contracts because it is contrary to general fraud laws. It simply indicates that an insurer, following the contestable period, may not claim that any misstatements in the application were made with the intent of the policyowner/insured to defraud.

2. The incontestable clause also assures that a named beneficiary will not have to substantiate any statements that were made on the application several years after the policy has been issued. In this situation, it would be extremely difficult for the named beneficiary and others to supply or substantiate information if the insurer contested the contract at the time of the insured's death.

3. The period of time after which the insurer can no longer contest a policy is two years from issue for most contracts.

T. ASSIGNMENT An assignment of a life insurance contract involves the transfer of some or all of the policyowner's legal rights under the contract to another party. The policy provisions concerning assignment do not usually grant the owner/insured any rights to assign, but do set out the procedures by which assignments may be made. When assignments are effected, the insurer must be notified.

The party receiving the assigned rights is known as the **assignee**. The person transferring these rights is known as the **assignor**. There are several types of assignments utilized, including the following.

1. Absolute assignment Under this type of assignment, the assignor transfers all rights to the assignee.

2. Collateral assignment This type involves the assignment of some but not all policy rights to an assignee. A lender may wish that a life contract be collaterally assigned so that it may draw upon the cash savings value if loan payments are not paid promptly.

U. SUICIDE CLAUSE When this clause is inserted in a life insurance contract, death by suicide is not covered during the policy's first two years.

1. If suicide occurs during this initial two-year period, premiums are refunded but no face amount (death benefit) is paid.

2. Following the two-year period, coverage is provided for suicide.

V. MISSTATEMENT OF AGE OR SEX Under this provision, the policy provides for an adjustment of benefits payable if it is discovered that, after an insured's death, or at time of claim, his age was misstated on an insurance policy application. Specifically, the benefit payable will be adjusted to an amount that the premium would have purchased at the correct age. An adjustment is involved whether the age was misstated higher or lower than it actually was.

1. Any inaccuracy regarding the applicant's sex would be treated in the same manner, since premiums for females may be less expensive than those for males.

W. SETTLEMENT OPTIONS At the time a life insurance contract is purchased, a policyowner should consider the manner in which the proceeds of the policy will be paid when it matures or when the insured dies. Any failure to adequately prepare for these contingencies may defeat the purpose for which the insurance was purchased. The policyowner may select from several settlement options to have the policy accomplish for the insured what he would like it to do. Death benefit settlement options are usually designated in the insurance contract and are used to define how the policy proceeds will be paid to the named beneficiary or the insured's estate.

1. Lump-sum payment Under this option, the proceeds of the policy are paid in a lump sum unless otherwise directed by the policyowner/insured during his lifetime. A lump-sum settlement is not really considered an option since life insurance contracts usually provide for a lump-sum settlement in the event of an insured's death. It is the most common form of policy proceeds distribution.

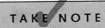

TAKE NOTE

Settlement options are the ways in which the death benefit proceeds from a life insurance policy can be paid to the beneficiary.

2. **Fixed amount option** Under this settlement option, the amount of income is the primary concern rather than a period of time (e.g., fixed-period) during which policy proceeds and interest earned are to be liquidated. Under this option, a fixed amount of income is designated to be paid at specific intervals (e.g., $2,000 per month). This amount is continued until the proceeds and any interest earned are exhausted.

   a. In most cases, this settlement option is more advantageous than the fixed-period option, since it is much more flexible. Insurers allow the insured to specify varying amounts of income at various times.

   b. The amount of each installment is the controlling factor under this option as the dollar amount to be paid is established and not the length of time for which installments are to be paid.

3. **Fixed-period option** This settlement option involves liquidating the proceeds and interest over a period of years, without reference to a life contingency (paid even if the beneficiary dies). It provides for the payment of policy proceeds in equal installments over a definite period of months or years.

   a. The amount of proceeds, the period of time, the guaranteed rate of interest, and the frequency of payments all determine the amount of each installment.

   b. The fixed-period option is valuable where the most important consideration is to provide income for a definite period of time.

4. **Life income option** This option distributes policy proceeds and interest with reference to life contingencies. Life income options are a form of life annuity and serve the same functions.

   a. The amount of each installment paid depends upon the type of life income selected, the amount of the proceeds, the rate of interest assumed, the age of the beneficiary when the income begins, and the sex of the beneficiary.

   b. Several life income options are available:
      - The pure life income option provides installment payments for as long as the primary beneficiary lives, with no return (refund) of principal guaranteed.
      - Refund life income options may take the form of a cash refund annuity or an installment refund annuity.
      - Life income with period certain (e.g., a specified number of years), occurs where installments are payable as long as the primary beneficiary lives, but should this beneficiary die before a predetermined number of years, the insurer will continue the installment to a second beneficiary until the end of the certain period.

✓

TAKE NOTE

Common exclusions found in most life insurance policies are death due to war and death due to aviation activities.

■ The joint and survivorship life income option occurs when, if at the death of the first party the second party is still living, installments are continued during the latter's lifetime.

5. **Interest only** Under this settlement option, the policyowner may leave policy proceeds with the insurer to earn interest. The proceeds are left with the insurer and the interest is paid to the beneficiary on an installment basis.

   a. This type of settlement option is generally selected when the policyowner wants to provide for contingent beneficiaries (such as children) after the death of the primary beneficiary (such as a parent).

   b. This option may also provide additional flexibility for the beneficiary since the proceeds are retained by the insurer until needed.

X. **CONVERSION OPTIONS** Policyowners have the ability to convert a term plan to a whole life plan if so desired. The most common conversion involves converting from a group term life policy to a whole life policy. (This will be discussed in a later Unit.)

III. COMMON POLICY EXCLUSIONS

Most life insurance contracts contain exclusions, or defined circumstances, that would not be covered if death occurs. Some of the more common exclusions are as follows.

A. **WAR EXCLUSION** This exclusion normally provides for the return of premium with interest in the event death occurs under conditions excluded in the policy. This clause is generally included in a life insurance contract that is issued during wartime or in time of impending military action. The purpose of this clause is to control adverse selection against the company by those individuals entering military service. Especially during wartime, an individual entering the military may purchase more insurance than he normally would. There are two basic types of war clauses.

   1. **Status type clause** If this clause is included in a life insurance contract, the policy will not pay in the event of death while the insured is in the military, regardless of the cause of death. This would hold true even if the insured were home on leave and his death had nothing to do with military action.

   2. **Results type clause** This type of clause is much less restrictive than the status type clause. A contract that includes this clause would not provide coverage for a member of the military if he were killed as a result of military exercises or service in general. However, if the individual was home on leave and fatally injured in an accident or died as a result of a nonservice related illness, the insurer would pay the face amount of the contract.

B. AVIATION EXCLUSION This exclusion restricts coverage in the event of death from aviation activities except when the insured is a fare-paying passenger. This exclusion is generally found in double indemnity (accidental death) provisions as well.

1. This exclusion generally restricts coverage for military pilots and crew members. Aviation-related deaths of test pilots, stunt pilots, student pilots, or crop dusting pilots are not covered (but may be covered for an additional premium). Commercial airline pilots and crew members are usually covered at standard rates.

   a. For example, a person who applies for life insurance coverage and is a private pilot, for example, may be issued a policy but an aviation rider or exclusion (excluding coverage for aviation activities) will be added to it.

U N I T   Q U I Z

1. How many months is the typical waiting period connected with the waiver of premium provision found in a life insurance contract?

    A. 1
    B. 2
    C. 3
    D. 6

2. The payor clause in a life insurance policy states that premiums will be

    A. waived until the insured child reaches age 30
    B. increased upon the death of the premium payor
    C. decreased upon the activation of the automatic premium loan provision
    D. waived until the insured child reaches the age of majority

3. All of the following information is included in the insuring clause EXCEPT the

    A. name of the insured
    B. name of the beneficiary
    C. dividend option selected
    D. insurer's promise to pay a benefit in the event of the insured's death

4. John Jones applies for a policy on September 1. It is received by the underwriting department on September 5, approved on September 7, and delivered to John on September 9. The 10-day free look period would expire on

    A. September 11
    B. September 15
    C. September 17
    D. September 19

5. With life insurance, the form of assignment where all rights are transferred to another person is known as

    A. collateral assignment
    B. absolute assignment
    C. consignment assignment
    D. split owner assignment

6. Gladys is the beneficiary of her husband Ben's life insurance policy. When Gladys dies, Ben neglects to name another beneficiary. At Ben's death five years later, the proceeds of his insurance policy will be paid to

    A. Gladys's heirs as named in her will
    B. Ben's heirs as named in his will
    C. Ben's estate
    D. the state in which Ben resided at the time of his death

7. All of the following statements are correct regarding beneficiaries EXCEPT

    A. irrevocable beneficiaries may be changed by the policyowner at any time if permission is granted by the beneficiary
    B. a tertiary beneficiary receives policy proceeds if the primary and contingent beneficiaries predecease the insured
    C. contingent beneficiaries share the policy proceeds with the primary beneficiary
    D. a spendthrift clause protects proceeds from the beneficiary's creditors

8. For a life insurance policy, the least expensive mode of premium is

    A. annual
    B. semiannual
    C. quarterly
    D. monthly

9. All of the following are types of nonforfeiture options EXCEPT

    A. fixed-period
    B. extended term
    C. reduced paid-up insurance
    D. surrender for cash

10. Which of the following insurance settlement options provides for the payment of proceeds over a specified time?

    A. Life income option
    B. Fixed-amount
    C. Fixed-period
    D. Interest only

ANSWERS

1. C   2. D   3. C   4. D   5. B
6. C   7. C   8. A   9. A   10. C

DISCUSSION QUESTIONS

1. Briefly discuss how the waiver of premium option functions.

2. Identify the two major components which make up the entire contract.

3. When does the free look period begin?

4. Contrast the primary and contingent beneficiaries. The revocable and irrevocable.

5. How does the automatic premium loan work?

6. What will occur when a policy loan is outstanding at the time of an insured's death?

7. Compare and contrast the three nonforfeiture options.

8. Discuss the concept of incontestability. Why is it important to an insured?

9. How would an incorrect age of the insured affect the policy proceeds of a life insurance contract?

10. Discuss the difference between the status and results clauses.

5

Taxes, Retirement Plans, and Social Security

KEY TERMS

Third-Party Ownership	Group Life	Conversion
Contributory Plans	Noncontributory Plans	Credit Life
IRA	SEP	Keogh Plans
TSA	Section 457	Defined Contribution
Defined Benefit	Key Employee	Buy-Sell Plans
Split-Dollar	Social Security	Quarter
PIA	Fully Insured	Currently Insured
1035 Exchange	Modified Endowment	

I. THIRD-PARTY OWNERSHIP

Third-party ownership refers to an arrangement in which a life insurance contract is owned by a party other than the insured. This type of ownership is usually used in business insurance settings and for estate planning purposes.

A. ESTABLISHMENT OF THIRD-PARTY OWNERSHIP Third-party arrangements need not necessarily be established at the time a contract is applied for, but may come about later as a result of a transfer or absolute assignment. A common example of third-party ownership involves a corporation purchasing a life insurance policy on a director or officer. In addition, wives who own policies covering the lives of their husbands and parents who own policies covering the lives of their children are other common examples of third-party ownership.

    1. Insurable interest Any third-party owner must have an insurable interest in the life of the person to be insured.

II. GROUP LIFE INSURANCE

Group life insurance differs from individual life insurance contracts in many areas including underwriting methods and some policy provisions. This life insurance coverage is concerned with the selection of risks by group factors rather than by individuals. Group life insurance protection involves a two-party contract (i.e., insurer and employer). An additional entity is also present—the covered employee. However, the covered employee does not receive a policy; instead, he is given a **certificate of coverage** which verifies that life insurance protection is in existence.

A. GROUP LIFE INSURANCE CHARACTERISTICS Characteristics of group life insurance include coverage that involves three parties and underwriting that focuses on the selection of risks by groups rather than by individuals. Another significant feature is that group life insurance coverage must be incidental to the purpose for which the group has been formed. This means that a group may not be formed for the specific purpose of providing insurance coverage for its members. Group life insurance coverage is generally issued without evidence of insurability being required by the individuals making up the group (though sometimes plans do require such proof). Since the employer is the policyowner and pays the premium, he receives the master policy. Most group life policies are term insurance.

B. CONVERSION PRIVILEGE An insured employee has the privilege of converting the face amount of his group term life insurance certificate to an individual policy of permanent (whole life) protection under various conditions.

    1. Within 31 days after termination of employment, a covered employee may convert to one of the insurer's standard individual permanent insurance plans at standard rates for the employee's attained age.

    2. No proof of insurability is required when a conversion takes place.

    3. Generally, the death benefit provided under a group life policy is continued during the conversion period. Again, this is the 31-day period from the date of termination of employment during which employees may convert their group coverage to an individual plan. Group life insurance coverage will continue in force for those 31 days, even though the conversion privilege may not be exercised.

C. CONTRIBUTORY VERSUS NONCONTRIBUTORY PLANS This refers to which party or parties will pay the group life insurance premiums. If the employer pays the entire premium, the plan is noncontributory. If the employee pays part of the premium (the premium is shared by both the employer and employee), the plan is contributory.

   1. If a plan is noncontributory, the group contract must cover 100% of the eligible persons in the group.

   2. If the plan is contributory, at least 75% of the eligible employees must be covered before the plan can become effective. For example, if 500 employees are eligible for a contributory group plan, at least 375 would have to enroll in the plan for it to be effective.

   3. Under contributory plans, the period of time during which the employee may enroll and receive coverage without evidence of insurability is known as the **eligibility period**.

D. TYPES OF GROUP LIFE INSURANCE Several types of contracts may be used in group life insurance. A group term contract has the same basic characteristics as an individual term life insurance policy. Most group life insurance contracts are issued on a group term basis. Group permanent life insurance is occasionally used in group insurance contracts.

E. ELIGIBILITY OF GROUP MEMBERS By its very nature, group insurance provides for participation by virtually all members of a given insurance group. Whether or not an individual member chooses to participate usually depends on the amount of premium he must pay, if the plan is contributory. If the plan is noncontributory and the employer pays the entire premium, full participation is the general rule.

   1. Employers and insurers are allowed some latitude in setting minimum eligibility requirements for employee participants. For instance, employees must be full-time workers and actively at work to be eligible to participate in a group plan. If the plan is contributory, the employee must authorize payroll deductions for their share of premium payments. In addition, a probationary period may be required for new employees, which means they must wait a certain period of time (usually from one to six months) before they can enroll in the plan.

   2. The probationary period is designed to minimize the administrative expense involved with those who remain with the employer only a short time. The probationary period is followed by the enrollment period, the time during which new employees can sign up for the group coverage. If an employee does not enroll in the plan during the enrollment period (typically 31 days), he may be required to provide evidence of insurability if he wants to enroll later. This is to protect the insurer against adverse selection.

F. GROUP CREDIT LIFE INSURANCE This coverage is available to protect a borrower and a lender. For example, if the borrower dies, the amount of the loan is paid by the insurance proceeds. In addition, the lender (creditor) will not be left with an uncollectible debt if the borrower (debtor) should die.

1. The creditor may not require the borrower to purchase coverage from a particular lender. In this case, the creditor may also purchase coverage on the life of the borrower.

2. Credit life insurance may not be written for an amount greater than the total indebtedness.

III. RETIREMENT PLANS

Various types of plans are available to individuals who wish to set aside funds for their retirement years. Depending on whether they have been approved by the IRS, these plans are referred to as tax-qualified or nonqualified plans.

A. TAX-QUALIFIED PLANS Retirement plans that are referred to as tax-qualified are those that receive special tax advantages. Generally speaking, qualified plans are classified as either defined contribution or defined benefit.

1. Defined contribution This type of plan has a separate account for each employee. The plan document states the amount that an employer will contribute to the plan, but it does not promise any particular benefit.

2. Defined benefit The plan document specifies the amount of benefits promised to the employee at his normal retirement date. It does not specify the amount that the employer must contribute annually to the plan to achieve the benefit.

a. Special rules for life insurance Life insurance benefits may be included in a qualified pension plan only on a basis that is incidental to the primary purpose of the plan. Life insurance is considered incidental if the cost of insurance is less than 50% of the employer contribution. Under a defined benefit plan, the requirement is that it be less than 50% of the employer contributions or that the life insurance death benefit not exceed 100 times the monthly retirement benefit.

The economic benefit of the life insurance (i.e., the cash value) included in a qualified plan is currently taxable to the employee. The economic benefit is the cost of the pure amount at risk (based on the Internal Revenue Service one-year term insurance rates, known as the **PS 58 rates**). This is the cost of the death benefit only. The total cost of term insurance would be taxable.

B. TYPES OF QUALIFIED PLANS Qualified plans may be established by an individual and by employers for the benefit of their employees. Some of the more common types of qualified plans include the following.

1. **Individual retirement accounts (IRAs)** Any individual who earns wages may participate in an IRA. A person may deduct the maximum contribution if he is a wage earner and does not actively participate in an employer-maintained retirement plan, or if he is a wage earner who actively participates in an employer-maintained retirement plan but has an adjusted gross income (AGI) of $50,000 or less if single and $70,000 or less if married and filing jointly.

   a. A single person whose AGI is between $50,001 and $60,000 is entitled to a partial deduction based on a formula. Married persons filing jointly whose AGI is between $70,001 and $80,000 are also entitled to a partial deduction. For married taxpayers, the range will increase in 2006 to $75,001–$85,000, where it will remain.

   b. The maximum annual contribution for any individual to an IRA is $4,000. In 2008, this limit is scheduled to increase to $5,000.

   c. Owners of IRAs must begin to receive payments from their accounts by the time they reach age 70½. In addition, if any withdrawals are made before the owner is 59½ years of age, a 10% penalty based on the amount received will be assessed in addition to income taxes.

   d. Following age 59½, any IRA distribution or payment made to the owner is subject only to ordinary income taxation.

   e. Individuals who are eligible to establish IRAs may create a spousal IRA with a nonwage earning spouse. The limit for a spousal IRA is based on the same schedule as the wage earner or 100% of the earned income of the wage-earning spouse, whichever is less.

   f. Individuals who are age 50 and older are allowed to contribute an additional amount in excess of the prescribed limit, up to $1,000.

   g. As mentioned previously, any benefits withdrawn from an IRA prior to age 59½ will be assessed a 10% penalty (note exceptions below). In addition, amounts withdrawn must also be added to the owner's taxable income for the year in which the withdrawals were received. However, if an individual wishes to roll over IRA funds into another IRA, this will be permitted if the proceeds are reinvested in the new IRA within 60 days following receipt of the distribution. Otherwise, the distributions will be taxable in the year received.

      1.) There are many exceptions to the 10% penalty. They include the following.

         a.) The 10% early withdrawal penalty will not apply if the distribution is used to pay medical expenses that exceed 7.5% of the owner's adjusted gross income.

         b.) Unemployed individuals receiving state or federal unemployment compensation for at least 12 consecutive weeks who take an IRA early distribution to pay health insurance premiums will not be subject to the 10% penalty.

2. **Roth IRAs** In addition to traditional IRAs, qualifying taxpayers have the option of establishing Roth IRAs. The primary difference between the two is that contributions to Roth IRAs are not deductible but distributions, if taken correctly, are entirely tax-free. Features of the Roth IRA include the following.

   a. Contributions are not deductible; however, qualified distributions are received tax-free. To be considered a qualified distribution, the IRA owner must have held the Roth IRA for at least five years *and* the distribution must be made:

      ■ on or after the date the owner reaches age 59½;

      ■ to the estate or beneficiary upon the owner's death (within five years of the owner's death);

      ■ as a result of the owner's disability; or

      ■ for first-time homeowner expenses, subject to a $10,000 lifetime limit.

   b. Limits on contributions to a Roth IRA are the same as traditional IRA; however, contributions may be made even after age 70½. Additionally, for those age 50 and over, additional amounts may be contributed. (This additional contribution limit is the same as for traditional IRAs.)

   c. The maximum contribution amount is reduced for joint filers with adjusted gross incomes (AGI) between $150,000 and $160,000 and single filers with AGIs between $95,000 and $110,000. Taxpayers with AGIs exceeding these amounts are not eligible to establish Roth IRAs.

   d. Individuals who set up a Roth IRA can still contribute to a traditional IRA; however, the maximum contribution to all IRAs is limited to the same contribution limit schedule.

   e. The traditional IRA required distribution rules do not apply; distributions need not start at age 70½.

   f. Taxpayers with AGI less than $100,000 can convert a traditional IRA into a Roth IRA without paying the 10% tax on early withdrawals.

3. **Education IRAs** With this type of IRA, more formally known as a **Coverdell IRA**, a taxpayer can pay for qualified higher education expenses (e.g., tuition, fees, books, and supplies.) Nondeductible annual contributions of up to $2,000 per child under age 18 can be made; the $2,000 limit cannot be circumvented by creating more than one IRA per child. (A 6% excise tax is imposed on excess contributions.)

   a. All build-up of earnings and withdrawals to pay qualified education expenses is tax-free.

   b. If the child does not attend college or there are any amounts remaining when the beneficiary (child) reaches age 30, the education IRA may be rolled over into the IRA of another child in the same family without penalty. Distributions not used for higher education expenses are added to the recipient's gross income and subject to a 10% penalty.

4. **Simplified employee pensions (SEPs)** SEPs are employer-sponsored IRAs. This type of plan offers corporations the opportunity to establish an employer-funded pension plan for eligible employees. Contributions must be made on behalf of employees ages 21 or older, who have performed service for the employer during the year for which the contribution is made and who, for at least three of the preceding five years, received a specified amount of compensation.

5. **Keogh plans** This type of retirement plan is also known as an **HR-10 plan**. This vehicle is provided for the self-employed individual who wishes to establish a retirement plan that will provide for tax deferral and a reduced tax liability.

   a. Like an IRA, annual contributions to a Keogh plan are tax deductible. Contributions may be made to a Keogh plan up to 100% of earned income or $41,000 per year, whichever is less. (The $41,000 limit is indexed for inflation and will increase each year.)

   b. Benefits from a Keogh plan may not be distributed to an owner before age 59½ without penalty, and they must begin no later than age 70½.

6. **Tax-sheltered annuities (TSA) or 403(b) plans** Employees of qualified 403(b) (tax-exempt) organizations are permitted, under the Internal Revenue Code, to contribute funds to individual retirement plans with before-tax dollars. Those eligible for TSAs include public, private, and parochial school teachers, school superintendents, college professors, clergymen, and social workers. For example, the pastor or minister of a church would be eligible for a tax-sheltered annuity. Government employees are not eligible.

   a. Before-tax dollars are subtracted from the individual's gross income by way of a **salary reduction**. This amount is deposited into an annuity or mutual fund and accumulates on a tax-deferred basis. In addition, since the individual's salary has been reduced, his tax liability is also reduced.

   b. The maximum contribution limit for a 403(b) plan is $15,000. The same limit applies to 401(k) plans.

   c. Catch-up contributions permit employees with 15 or more years of service to make up for prior contributions that could have been made under the plan, but were not.

7. **Section 457 plans** Section 457 plans are similar to TSAs, but they are reserved for employees of other public bodies, such as states, counties, and municipalities. Under these plans, the employer agrees with each employee to reduce salary by a specified amount and invest the deferrals in one or more vehicles that may include insurance products. The principal difference between Section 457 plans and 403(b) plans is that the investments in Section 457 plans are owned by the employer; those in 403(b) plans are owned by the employee.

8. **Annual premium retirement (tax-deferred) annuities** This type of vehicle is a tax-deferred device but not a tax shelter in its true sense. Tax-deferred annuities provide tax-deferred income. The income earned on the money placed in the tax-deferred annuity is not currently taxable to the owner, until it is withdrawn.

   a. Unlike a tax shelter, the owner does not receive a tax deduction in the amount of a contribution (as with an IRA or Keogh plan). The owner only receives a deferral of taxation on earned income.

9. **401(k) plans** An increasingly popular form of qualified plan, a **401(k) plan** allows employees to elect to contribute a portion of their income into an account in their name and instruct their employer to make contributions on their behalf. Amounts the employee elects to contribute (deferring a portion of current income) are treated for tax purposes as contributions made by the employer. This makes all monies set aside in the plan deductible by the employer, and the contribution plus its earnings are tax-deferred to the employee until withdrawal.

   a. A 401(k) plan provides current and future tax savings since an employee agrees to defer a percentage of his pretax income by way of a salary reduction. The employee's salary is reduced by the amount of the contribution, and therefore, his tax liability is reduced (since contributions are considered to have been made by the employer). All interest earned on contributions accumulate on a tax-deferred basis.

   b. Employers also save money on unemployment taxes and workers' compensation premiums by contributing to 401(k) plans since these taxes and premiums are, in whole or in part, based upon employee salaries.

   c. Current contribution limits to 401(k) plans are $15,000 ($15,500 as of 2007). Those ages 50 and over may make additional contributions up to $5,000.

   d. The IRS has established strict withdrawal provisions for 401(k) plans including no withdrawals before age 59½ are allowed except for death, disability, retirement, job change, or proof of financial hardship. Loans, however, are permitted based on specified limitations (i.e., the lesser of $50,000 or 50% of the vested value of the account).

10. **SIMPLE (Savings Incentive Match Plans) plans** A SIMPLE **plan** is a tax-favored means for providing a retirement option that does not have to satisfy many of the qualified plan requirements.

    a. Plan assets are not taxed until distributed and contributions are tax deductible by the employer.

    b. SIMPLE plans need not satisfy nondiscrimination requirements.

    c. Eligible employers for SIMPLE plans are those with no more than 100 employees who received at least $5,000 in compensation for the preceding year. The employer must not maintain another employer-sponsored retirement plan to which contributions were made or benefits accrued.

d.   SIMPLE plans can take the form of an IRA plan or a 401(k) plan.

1.)   **SIMPLE IRAs**   Under SIMPLE plans structured as an IRA, an employee may make elective contributions up to a maximum limit annually (this limit was $10,000 in 2006, plus cost of living, or COLA increases); the employer is required to match the employee contribution which greatly increases the amount deposited in the plan.

a.)   **Vesting**   All contributions to a SIMPLE IRA are nonforfeitable; employees are vested immediately.

b.)   **Participation requirements**   A SIMPLE plan must be open to every employee who (1) received $5,000 in compensation during any two preceding years and (2) is expected to receive at least $5,000 during the current year.

c.)   **Contribution elections**   Eligible employees may elect to participate in a SIMPLE plan by making elective deferrals during the 60-day period before the beginning of the year or the 60-day period before the employee becomes eligible to participate; contribution amounts elected by the employee may be changed during this period; and participation may be terminated by the employee by simply stopping the contributions.

d.)   **Taxation of SIMPLE IRA distributions**   Distributions are taxable upon distribution and includable in income.

e.)   **Rollovers**   Distributions from one account may be rolled over into another SIMPLE account; after two years, they may be rolled over from a SIMPLE account into an IRA without penalty.

f.)   **Early withdrawal penalty**   Withdrawals before age 59½ are subject to the 10% early withdrawal penalty applicable to IRAs; for early withdrawals made during the first two years, a 25% penalty will be assessed.

2.)   **SIMPLE 401(k) plans**   An employer that does not employ more than 100 employees or maintain another qualified plan may provide a SIMPLE plan as part of a 401(k) arrangement. The nondiscrimination tests applicable to elective deferrals and employer matching contributions under a 401(k) plan will be satisfied if the plan meets the contribution and vesting requirements applicable to SIMPLE plans discussed above.

      a.) An employer can take a tax deduction equal to the greater of:

- 15% of the compensation paid or accrued during the tax year to participants in a stock bonus or profit sharing plan; or
- the amount that it must contribute to the simple 401(k) plan for the year.

      b.) All eligible employees must be notified that they have right to make or modify an elective deferral during the 60-day period before every January 1.

C. NONQUALIFIED PLANS Because all retirement plans approved by the IRS are considered qualified, all others are viewed as nonqualified.

    1. Nonqualified deferred compensation plans represent an important fringe benefit for executives and other highly paid employees.

    2. Nonqualified plans permit the employer to choose the individuals he wants covered by the plan. In other words, the employer may discriminate with a nonqualified plan.

    3. These plans are used to provide additional benefits to key employees.

IV. BUSINESS INSURANCE

Life insurance is a useful tool in business situations. It helps to ensure business continuation and protect business owners as well as their dependents. There are various forms of business life insurance which help protect a corporation from economic loss if, for example, a key employee should die prematurely. Some of the more common forms of business life insurance are described below.

A. KEY-EMPLOYEE LIFE INSURANCE This type of coverage protects a business against loss of one of its most valuable assets—a key employee. A life insurance program would provide the corporation or employer with funds necessary to replace a critical individual (or otherwise compensate the business for any financial loss sustained) if a key employee were to die and his contribution to the company was terminated. Obviously, the loss of a key employee may not be recovered, but the proceeds of the policy will permit the employer to reduce his financial loss. Policy proceeds may be used to hire a new key person, hire temporary help, or train new employees.

    1. Various types of key employees include directors and officers of a firm, key sales or marketing personnel, supervisors, and foremen.

    2. The primary purpose is to indemnify a business for financial losses caused by the death of a valuable employee.

    3. Key-employee life insurance also receives favorable tax treatment. The death proceeds of key-employee life insurance are not taxable. However, premiums are not deductible for business income tax purposes. In most cases, premiums paid are not deductible and the benefits received are usually not taxable. However, in cases where premiums are deductible, benefits received are usually taxable to the recipient.

B. BUY-SELL AGREEMENTS Buy-sell agreements help with the orderly continuation of a business where survivors receive a fair cash settlement for a deceased owner's interest. The most common way in which to fund a buy-sell agreement is through the use of life insurance. Funding the agreement with life insurance proceeds guarantees that the necessary cash to pay for the deceased owner's interest in the business will be available. It allows another individual to purchase the deceased owner's interest so the business will continue without further disruption.

1. Legal contracts (the buy-sell agreement) are drawn which set a predetermined value on each person's portion of ownership in the business.

2. Buy-sell arrangements may be used in any form of business whether it is a sole proprietorship, partnership, or corporation. However, there must be a potential buyer for a buy-sell agreement to be created.

3. When a buy-sell agreement is funded by permanent life insurance, the plan may also call for a transfer of ownership should the proprietor prefer to retire at some future time. The retiring employee would use the policy's cash value to make a substantial down payment on the purchase price of the business.

4. The two most common types of buy-sell funding agreements are the (1) entity plan (this is where the business purchases the life insurance coverage) and (2) the cross-purchase plan (with this plan, the individuals purchase coverage on each other). For example, an entity plan may be used by three partners where the partnership purchases and owns a life insurance policy covering each partner (a total of three policies). In a cross-purchase plan with three partners (i.e., Partners A, B, and C), each partner purchases and owns a life insurance policy covering the other two partners. Therefore, Partner A owns policies covering B and C; Partner B owns policies covering A and C; and Partner C owns policies covering A and B (a total of six policies).

C. SPLIT-DOLLAR INSURANCE Split-dollar life insurance is a special form of life insurance funding agreement most commonly used in business situations (and occasionally used in family situations) to provide life insurance coverage as a benefit for a valued employee with a minimum cash outlay.

1. This plan requires a cash value type of permanent life insurance.

2. For example, assume a key or valued employee has a definite need for life insurance protection but lacks the funds necessary to the coverage. With a split-dollar plan, the employer contributes to the premium each year in an amount equal to the increase in the policy's cash value and the employee pays only the balance of the premium. If the policy is surrendered at any time, the cash savings value amount is returned to the employer. If the insured dies, the employer gets back the money paid out for the premiums (the employer is generally listed as beneficiary for an amount of the death proceeds equal to the premiums paid) and the balance is paid to the deceased's beneficiary.

3. A split dollar plan involves a single life insurance contract that utilizes cash savings value and term insurance protection to guarantee the return of premiums paid by one party (generally the employer) and assures a death benefit to be paid to a named beneficiary.

TAKE NOTE

Equity buy-sell   The business purchases life insurance on the lives of each partner or owner.

Cross purchase buy-sell   Each partner or owner purchases life insurance on the lives of their co-partners or co-owners.

V. SOCIAL SECURITY BENEFITS

Social Security (also referred to as OASDI—old age, survivors, and disability insurance) benefits are determined by a formula based on earnings. The Social Security Administration is responsible for administering benefits and collecting premiums.

A. SOCIAL SECURITY SURVIVOR BENEFITS   There are several types of survivor benefits provided under Social Security.

1. **Lump-sum death benefit**   This benefit helps the deceased's survivors to pay for funeral costs. The lump-sum death benefit provided by Social Security may not exceed $255. Payment is made to a surviving spouse who was living with the deceased. If no surviving spouse is present, the benefit may be paid to an eligible child.

2. **Surviving spouse's benefit**   The eligible surviving spouse of a fully insured worker is entitled, at the spouse's normal retirement age, to a monthly life income equal to the worker's primary insurance amount (PIA) at death. Or, if the spouse wishes to receive these benefits early, she can elect reduced benefits, starting as early as age 60.

    a. If the surviving spouse has a dependent child under age 16 (or age 22, if disabled), and the child was a dependent of the deceased worker, an additional benefit of 75% of the worker's PIA is payable, regardless of the spouse's age, until the child reaches age 16. Disabled children will entitle the surviving spouse to this benefit indefinitely, as long as the child remains disabled and under the care of the surviving spouse.

    b. The **blackout period** is the period of years during which no Social Security benefit is payable to the surviving spouse of a deceased, fully insured worker. It is between the time the youngest child of the worker (in the spouse's case) attains the age of 16 and the spouse's age 60.

3. **Child's benefit**   A child who is under age 18 (or disabled before age 22) whose parent is a deceased worker may receive a benefit equal to 75% of the worker's PIA until the child turns age 18 (age 19 if still in high school). If the child marries before age 18, the benefit ends.

4. **Other death benefits**   Death benefits may also be provided for dependant parents if a deceased child provided at least half of the parent's support.

B. **SOCIAL SECURITY DEFINITIONS** There are several definitions that are relevant to Social Security benefits, including the following.

1. **Quarter of coverage** This is a unit of coverage credited to a worker for each portion of a calendar year's covered wages or a self-employed income which equals or exceeds an amount specified for that year by law.

2. **Primary insurance amount (PIA)** This is an amount equal to the worker's full retirement benefit at his normal retirement age.

3. **Fully insured** A person becomes fully insured by acquiring a sufficient number of quarters of coverage to meet either of the following two tests.

   a. A person is fully insured if they have 40 quarters of coverage (10 years of covered employment). Once a person has acquired 40 quarters of coverage, they are fully insured for life, even if they spend no further time in covered employment (or covered self-employment).

   b. A person is fully insured if: (1) he has at least six quarters of coverage, and (2) he has acquired at least as many quarters of coverage as there are years elapsing after 1950 (or, if later, after the year in which he reaches age 21) and before the year in which he dies, becomes disabled, or reaches, or will reach age 62, whichever occurs first.

4. **Currently insured** A person is currently insured if he has acquired at least six quarters of coverage during the full 13-quarter period ending with the calendar quarter in which he (1) died, (2) most recently became entitled to disability benefits, or (3) became entitled to retirement benefits.

VI. TAX TREATMENT OF INSURANCE PREMIUMS AND PROCEEDS

For the most part, life insurance has been granted favorable tax treatment by the Internal Revenue Service.

A. **PREMIUMS** Premiums paid on an individual plan of life insurance are viewed as a personal expense and are not deductible. Those paid on group life plans are deductible by the employer if a noncontributory type plan is involved. These premiums are viewed as a business expense. If the group plan is contributory, premiums paid by the employee are usually not deductible.

1. The premium for the first $50,000 of coverage under a group plan (noncontributory) is not included in the employee's income for tax purposes. When an individual's group coverage exceeds $50,000, the value of the premiums on the additional face amount is reportable as income by the employee.

B. PROCEEDS Life insurance policy death proceeds are generally exempt from income taxation, even though they may exceed the cost of the insurance (the premiums paid).

    1. Any payment made to a beneficiary out of policy proceeds (death benefit) is not taxable. Any interest accrued and paid is taxable. For example, if the proceeds are left with the insurer under the interest-only settlement option, the interest payments would be taxable.

    2. Policy dividends paid to the policyowner are not taxable since they are considered a return of overpaid premiums.

C. 1035 EXCHANGE This involves Section 1035 of the Internal Revenue Code regarding certain exchanges of insurance policies and affords the postponement of tax on certain exchanges of insurance contracts. The law states that:

- an ordinary life contract may be exchanged tax-free for another life contract or for an endowment or annuity contract;
- an endowment may be exchanged tax-free for another endowment; and
- an annuity may be exchanged tax-free for another annuity contract.

U N I T   Q U I Z

1. Of the following policies owned by Bill, which one would be considered a third-party ownership arrangement?
   A. A $500,000 policy on his life, with the benefit payable to his wife
   B. A $40,000 policy on his life, with the benefit payable to the United Way
   C. A $25,000 policy on his wife, with the benefit payable to his children
   D. A $75,000 policy on his life, with the benefit payable to his estate

2. All of the following statements concerning group life insurance are correct EXCEPT
   A. evidence of insurability is not required
   B. individuals covered by the plan are not parties to the contract
   C. a covered employee is the policyowner
   D. group coverage must be incidental to the formation of the group

3. In a contributory plan, what percentage of employees must participate in the plan before a policy will be issued?
   A. 50%
   B. 75%
   C. 90%
   D. 100%

4. A conversion privilege is an element of all group life contracts. An insured employee has how many days to convert to an individual plan once employment is terminated?
   A. 10
   B. 20
   C. 28
   D. 31

5. A group life insurance plan where an employer pays the entire cost is known as a
   A. contributory plan
   B. noncontributory plan
   C. credit life plan
   D. risk-sharing plan

6. Which of the following affects the deductibility of contributions made to a traditional IRA?
   A. The IRA owner's age
   B. Whether or not the IRA owner participates in a qualified employer plan
   C. The type of investments the IRA purchases with the contributions
   D. The IRA owner's marital status

7. Keogh plans are designed for and available to
   A. an employer with more than 100 employees
   B. a self-employed professional
   C. a businessowner who becomes disabled
   D. an employee without a qualified plan

8. Bill is a school teacher who is participating in a TSA. Bill's contribution will be treated as
   A. a tax deduction
   B. a tax credit
   C. a salary reduction
   D. nontaxable income

9. Which of the following statements concerning split-dollar life insurance is CORRECT?
   A. This type of plan may utilize any form of life insurance contract.
   B. It is useful to the key employee who needs protection but has insufficient funds to meet his needs.
   C. Two life policies are required; one for the employee and one for the employer.
   D. All policy death proceeds are paid directly to the employer.

10. Premiums paid on an individual life insurance policy are generally
    A. not deductible
    B. deductible until cash values exceed premium payments
    C. deductible once they exceed 7.5% of AGI
    D. deductible as long as the policy is less than $100,000

ANSWERS

1. C	2. C	3. B	4. D	5. B
6. B	7. B	8. C	9. B	10. A

DISCUSSION QUESTIONS

1. Discuss some of the important characteristics of group life insurance.

2. Compare contributory and noncontributory plans.

3. Briefly describe the purpose of group credit life.

4. Briefly describe the following:
   A. IRA
   B. Keogh plan
   C. TSA

5. Compare and contrast a defined benefit and defined contribution plan.

6. Why would a buy and sell agreement be important to a key employee? What is the best way in which to fund such an agreement?

7. Provide an example illustrating how split-dollar life insurance works.

8. List several types of death benefits provided by Social Security.

9. Compare fully and currently insured status.

10. Compare the deductibility of premiums payable and proceeds receivable on individual and group life insurance plans? How are dividends on individual policies treated?

6

Life Insurance Practice Final Examination

Following your thorough study of Units 1 through 5, take this 50-question practice final on life insurance principles. Grade your performance using the answer key provided. Carefully review the information in this book regarding those questions answered incorrectly.

LIFE INSURANCE
PRACTICE FINAL EXAMINATION

1. Jason is the insured in a $100,000, 10-year renewable term policy. Soon after taking out the policy, he develops a serious heart condition. Which of the following statements is CORRECT?

   A. Since the condition manifested after the policy was issued, he will not be able to renew his policy.
   B. Jason will be able to renew his policy.
   C. It will be necessary for Jason to show evidence of insurability in order to renew the policy.
   D. If Jason renews his policy, it will be rated for his health condition.

2. Jane buys a $25,000 policy and her agent tells her that as long as she is approved, the coverage goes into effect immediately. What did Jane's agent give her?

   A. Consideration
   B. Conditional receipt
   C. Return of premium
   D. Binding receipt

3. The primary purpose of an annuity is to

   A. liquidate the separate account of an investment portfolio
   B. provide income for an individual's retirement
   C. provide income for a beneficiary
   D. create an estate immediately

4. Under what circumstance would an insurance applicant be asked to submit a signed statement of continued good health?

   A. When the initial premium is not submitted with the application
   B. When the policy is underwritten as substandard
   C. In order to receive a preferred rating
   D. When an inspection report is ordered

5. When a firm establishes a contributory group term life insurance contract, what percentage test must be met for the participation?

   A. 50%
   B. 60%
   C. 75%
   D. 100%

6. Louis owns a $10,000 term life policy. He paid the $200 annual premium on February 1. Louis fails to pay the second annual premium and dies on February 28 of the following year. How much will the beneficiary receive from Louis' insurance company?

   A. $0
   B. $10,000
   C. $9,800
   D. None of the above

7. All of the following statements are true with regard to the 10-day free look provision in a life insurance policy EXCEPT

   A. the 10-day free look period begins when the insured receives the contract
   B. an insured who returns the policy within the 10-day free look period will receive a full refund of premiums paid
   C. if a conditional receipt was issued, a *pro rata* refund will be made if the insured returns the policy within the free look period
   D. to get a refund, the policyholder must return the policy within 10 days from the date the policy was received

8. All of the following are common life insurance policy provisions EXCEPT a(n)

   A. entire contract clause
   B. insuring clause
   C. free look period
   D. premium deductibility option

9. Which of the following statements concerning the Fair Credit Reporting Act is CORRECT?

   A. It provides that credit life insurance will be available to an applicant on an attained age basis.
   B. It provides additional funding for the cash savings value of a whole life policy.
   C. It requires that the applicant for insurance coverage will be informed if a consumer report is requested.
   D. It offers protection against creditors if the applicant defaults on a loan.

10. The underwriting department of a life insurance company acquires information on an applicant for life insurance coverage from all of the following sources EXCEPT

    A. an agent's report
    B. the life insurance application
    C. Department of Motor Vehicles records
    D. the Medical Information Bureau

11. To cover the contingency of a family breadwinner's death, all of the following would be appropriate applications for a decreasing term insurance policy EXCEPT to

    A. ensure that the family's 5-year-old son will have a source of funds for his college education
    B. cover the family's mortgage
    C. cover the family's car payments
    D. ensure that the family's home improvement loan is covered

12. Pearl takes out a $100,000 permanent insurance policy on her life, naming her daughter, Juanita, as the beneficiary. Five years after the policy was issued, Pearl dies and Juanita submits a claim to the insurer for the death benefit. Upon reviewing the claim, the insurer discovers that Pearl had made a number of misstatements on the original application. The insurer will

    A. deny the claim entirely
    B. pay the full $100,000 to Juanita
    C. calculate any additional costs the company incurred due to the misstatements, deduct them from the death proceeds, and pay Juanita the balance
    D. require Juanita to substantiate the misstatements in order to be paid the full $100,000

13. An insured may receive protection against the unintentional lapse of his life insurance contract by requesting the

    A. cash savings amount
    B. extended term option
    C. at-interest option
    D. automatic premium loan

14. Under a group life insurance policy, an employee demonstrates her evidence of participation by producing a

    A. master policy
    B. certificate of insurance
    C. group policy
    D. premium receipt

15. Kevin takes out a loan from the cash value of his life policy, and subsequently dies. The insurance company will typically pay

    A. the face amount minus the interest and loan amount
    B. the full death benefit of the policy
    C. no less than $10,000
    D. the full death benefit after receiving the loan balance from the beneficiary

16. Which of the following is the most likely outcome if an individual who engages in a hazardous occupation applies for a life insurance policy?

    A. The application will be rejected.
    B. Dividends normally paid will be withdrawn.
    C. The policy will be issued but rated-up.
    D. A fixed-period option must be implemented in order for the policy to be issued.

17. A retired person purchases an annuity for $90,000. One month later, he starts to receive payments. Based solely on these facts, what type of annuity does he have?

    A. Immediate
    B. Cash payment
    C. Life only
    D. Interest-only

18. An agreement to purchase a deceased partner's share of a business which is usually funded by life insurance best describes a

    A. Keogh plan
    B. split-dollar plan
    C. buy and sell agreement
    D. key-employee life insurance

19. John owns a $100,000 whole life insurance policy with an additional $100,000 accidental death rider attached to it. While driving to work, John suffers a heart attack and dies instantly. His auto then runs off the road and crashes down an embankment. How much will his policy pay to the beneficiary?

    A. $0
    B. $100,000
    C. $150,000
    D. $200,000

20. Darren owns a $50,000 whole life policy. He wishes to discontinue paying premiums, but wants to continue having insurance protection for the remainder of his life. Which of the following options should he select?

    A. The reduced paid-up insurance nonforfeiture option
    B. The contract's policy loan option
    C. The extended term nonforfeiture option
    D. The paid-up additions dividend option

21. Tim submits his initial premium to his agent. Tim's agent gives him a conditional receipt. When will Tim's policy go into effect?

    A. When his check is received by the insurance company's home office
    B. When the policy is delivered to Tim
    C. When Tim's check clears his bank
    D. When Tim takes his required medical exam, the premium is received, and the policy is approved by underwriting

22. Laura is 27 years old. She wants the opportunity for market-linked interest rates, plus she wants to be able to make additional premium contributions throughout the year. What would be the best type of insurance policy for her?

    A. Modified endowment
    B. Straight whole life
    C. Variable universal life
    D. Current assumption whole life

23. An applicant for a whole life insurance policy applies for an accidental death provision in addition to the basic contract. The underwriting department lists this applicant as a standard risk. Assuming that coverage is issued, all of the following statements are correct with regard to the benefits that will be paid by the policy in the event of the applicant's accidental death EXCEPT

    A. if the insured dies in an accident at age 60, the accidental death benefit is payable
    B. the accidental death benefit amount is usually twice the face amount of the policy
    C. the benefit will be paid even if death resulted from an act of war
    D. death must occur within 90 days of the accident

24. Which of the following is accurate with regard to the misstatement of age provision?

    A. If an applicant unintentionally misstates his age on the application, no action will be taken by the insurer.
    B. Any misstatement of age on an application will result in a benefit adjustment.
    C. If a misstatement of age occurs on an application for life or health insurance, a pro rata refund of premium will be made to the insured or be paid to the insurer.
    D. Any of the above could apply.

25. Gavin purchases a whole life contract with a face amount of $100,000. Gavin may name which of the following as a beneficiary?

    A. His wife
    B. His niece
    C. A favorite charity
    D. All of the above

26. If an insured understated her age and this error is discovered upon her death, the insurer will

    A. refund all past premiums paid with any accumulated interest
    B. refuse to pay the face amount of the contract
    C. pay an amount equivalent to that which the premium would have purchased at the correct age
    D. pay the face amount of the contract with a deduction for the amount of the underpaid premium

27. The most common method for the payment of life insurance death benefits is
    A. the fixed-amount option
    B. the life income option
    C. the fixed-period option
    D. the lump-sum cash option

28. Frank, age 39, buys an endowment-at-age-65 policy and names his wife as his only beneficiary. His wife dies 10 years later. Frank dies at age 61, leaving a 32-year-old son and a 30-year-old daughter. The policy proceeds will go to
    A. his son, who is the first-born child
    B. both children equally on a per capita basis
    C. his wife, or her estate
    D. his estate

29. Lon owns a $50,000 whole life policy. At age 47, Lon decides to cancel his policy and exercise the extended term option with the policy's cash value. He will receive a term policy with a face value of
    A. $25,000
    B. $50,000
    C. $100,000
    D. The face amount cannot be determined with the information presented.

30. The insuring clause found in a life insurance contract states
    A. the promise that the insurer will pay a stated amount to a named beneficiary after receiving proof of the insured's death
    B. the location where the insurance company is domiciled
    C. the date coverage is to take effect
    D. that coverage is effective with payment of the first premium

31. The term used to indicate that a policy beneficiary cannot be changed is
    A. tertiary
    B. contingent
    C. irrevocable
    D. permanent

32. If a primary beneficiary predeceases an insured, the individuals to whom the proceeds are paid are referred to as
    A. contingent beneficiaries
    B. collateral beneficiaries
    C. revocable beneficiaries
    D. subsequent beneficiaries

33. The waiver of premium provision in a life insurance policy applies
    A. if the insured becomes disabled
    B. if the policyowner becomes disabled
    C. if the policyowner suffers a financial hardship
    D. when premiums paid exceed the policy's face amount

34. The settlement option that provides for payments to be made in regular installments to a beneficiary until the principal and interest are exhausted best describes
    A. life income
    B. interest-only
    C. fixed-income
    D. fixed-amount

35. Which of the following statements regarding taxation of life insurance is NOT correct?
    A. Dividends themselves are not taxable, but any interest paid on the dividends is taxable as received.
    B. The interest paid on policy loans is tax deductible in the year or years paid.
    C. A lump-sum benefit received by a beneficiary upon death of the individual insured is not taxable as income.
    D. Upon surrender of a policy, the policyowner is taxed on the amount by which the cash value exceeds the sum of premiums paid.

36. In order to reinstate a lapsed whole life insurance policy, all of the following may be required EXCEPT
    A. all back premiums must be paid
    B. all cash values taken from the lapsed policy must be repaid
    C. the insured may have to provide proof of insurability
    D. a new contestable period may apply to the reinstated policy

37. All of the following statements regarding a 403(b) plan are correct EXCEPT

    A. employees of nonprofit organizations qualify for this type of plan
    B. this type of plan involves a salary reduction rather than a deduction
    C. government employees are eligible for this type of plan
    D. parochial school teachers qualify for participation

38. In a policy insuring the life of a child, which of the following allows the premiums to be waived in the event of the death or disability of the person responsible for premium payments?

    A. Waiver of premium provision
    B. Reduction of premium option
    C. Payor provision
    D. Reduced paid-up option

39. An insured died during the grace period of her life insurance policy and had not paid the required annual premium. The insurance company is obligated to pay which of the following to the beneficiary?

    A. The cash value of the policy, if any
    B. The full face amount of the policy
    C. The face amount of the policy less the annual payment
    D. A refund of all prior paid premiums

40. All other factors being equal, which of the following lists from the largest annual premium to the smallest annual premium?

    A. 20-pay life, 20-year level term, 20-year decreasing term, 20-year endowment
    B. 20-year endowment, 20-year level term, 20-year decreasing term, 20-pay life
    C. 20-year endowment, 20-year decreasing term, 20-year level term, 20-pay life
    D. 20-year endowment, 20-pay life, 20-year level term, 20-year decreasing term

41. A 20-year family income policy was purchased effective April 1, last year. The insured died on August 1, last year. The beneficiary receives monthly income for

    A. 20 years
    B. 10 years
    C. 19 years and 8 months
    D. 9 years and 8 months

42. Generally, premiums paid on an individual life insurance policy are

    A. deductible
    B. not tax deductible
    C. assignable
    D. nonqualified

43. Andrew is the insured under a $150,000 life insurance policy. He has designated his wife as the primary beneficiary of the policy, his two children as contingent beneficiaries, and his Alma Mater, Homestead U., as tertiary beneficiary. Which of the following correctly describes how the proceeds will be distributed at his death?

    A. Wife—$50,000; children—$25,000 each; Homestead U.—$50,000
    B. Wife—$100,000; children—$12,500 each; Homestead U.—$50,000
    C. Wife—$100,000; children—$25,000 each
    D. Wife—$150,000

44. Under what type of life insurance policy will the death benefit vary, based on the performance of an underlying portfolio of securities?

    A. Variable life
    B. Universal life
    C. Current assumption whole life
    D. All of the above

45. All of the following are typical requirements imposed on those who participate in a group life insurance plan EXCEPT

    A. submitting to a medical exam
    B. full-time employment status
    C. contributing to any premium requirement through a payroll deduction arrangement
    D. satisfying a probationary waiting period before enrolling in the plan

46. If the beneficiary of a life insurance policy predeceases the insured two hours before his death and the insured has named no other beneficiary, the common disaster clause would

    A. prevent the proceeds from going into the estate of the beneficiary
    B. provide that the proceeds go directly to the estate of the beneficiary
    C. allow the probate court to decide where the proceeds should go
    D. provide that the proceeds be shared equally between the insured's estate and the beneficiary's estate

47. Which of the following statements regarding a renewable term life insurance policy is CORRECT?

    A. An insurer must renew a renewable term policy at the policyowner's request regardless of the insurability status of the insured.
    B. When a renewable term insurance policy is renewed, the statements on the application once again become contestable for a 2-year period.
    C. Renewal premiums are based on the insured's age at the time of the original application.
    D. The cost of this type of term policy is lower due to a decrease in the chance of adverse selection.

48. Which of the following statements regarding a revocable beneficiary is CORRECT?

    A. A revocable beneficiary may not be changed by the policyowner without the consent of that beneficiary.
    B. A revocable beneficiary receives policy proceeds in the event that the primary beneficiary predeceases the insured.
    C. All policy rights are relinquished when a revocable beneficiary is named.
    D. The policyowner may change the beneficiary without his knowledge or approval.

49. Denise has decided to cash in her $50,000 life insurance policy and use the $15,000 in surrendered cash values to purchase a single premium annuity. Which of the following correctly describes the income tax treatment of this transaction?

    A. Under Section 1035, the transaction will require Denise to recognize $15,000 as taxable income in the year the transaction takes place.
    B. Under Section 1035, the transaction requires Denise to recognize $15,000 as taxable income, but allows her to spread the tax liability over the next 5 years.
    C. Under Section 1035, the transaction requires Denise to recognize $15,000 as a capital gain in the year the transaction takes place.
    D. Under Section 1035, the transaction is considered a nontaxable event.

50. The following are an agent's duties and responsibilities at the time of the application EXCEPT

    A. to probe beyond the specific questions if he feels the applicant is misrepresenting or concealing information
    B. to check to make sure that there are no unanswered questions on the application
    C. to change an incorrect statement on the application by personally initialing next to the corrected statement
    D. to explain the nature and type of any receipt he is giving to the applicant

ANSWERS TO LIFE INSURANCE PRACTICE FINAL EXAMINATION

1. **B**   Under term life insurance, the option to renew allows the policyowner to renew the policy without evidence of insurability. The renewal is then effected by the policyowner paying the premium for the age attained, not per the basis of his health.

2. **B**   Under a conditional receipt, coverage becomes effective on the date the application is approved for the plan applied for, the amount of coverage applied for, and the premium rate applied for. Coverage may also depend on the results of a medical exam which, if acceptable to the insurer, mark the effective date of coverage.

3. **B**   An annuity provides income to a person (the annuitant) while he is alive and thus is an effective way to provide for a person's retirement. It differs from life insurance, which provides income to survivors upon the death of the insured.

4. **A**   A signed statement of continued good health is normally required when the initial premium is not submitted with the insurance application. The purpose is to ensure the insured has remained in good health during the underwriting period.

5. **C**   If the premium is shared by the employer and employee, at least 75% of all eligible employees must participate in the plan before the policy may be issued.

6. **C**   The grace period in life insurance contracts is usually 31 days. If proceeds are paid during the grace period, any outstanding premium owed to the insurer will be deducted from the face amount of the contract.

7. **C**   The free look period is granted whether or not a conditional receipt was issued. Furthermore, if the policy is returned within the period, the insured is entitled to a full refund, not to a *pro rata* portion of it.

8. **D**   There is no provision that allows for the deductibility of insurance premiums. In fact, as a general rule, premiums for individual life policies are not deductible. They may be deductible for certain forms of business-owned insurance, but not through a clause in the policy.

9. **C**   The Fair Credit Reporting Act states that when an applicant is denied coverage due to information obtained from a third-party source, the applicant will be informed of the source.

10. **C**   Life insurance companies may draw upon primary sources to compile information on applicants for life insurance coverage. These include the application, medical examinations, inspection reports, and the agent's report.

11. **A**   Decreasing term insurance provides for a declining amount of insurance over its term. It is appropriate to cover loans or obligations that decrease over time; it is not appropriate to provide for amounts that will not decrease over time (such as a future amount to cover a college tuition).

12. **B**   Due to the standard incontestability clause included in all insurance policies, the insurer has only a limited period of time from issue to dispute the statements in an insurance application. After that time (typically 2 years from issue), the insurer cannot challenge any statements made by the applicant on the application nor require the beneficiary to substantiate any statements.

13. **D**   The automatic premium loan provision protects the policyowner against the inadvertent lapse of the contract. If the cash value is sufficient, a loan in the amount equal to premium due is subtracted from the cash value to pay the premium.

14. **B**   Since the employer is the policyowner and pays the premium, it receives the master policy. Employees covered by the group life insurance policy do not receive a policy. They are given a certificate of coverage instead.

15. **A** Any policy loan outstanding at the time of the insured's death reduces the policy proceeds. The outstanding loan is subtracted from the face amount of the contract and the remainder paid to the beneficiary.

16. **C** Substandard risks present the insurer with additional exposures to loss that may be due to adverse health conditions, moral hazards, or hazardous occupations or avocations. These risks are usually issued rated policies (policies that are issued with a higher-than-standard premium).

17. **A** An immediate annuity will make its first benefit payment one payment interval from the date of purchase.

18. **C** Buy-sell agreements help with the orderly continuation of a business where survivors receive a fair cash settlement for a deceased owner's interest. Life insurance is the most common way to fund these agreements. The proceeds guarantee that the necessary cash to pay for the deceased owner's interest will be available.

19. **B** The accidental death rider pays its benefit if the insured dies from an accident. In this case, John died from the heart attack before his auto crashed. Therefore, his estate is entitled only to the $100,000 death benefit of the base policy.

20. **A** Under a life insurance policy's reduced paid-up insurance nonforfeiture option, the cash value of an existing policy is used as a single premium payment to purchase a (lesser face amount) paid-up permanent policy. The paid-up policy will remain in force without any additional premium payments.

21. **D** Under a conditional receipt, coverage becomes effective on the date the application is approved for the plan applied for, the amount of coverage applied for, and the premium rate applied for. Coverage may also depend on the results of a medical exam which, if acceptable to the insurer, mark the effective date of coverage.

22. **C** A variable universal life insurance policy is a hybrid of variable and universal life insurance. It offers a combination of investment options, a flexible premium and expense deduction method, and a guaranteed death benefit. It is considered to be the ultimate interest-sensitive product, in part because it combines the marketable features of both variable and universal life insurance.

23. **C** An accidental death benefit clause or rider will not pay a multiple death benefit if the insured died from certain illegal activities; aviation activities, except as a passenger traveling on commercial airlines; where an accident was involved with illness, disease, or mental infirmity; or from an act of war.

24. **B** Under the misstatement of age provision, if the insured's age is stated incorrectly in the application, amounts payable will be adjusted to an amount that the premium would have purchased at the correct age. An adjustment is involved whether the age was misstated to be higher or lower than the insured's actual age.

25. **D** One of the rights of policy ownership is the right to name a beneficiary. Any person, natural or legal (such as a corporation), may be named a beneficiary of a life insurance policy.

26. **C** Under the misstatement of age provision, if the insured's age is stated incorrectly in the application, amounts payable will be adjusted to an amount that the premium would have purchased at the correct age. An adjustment is involved (benefit or premium) whether the age was misstated to be higher or lower than the insured's actual age.

27. **D** The most common way in which life insurance proceeds are paid is as a single, lump-sum cash settlement.

28. **D** Frank's wife was the sole beneficiary named in his policy. When she died, the policy was left without a beneficiary. Frank would have been wise to name their son and daughter contingent beneficiaries in the event his wife predeceased him. Because he did not, the death benefit will be paid to his estate.

29. **B** As a nonforfeiture option, extended term insurance permits the policyowner to have the insurer use the existing cash value to buy term insurance equal to the face amount of the original policy with a single net premium. Therefore, Lon's cash

value will buy a term insurance policy with a face amount of $50,000, the same as the face amount of the whole life policy he cancelled.

30. **A** The insuring clause in a life insurance policy states that the insurer will provide life insurance protection for the named insured which will be paid to a designated beneficiary when proof of death is received by the insurer.

31. **C** When an insured makes a beneficiary designation that is irrevocable, the designation cannot be changed without the consent of the named beneficiary. Regardless of the designation, the policyowner retains all other rights of ownership.

32. **A** The contingent beneficiary receives the face amount of the insured's life insurance policy if the primary beneficiary predeceases the insured. This secondary beneficiary will receive the face amount of the policy if the primary beneficiary is not living at the time the insured dies.

33. **A** The waiver of premium provision in a life insurance policy, available for an additional premium, provides for the discontinuance of premium payments if the insured becomes totally disabled for a specified period of time (typically 90 days).

34. **D** Under the fixed-amount settlement option, a fixed amount of income is designated to be paid at specific intervals. This amount is continued until the proceeds and any interest earned are exhausted.

35. **B** Life insurance policy proceeds are generally exempt from income taxation, even though they may exceed the cost of the insurance (the premiums paid). Any payment made to a beneficiary out of policy proceeds (such as a death benefit) is not taxable. Any interest accrued and paid is taxable. Policy dividends paid to the policyowner are not taxable since they are considered a return of overpaid premiums. Policy loans are not deductible.

36. **B** In order to reinstate a lapsed whole life insurance policy, the cash values must be intact. If the policy's values had been taken, the policy would have been cancelled. If the policy is a universal life policy, cash values could have been withdrawn; they do not have to be repaid in order to reinstate the policy.

37. **C** Employees of qualified, tax-exempt organizations are permitted, under the Internal Revenue Code, to contribute funds to 403(b) with tax-free dollars. Those eligible for tax-sheltered annuities include public, private, and parochial school teachers, school superintendents, college professors, clergy, and social workers. Government employees are not eligible.

38. **C** For an additional premium, the payor benefit, provision, or clause may be added as a rider to a life insurance contract. It provides for the continuance of coverage on the life of a juvenile in the event or total disability of the individual responsible for paying the premiums (a parent or guardian).

39. **C** The grace period continues coverage after the date on which the premium is due. Since coverage continues, the face amount of the policy will be paid to the beneficiary if the insured dies during this period. However, any outstanding premium owed to the insurer will be deducted from the face amount of the policy.

40. **D** A 20-year endowment leaves a relatively short time span in which to endow the policy, and therefore the highest annual premiums. A 20-pay whole life insurance policy similarly requires the insured to pay all of the premiums within 20 years, a relatively short time. A 20-year level term policy provides a straight, level benefit amount for a level premium subject to increase as the insured ages. A 20-year decreasing term policy has the lowest premium due to the fact that the face amount decreases as the rate per unit of insurance increases. The premium remains constant through the term of the policy.

41. **C** Family income policies provide for monthly income payments to the beneficiary, beginning at the death of the insured and continuing to the end of the original policy period. The monthly benefit period is measured from the date on which the coverage began. In this case, the insured died 4 months after coverage began, so the beneficiary will receive monthly income from the policy for 19 years and 8 months.

42. **B**   Premiums paid on an individual life insurance policy are considered personal expenses by the IRS and are not deductible from the individual's ordinary income.

43. **D**   The primary beneficiary (or beneficiaries) of a life insurance policy stand first in line to receive the proceeds at the insured's death. Only if the primary beneficiary predeceases the insured will the contingent beneficiary receive any proceeds; and only if both the primary and contingent beneficiary both predecease the insured will a tertiary beneficiary receive any proceeds.

44. **A**   Variable life insurance is a combination of insurance products and securities products whose cash values are invested in an underlying account comprised of securities. The performance of the securities—up and down—determines the product's values (death benefit as well as cash value).

45. **A**   Full-time employment status, satisfying a probationary period, and contributing to any premium, if the group plan is contributory, are all common requirements for participating in a group life insurance plan. Submitting to a medical exam or providing proof of insurability are not.

46. **A**   The common disaster clause of a life insurance policy stipulates that, in case of death in a common accident, the insured is presumed to have survived the beneficiary. This prevents the payment of the insurance proceeds to the estate of the beneficiary and thus permits the proceeds to be distributed to any contingent beneficiaries or wherever else provided for by the policy. This clause also reduces estate taxes because the proceeds will not be taxed in both estates.

47. **A**   A renewable term life insurance policy allows the insured to renew the policy at the end of the term without providing evidence of insurability. Renewal premiums are based on the insured's attained age. An age limitation is usually included, so that the insured may not renew the policy indefinitely.

48. **D**   A revocable beneficiary may be changed by the policyowner at any time and for any reason without the beneficiary's knowledge or consent.

49. **D**   Section 1035 of the Internal Revenue Code allows for the exchange of the following as nontaxable transactions: a life insurance policy exchanged for another life insurance policy or for an endowment or an annuity; an endowment policy exchanged for another endowment policy; and an annuity exchanged for another annuity.

50. **C**   Any changes made to an insurance application after it is completed by the applicant must be initialed by the applicant. Some insurers also require that the agent initial changes made to the application. These signatures protect the insurer in the event a dispute arises and the applicant or the agent does not recall the changes that were made.

7

Introduction to Health Insurance and Types of Policies

KEY TERMS

Disability

Key Employee

Accidental Death

Surgical Expense

Corridor Deductible

Comprehensive

MEWA

Group Health

Long-Term Care

Monthly Benefit

Buyout

Dismemberment

Major Medical

Initial Deductible

HMO

Service Organizations

Conversion

PPO

Business Overhead

Group Disability

Basic Hospital

Coinsurance

Stop Loss

MET

Medigap

COBRA

I. TYPES OF ACCIDENT AND HEALTH INSURANCE POLICIES

Accident and health insurance refers to the broad field of insurance plans that provide protection against the financial consequences of illness, accidents, injury, and disability. Health insurance claims payments to insureds amount to billions of dollars every year.

Within the health insurance arena, three distinct categories of insurance exist: **disability income insurance**, **medical expense insurance**, and **accidental death and dismemberment insurance**.

A. DEFINITIONS OF DISABILITY

1. Total disability Under individual or group disability insurance policies, insureds are considered to be **totally disabled** if they cannot perform the duties of their own occupation for a specific period of time. In previous years, many disability income contracts specified this period of time as two years. After this two-year period expired, an individual would be considered totally disabled only if he were unable to engage in any occupation for which he was suited by training, education, and experience.

  a. Many insurers now offer total disability coverage in an individual's own occupation for up to five years, 10 years, to age 65, or life, depending upon the insured's occupation classification.

2. Partial disability According to health insurance contracts, **partial disability** is the inability to perform one or more important duties of an insured's occupation. Partial disability benefits are usually 50% of the total disability monthly benefit. An extra premium is charged for this type of coverage if it is added to the policy.

  a. An individual who purchases a disability income contract paying $2,000 per month, if disabled, would receive 50% of this amount, or $1,000 per month for partial disability.

  b. In addition, the maximum benefit period allowed for partial disability is short in comparison to total disability. The most common benefit periods are three and six months.

3. Residual disability A residual disability benefit provides a reduced monthly benefit in proportion to an insured's loss of income when he has begun working again after (or during) a disability, but at reduced earnings (income). In most policies, this benefit is payable only when the insured has returned to his job, engaged in his normal occupation. An additional premium is charged for this benefit.

  a. An individual owns a disability income policy with a residual disability rider included, and incurs a 60% loss of income while disabled. The policy would pay 60% of the insured's specified maximum benefit. If the contract paid $2,000 per month for a total disability, the insured would receive $1,200 per month for residual disability.

  b. In most cases, no benefits are paid with a residual benefit if the loss of income is less than 20% or 25%.

B. DISABILITY INCOME INSURANCE Disability income insurance is intended to replace a portion of an insured's earned income (typically 70%) by providing periodic indemnity payments (monthly benefits) while the insured is disabled due to accident or illness. The determination of total benefits paid is based upon the monthly dollar benefit amount selected by an insured, the elimination or waiting period involved, and the maximum benefit period applied for, such as two years, five years, 10 years, to age 65, or for life.

1. **Individual disability income policy** An **individual disability income contract** is one whose premium is paid by the individual insured. This type of policy protects against economic loss that an individual or family may suffer due to the total disability of a wage earner. It protects a family if the insured is unable to work and earn an income. Disability has sometimes been termed a "living death" due to the fact that it can create additional expenses for an individual and family.

   a. Premiums payable on an individual disability income contract are generally not tax deductible.

   b. Premium rates are determined per $100 of monthly income benefit, the waiting period selected, the length of the benefit period, the applicant's age, sex (in some states), income, occupation, and whether or not the applicant has any other current disability income policies in force.

   c. The **elimination period** under a disability income policy is the time immediately following the onset of a disability when benefits are not payable. Elimination periods eliminate claims for very short-term disabilities for which the insured usually can manage without financial hardship. These periods vary by policy, from one week to one year. The elimination period under most policies is typically 30 to 90 days.

   d. Many riders are available which may be added to an individual disability income contract to provide additional coverage for risks such as partial disability, residual disability, guaranteed insurability, disabling injury benefits, cost of living adjustments, and many more.

   e. **Computation of monthly benefit** For example, assume that an individual owns a disability income contract paying $2,000 per month for five years in the event that the insured is totally disabled. This contract also has a 30-day waiting period. The insured becomes disabled for 45 days. Therefore, he would collect $1,000. In other words, he would collect one-half of the monthly benefit because he was disabled for one-half of one month following the waiting period.

   f. **Exclusions** Common exclusions found in a disability income contract are similar to those that appear in other accident and health policies. The more common ones involve disability due to:
      - intentionally self-inflicted injuries;
      - war;
      - occupational injuries (those covered by workers' compensation); and
      - pregnancy (although many companies are now providing this coverage).

> ## TAKE ✓ NOTE
>
> The amount of coverage under a group credit health insurance plan for any single insured/debtor cannot be more than the total amount of his debt.

2. **Business overhead expense (BOE) policy** Another form of disability income insurance is a **business overhead expense contract**. This policy does not provide income replacement in the same sense as an individual disability income policy. Its intent is not to replace earned income when an insured is disabled. Rather, a BOE policy is designed to cover the business overhead expenses which continue when the businessowner is disabled.

   a. Examples of covered business expenses include the reimbursement of actual expenses for rent, employee benefits, utilities, depreciation, and other normal fixed expenses.

   b. Most BOE contracts have 30-day elimination periods and benefit periods between one and two years.

   c. Business overhead expense policies are written on a reimbursement basis. This is in contrast to individual disability income contracts which are written on an indemnity basis. (These concepts are explained shortly.)

   d. BOE policies provide monthly payments based on the actual expenses incurred by the business.

3. **Business health insurance** The various forms of business disability insurance are closely related to the business uses of life insurance. Some of the more common types include the following.

   a. **Key-employee disability insurance** When a key employee of a business becomes totally disabled, the business may suffer serious economic losses. These loss exposures may be offset by purchasing key-employee disability income insurance. This type of contract protects the business against the inability of the key employee to perform his regular duties and eases any economic burden that may exist if the disabled employee's salary and other benefits continue during a period of disability.

      1.) Some companies handle this exposure by instituting salary continuation programs where a company funds the disability income plan out of its earnings. Disability income plans may be funded by individual policies or group disability income contracts.

      2.) **Premiums** When an employer pays the premium on a disability income contract covering a key employee, the premiums paid are not tax deductible to the employer, but benefits received are tax-free.

b. **Group credit health insurance** This type of coverage is also referred to as **group credit disability income insurance**. It is the health insurance equivalent to group credit life insurance. It is primarily used in debtor/creditor relationships where large amounts of funds are borrowed. This health contract will protect a lender in the event that borrowers become disabled and cannot meet their monthly payments. This policy would be issued and paid for by the lender. The amount of coverage may not be more than the total sum of payments due from the borrower. A debtor or borrower is not required to purchase this type of coverage. This will usually be done by the creditor or lender.

c. **Business disability buyout policy** These policies provide funds for a business to purchase the interest of a totally disabled partner or stockholder. Policies are arranged so that benefits are not payable until after 12, 18, or 24 months of a disability. That duration is selected to correspond to a trigger point, which is the date designated in the formal buy-sell agreement at which the nondisabled persons must buy out the totally disabled individual. Although benefits may be paid on a monthly basis, more commonly benefits are paid as a lump sum or under a periodic settlement arrangement as reimbursement for the actual amount paid by the buyers to purchase the disabled person's interest in the business.

4. **Group disability income** Disability income coverage is available to members of a group. Group long-term disability (LTD) or short-term disability (STD) is available. The definitions of disability in group disability income policies are generally more restrictive than those found in an individual policy. The cost of LTD or STD policies is less than individual policies due to the larger number of insureds. Benefit periods available under STD plans are generally six to 18 months. Benefit periods for LTD plans are similar to those available under an individual plan (i.e., two years, five years, 10 years, age 65, life).

a. Benefits payable by group disability plans are generally reduced by any benefits received from social insurance plans (e.g., Social Security, workers' compensation, etc.).

C. **ACCIDENTAL DEATH AND DISMEMBERMENT (AD&D)** This type of coverage provides protection from the accidental death of an insured or pays a specific benefit if an insured suffers a dismemberment covered under the terms of the contract.

1. **Accidental death** This coverage may be purchased as a separate policy or as an added benefit to a health insurance contract. These policies or riders provide a specific amount to be paid to a named beneficiary in the event that an insured dies as the result of an accident.

a. The benefit amount payable as a result of accidental death is referred to as the **principal sum**.

2. **Accidental dismemberment** Accidental dismemberment provides that an insured will be paid a specific benefit amount if he suffers the accidental loss of a limb, sight, speech, or hearing. Coverage refers to the actual severance of limbs such as a hand, arm, or leg though some insurers consider the loss of use of these members as a dismemberment loss. It generally does not apply to the severance of a finger or toe, although some contracts pay a lower percentage of benefit in this event.

a. The benefit amount payable for an accidental dismemberment is referred to as the **capital sum**. The capital sum is generally a percentage (e.g., 50%) of the principal sum.

D. MEDICAL EXPENSE INSURANCE Unlike disability insurance, which provides income in the event of a disabling illness or injury, medical expense insurance is designed to cover the cost of treating an illness or disability by reimbursing the insured, fully or in part, for these costs. Several forms of coverage are available under medical expense insurance policies including hospital expense, surgical expense, miscellaneous medical expenses, major medical expense, comprehensive medical expense, dental care expense, and other limited medical expenses. Today, most health insurance companies provide contracts which include all or most of these coverages.

1. **Basic hospital expense** Basic hospital expense coverage provides benefits such as room and board expenses. For example, the contract might pay $100 per day for room charges up to a maximum of 180 days. Also provided is coverage for miscellaneous medical expenses (which are expressed as a multiple of the daily hospital benefit) including the cost of x-rays, diagnostic tests, ambulance services, laboratory fees, drugs, medicines, operating room charges, nursing services, and doctor visits in the hospital. Hospital expense coverage may be written on an indemnity basis or on a reimbursement basis.

   a. If a policy is written on an **indemnity basis**, it means that the insurer will pay a specified amount per day as provided by a schedule appearing in the policy (with a maximum number of days paid).

   b. If the coverage is written on a **reimbursement** or **expense-incurred basis**, payment is made by the insurer for all or a percentage (such as 80%) of the expenses incurred, regardless of the daily amount involved.

2. **Surgical expense** This coverage helps offset the cost of surgery and is usually covered along with hospital and miscellaneous medical expenses. Surgical expense benefits pay for the charges assessed by a surgeon for an operation. Surgical expense coverage lists (or schedules) surgical procedures and the corresponding reimbursable amounts in the contract. The most common approach used by surgical expense coverage is to establish a maximum limit for coverage. The amount of the benefit schedule is typically expressed in terms of the maximum benefit payable. In addition, many other surgical procedures are listed with a dollar amount or a percentage of the maximum shown. These listings are referred to as surgical schedules and provide payment for the usual and customary charges extended for various surgical procedures.

   a. For example, assume that a surgical expense policy has a $5,000 schedule. The $5,000 figure is the maximum for heart bypass surgery. Furthermore, the schedule may provide a percentage of the maximum for less complicated surgical procedures.

3. **Miscellaneous coverage provided by basic medical expense insurance** Several types of benefits may be provided by basic medical expense contracts including maternity, mental illness, private duty nursing charges, nursing home care, and physicians' expense benefits other than surgical expenses. Exclusions in this policy are similar to those in most health contracts.

> ## TAKE NOTE
>
> **Coinsurance**   The concept of both the insured and the insurer sharing the costs of the insured's medical care. After a deductible is paid by the insured, the insurer's share of the costs is typically 70% to 80%; the insured pays the remaining 20% or 30%.

4. **Major medical policies**   Major medical expense contracts were developed as a result of the increased sophistication and expense involved with medical procedures and techniques. Major medical and most other health plans providing hospitalization coverage rarely, if ever, include a noncancellable renewability provision. Major medical expense contracts are characterized by high maximum limits, blanket coverage, coinsurance or percentage participation, and a deductible.

    a. **High maximum limits**   This is one of the primary characteristics of major medical expense insurance. High maximum limits such as $250,000, $500,000, or $1 million are provided by the contract.

    b. **Blanket coverage**   This coverage provides protection for all types of medical expenses incurred whether the insured is in or out of the hospital.

    c. **Percentage participation**   Also known as **coinsurance**, this stipulates that after a deductible is satisfied, a certain percentage of costs incurred will be paid by the insurer with the remaining amount being the responsibility of the insured. The most common coinsurance ratio is 80/20. This means that the insurer will pay 80% of incurred expenses after the deductible and the insured is responsible for the remaining 20%. The coinsurance clause motivates the insured to minimize unnecessary care.

        1.) For example, if an insured owns a major medical expense policy with a $500 deductible and an 80% coinsurance clause, and he incurs a medical bill of $5,000, the insurer will be responsible for $3,600. This is calculated by subtracting the deductible from the total medical bill ($5,000 − $500 = $4,500) and multiplying this figure by 80%. Thus, the insurer pays $3,600 of the total bill and the insured is responsible for $1,400 (the $500 deductible + 20% of $4,500 or $900).

    d. **Deductibles**   The basic purpose of a deductible in major medical expense contracts is to aid in reducing costs by eliminating small claims. As illustrated by the previous example, to determine the amount of a claim to be paid by the insurer, the deductible must first be subtracted from the total medical bill. The remaining amount will then be multiplied by the coinsurance percentage to arrive at the amount which must be paid by the insurer and the amount which remains the responsibility of the insured. Deductibles are generally expressed as a fixed dollar amount.

        1.) **Corridor deductible**   This is a deductible that exists between where basic medical expense benefits leave off and major medical begins.

TAKE ✓ NOTE

Stop-loss provisions included in medical expense policies serve to stop the losses the insured incurs once medical costs reach a certain limit. Beyond that limit, the insurer pays 100% of the costs.

2.) Initial deductible This is the most common form of deductible used in major medical expense contracts. With this deductible, an insured will pay the first $100, $500, or $1,000 of incurred medical bills.

Initial Deductible

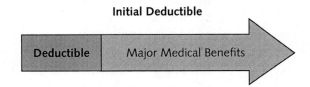

Typically used with comprehensive policies, an initial deductible is a stated amount that the insured must pay before any policy benefits are paid.

Corridor Deductible

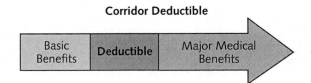

Typically used with supplemental plans, a corridor deductible is the deductible imposed after all basic benefits have been paid but before any major medical benefits will be paid.

e. Exclusions Normal exclusions found in a major medical policy include injuries sustained due to war, intentionally self-inflicted injuries, eye examinations, regular dental care, any injuries covered by workers' compensation, and in some cases, injuries sustained in private aircraft if an insured is the pilot, co-pilot, or crew member.

f. Stop-loss feature Several major medical policies have a stop-loss provision which states that an insurer will pay 100% of covered expenses after the insured's out-of-pocket payments for eligible expenses reach a certain level.

Benefits under major medical are expressed as a percentage of eligible expenses. A benefit period begins only after a specified amount of expenses have been accrued during the accumulation period (a specified period of time, such as 90 days), during which the insured must incur eligible medical expenses at least equal to the deductible.

5. Comprehensive major medical policies This type of coverage is similar to major medical insurance, although it provides broader benefits. It combines all of the basic medical expense benefits into a single package ranging from hospital and surgical expenses through major medical type coverage.

a. This policy provides large maximum benefit limits. It is also characterized by a deductible and coinsurance provisions.

b. A comprehensive major medical policy may provide first dollar basic medical expense coverage up to a specified limit such as $1,000; a corridor deductible; and then 80/20 coinsurance. This policy may also be characterized by a single deductible per person and per family. All expenses incurred above the deductible amount are covered on a percentage participation basis up to the policy limit. For example, this policy may have a $50 per person, $250 per family annual deductible. After these deductible amounts are satisfied, the policy then pays 80% of all covered expenses up to the policy limits.

6. **Health maintenance organization (HMO)** This form of health care coverage is a relatively recent development in the financing and delivery of prepaid physician and hospital care. More of a method of delivering health care, an HMO covers a wide range of comprehensive health care services for members who are enrolled on a group basis and who pay a fixed periodic type premium in advance for the services of participating physicians and hospitals.

   a. HMOs emphasize preventive medicine with early treatment and diagnosis by way of prepaid routine physical examinations and diagnostic screening techniques.

   b. These organizations are basically prepaid group practice plans that have an agreement with one or more hospitals for admission of enrolled members on a service-type basis.

   c. HMOs may be sponsored by hospitals, employees, government, medical schools, insurance companies, or other organizations.

   d. An HMO functions on a different basis than the traditional methods for delivering health care. The traditional system is based on a fee-for-service concept. Under an HMO, health care is provided in return for a pre-negotiated lump-sum or periodic payment.

7. **Preferred provider organization (PPO)** These are groups of health care providers that contract with employers, insurers, or third-party organizations to provide medical care services at a reduced fee.

   a. PPOs may be organized by the providers themselves or by other organizations such as insurers or groups of employers.

   b. Like HMOs, they may take the form of group practices or specific individual practices.

   c. PPOs can provide a wide range of diverse services but may also provide limited benefits such as hospital care only in one hospital.

   d. They differ from HMOs in two ways, as outlined below.

1.) They do not provide benefits on a prepaid basis. Participants (physicians) are paid on a fee-for-service basis.

2.) Employees (subscribers) are not required to use the practitioner, physician, or facility of the PPO that contracts with their group insurer or employer. Incentives, however, are provided for subscribers to use the PPO, such as lower or reduced deductibles.

e. PPOs are utilized by commercial insurers, Blue Cross and Blue Shield, employer self-funded groups, etc.

1.) Commercial carriers utilizing PPOs may be organized on a mutual or stock basis. They also offer individual or group type plans.

2.) With employer plans that are partially self-funded, group plans for employees and dependents are utilized. They are generally administered by third-party administrators. Self-funding arrangements may also be used by a union trust fund. In any event, the employer or union trust fund assumes a portion (or all) of the financial risk rather than transferring it to an insurer.

f. Utilization review establishes control over providers of service in the PPO. This involves procedures such as second surgical opinions, pre-certification of patients, concurrent review, and ambulatory services.

8. **Point-of-service plan** As a hybrid of HMOs and PPOs, point-of-service plans (POS) combine aspects of a traditional medical expense plan with an HMO or a PPO. Participants in a POS plan decide whether they want to receive treatment from an HMO or PPO network physician at the time they seek care.

a. **Open-access plan** An open-access POS can take the basic form of any type of HMO. However, it allows a subscriber to go outside the HMO network of medical care providers at any time.

b. **Network plan** A network plan POS requires the participant to choose a primary care physician the same way an HMO does. This physician acts as a gatekeeper to control utilization and refers members to specialists within the network. Again, however, the subscriber may elect to go outside the network of providers for specific services as desired.

9. **Flexible Spending Account** Flexible Spending Accounts (FSAs) are often offered with a cafeteria plan that allows employees to pick from a menu of qualified fringe benefits. There are two basic types: health-care accounts and dependent-care accounts.

a. **Operation** The employer generally limits the amount a participating employee can contribute for the year. These contributions are used to pay qualified health care costs, including nonreimbursed medical and dental expenses, deductibles, and co-payments. FSA contributions are generally made through regular payroll deductions.

b. Taxation FSA funds may be used to pay for qualified medical expenses without any tax consequences. Qualified expenses include those that normally would be eligible for a medical expense deduction on a personal tax return as well as expenses for nonprescription medicine or drugs to treat personal injuries or sickness. However, an FSA cannot be used to reimburse health insurance premiums costs, including premiums for a long-term care policy.

10. **Health Reimbursement Account** Health Reimbursement Accounts (HRAs) are patient-directed health plans, or defined contribution health plans. Through HRAs, employees can control reimbursements for qualified health care expenses.

   a. The employer determines the amount it is willing to pay for medical benefits and shifts the allocated dollars to the employees. Then each employee decides how much should be spent on health insurance and other qualified expenses.

   b. An HRA can cover medical expenses that would normally be deductible on an individual's tax return, including insurance premiums for eligible health insurance plans and long-term care plans. It can also be used to cover expenses for nonprescription medicine or drugs to treat personal injuries or sickness.

11. **Health Savings Account** Health Savings Account (HSAs) are designed to offer individuals a tax-advantaged means of accumulating savings to pay for qualified medical expenses. An HSA may be established by any employer or nonprofit organization. There is no limit on the minimum or maximum number of employees who can participate in the plan. An individual can set up an HSA without being associated with a particular employer.

   a. Eligibility To participate in an HSA, an individual must meet all of the following four requirements:

   1.) Have a qualifying high-deductible health insurance policy in effect before opening the HSA account

   2.) Not be entitled to receive benefits under Medicare (generally, not having reached the age of 65 years)

   3.) Not be claimed as a dependent on another person's income tax return

   4.) Not be covered by any other health insurance plan that is not a qualifying high-deductible health insurance plan (other than certain types of policies)

   b. Permitted health insurance plans Although an individual generally cannot participate in an HSA if he is covered by a health insurance plan that is not a high-deductible plan, there are certain exceptions for other types of policies:

   1.) Separate dental or vision care insurance

   2.) Separate long-term care insurance

3.) Workers' compensation insurance

4.) Disability income insurance

5.) Business interruption insurance

6.) Insurance paying a fixed amount for hospitalization

7.) Travel insurance

8.) Automobile insurance

12. **High-deductible health plan** A high-deductible health plan provides the catastrophic insurance coverage that may be combined with an HSA. The HSA works best for the insured when it pays other expenses that are not covered by the catastrophic insurance.

   a. **Family coverage** In the case of family coverage, a plan qualifies as a high-deductible health insurance plan only if no benefits are payable until the minimum family deductible has been exceeded, regardless of the amount of expenses incurred by individual family members.

   b. **No first-dollar coverage** A qualifying health insurance plan may not provide for first dollar coverage of most health care expenses. Apart from an exception for preventive care, the insurer is not allowed to pay or reimburse amounts spent on health care until the deductible limit has been met.

13. **Consumer Driven Health Plan** A Consumer Driven Health Plan (CDHP) is a health benefit plan in which individuals select their health care providers, manage their health expenses, and assume more control in protecting their health. CDHPs are characterized by:

   a. Tax-exempt health account that pays for health expenses up to a limit, a high-deductible health insurance policy that covers expenses beyond the deductible, and a "corridor" between them in which the insured pays for health care expenses

   b. An opportunity to apply funds that are not spent in a current year to medical expenses of a future year

   c. Support for insureds in selecting health care providers, comparing policies and prices, and managing health care expenses

14. **Multiple employer trust (MET)/multiple employer welfare association (MEWA)** The **multiple employer trust** (also referred to as multiple employer welfare associations) is a popular method to market group benefits to employers who have a small number of employees. METs/MEWAs are legal entities in form of trusts that may be sponsored by an insurance company, an independent administrator, or some other organization, and are established for the purpose of providing group benefits to participants.

a. Each trust must have an administrator and a trustee. The administrator may be an insurance company or a professional administrator. The trustee involved is usually a commercial bank.

b. METs/MEWAs may provide either a single type of insurance or a wide range of coverage. It may provide benefits on a self-funded basis or fund benefits with a contract purchased from an insurance company.

c. Categories of METs/MEWAs METs/MEWAs may be categorized according to how they are administered, whether by an insurer or a third-party administrator. There are three basic categories.

> **1.) Fully insured MET/MEWA** Here benefits are insured and the MET/MEWA is administered by an insurance company.

> **2.) Insured third-party administered METs/MEWAs** In this case, benefits are insured and the MET/MEWA is administered by a third party.

> **3.) Self-funded MET/MEWA** With this type, benefits are self-funded and the MET/MEWA is administered by a third party.

15. Service organizations (Blue Plans) The most common types of service organizations include Blue Cross and Blue Shield plans. The "Blues" have been organized under special legislation and established at the state level by hospitals and other medical professionals as a means of providing health care to the public.

a. Blue Cross and Blue Shield are nonprofit organizations (in most cases) which are exempt from many state regulations. These organizations also receive favorable income and state tax treatment. Blue Cross and Blue Shield have contractual agreements with hospitals and participating physicians that provide services to subscribers (insureds). Coverage is offered on both a group and individual basis.

b. Blue Cross and Blue Shield organizations are not the same as private insurance companies, not federally sponsored, and are not owned by hospitals and physicians.

c. Blue Cross Blue Cross provides coverage for hospital benefits. Under this plan, the insured is billed only for services not covered by the particular plan, while the member hospital providing the services is paid directly by Blue Cross. Blue Cross plans were originally organized by individual hospitals to permit and encourage prepayment of hospital expenses.

d. Blue Shield Blue Shield insurance provides coverage for physicians expenses, including surgical expenses. Blue Shield pays its benefits either to the hospital or directly to the physician. Assessed charges are typically made on a usual, customary, and reasonable (UCR) basis for an identified geographical area.

e. Service vs. indemnity approach Blue Cross and Blue Shield operated on a **service approach** where an insured receives the benefits stipulated in the contract, such as "coverage for daily room and board." Under an **indemnity approach**

(used by private insurance companies), an insured is provided with a specific dollar amount of coverage for each benefit, such as "$125 per day for daily room and board charges."

    1.) Service approach Insured receives the service; no cost is stipulated in the contract.

    2.) Indemnity approach Insured receives a dollar amount to cover the costs of covered services.

E. GROUP HEALTH INSURANCE This is a plan of insurance coverage that protects a group of individuals (employees) under one contract. This insurance is usually based on an employer-employee relationship but may be offered to groups who join together out of a common interest, such as trade associations or unions.

  1. Characteristics and concepts of group coverage As in group life insurance, employees covered by a group health plan do not receive a policy. The employer is the policyowner and receives the master contract. The employee receives a certificate of coverage. There are two parties to the contract, the insurer and the employer. The employee is not a party to the contract; instead, he receives a **certificate of insurance** as evidence of participation in and coverage under the program.

    a. Group plans may be contributory (where the employee pays a portion of the cost) or noncontributory (where the employer pays the full cost).

      1.) If noncontributory, 100% of the eligible employees must be covered under the plan.

      2.) If contributory, at least 75% of the eligible employees must participate before the group policy can be put into effect.

    b. Group underwriting Underwriting a group health policy requires no medical examination or statement concerning a person's health. There is no individual underwriting since it is the group that is underwritten, not the individual member of the group. However, if a person declines coverage under a group plan and later changes his mind and wants coverage under the plan, the insurer may require proof of insurability, such as a medical examination.

    c. A group of persons cannot band together for the sole purpose of purchasing group health insurance coverage. The group insurance coverage must be incidental to the group.

  2. Group conversion Group policies contain a conversion privilege permitting the employee to convert his coverage to an individual health plan when that person's employment is terminated.

    a. The employee has 31 days to convert to an individual plan once employment is terminated without providing evidence of insurability. This privilege is not available to employees who are retiring.

TAKE NOTE

COBRA is a federal act that amended ERISA, the Internal Revenue Code, and the Public Health Service Act to provide continuation of group health coverage that otherwise might be terminated.

3. **Individual and group health differences** One primary difference between these individual and group health plans is that group insurance provides benefits for nonoccupational illnesses and injuries, occupational illnesses and injuries are covered by workers' compensation insurance. Individual policies cover both occupational and nonoccupational. Other differences include the following.

   a. An individual contract is a two-party contract between insurer and insured. Group coverage continues to be a two-party contract (insurer and employer) but an additional entity (i.e., covered employee) is now included.

   b. An insurer may cancel an individual insured's policy if it is an optionally renewable or cancellable contract. Under group insurance, an individual cannot be cancelled unless the contract for the entire group is cancelled.

F. **CONSOLIDATED OMNIBUS BUDGET RECONCILIATION ACT (COBRA)**
COBRA was created in 1985 and stipulated that employers must offer continuation of group health coverage for a specified period of time to qualified employees and their beneficiaries who would not otherwise be eligible for continued coverage because of a particular qualifying event involving the covered employee. Such events would include death, divorce, or termination of employment.

   1. **Qualified beneficiaries** Qualified beneficiaries under COBRA include the spouse and dependent children of an employee entitled to coverage under the terms of a group health plan.

   2. **Employer penalties** An employer that fails to meet the continuation requirements may not take a federal income tax deduction for its group health plan contributions.

      a. For example, if an employer has 1,000 employees and the cost per employee for group health coverage is $2,000, the employer will lose a $2 million business expense deduction if it does not comply with COBRA.

      b. In addition, if an employer fails to meet the requirements, highly compensated individuals must include in their income the cost of employer group health plan contributions (e.g., the cost per employee of $2,000) made on their behalf. These at-risk employees are usually those who are in the top 25% of the highest-paid employees.

   3. **Type of coverage under COBRA** The continued health coverage provided for plan beneficiaries must be identical to that being provided under the plan for similarly situated beneficiaries.

4. **Maximum period of continuation coverage** A qualified beneficiary (i.e., surviving spouse) may have more than one qualifying event that entitles the beneficiary to continued coverage, but in no event may the coverage period exceed a 36-month period. If an individual is laid off from a job, he may continue coverage for a period not to exceed 18 months.

    a. Continuation coverage may terminate once a beneficiary becomes covered by another plan or Medicare. Continuation coverage does not apply if the employer terminates the entire health plan.

5. **Notification required** Each covered employee or qualified beneficiary is responsible for notifying the plan administrator of the occurrence of qualifying events within 60 days after the event in order to take advantage of continued coverage.

6. **Premiums** COBRA allows employers to charge those who elect to continue coverage 102% of the premiums the employer pays for each employee. The additional 2% covers administrative duties and paperwork required of the employer.

    a. A grace period exists for the failure to pay premiums. It is the longest of (1) 30 days; (2) the period the plan allows employees for failure to pay premiums; or (3) the period the insurance company allows the plan or the employer for failure to pay premiums.

G. **HEALTH INSURANCE PORTABILITY AND ACCOUNTABILITY ACT (HIPAA)** In 1997, Congress passed the Health Insurance Portability and Accountability Act. In part, the purpose of the act was to improve portability and continuity of health insurance coverage in the group and individual markets, and to improve access to long-term care services and coverage. Major provisions of the legislation include the following.

1. There is an exemption from the 10% penalty on premature IRA withdrawals if they are used to pay medical expenses in excess of 7.5% of adjusted gross income. Also exempt from the 10% penalty are early IRA withdrawals to pay for medical insurance if an individual has received unemployment compensation under federal or state law for at least 12 weeks. (The latter is without regard to the 7.5% floor.)

2. Qualified long-term care insurance for chronically ill individuals will be treated as accident and health insurance contracts so that amounts received under contracts issued after 1996 will be considered reimbursements for medical care expenses and therefore generally excludable from income.

3. Portability of health insurance coverage has been enhanced by restricting certain group health plans' ability to exclude individuals from coverage based on preexisting conditions or health status after June 30, 1997. The term *portability* refers to credible coverage certificates, which must be issued by employers, upon request, to previously covered employees, beginning July 1, 1997. To qualify, any individual (including family members) must have been covered under another group plan with no gaps in coverage longer than 63 days.

4. Another health insurance innovation introduced by HIPAA was the **medical savings account (MSA),** which enabled small businesses, self-employed persons, their employees, and their families who were covered by a high deductible health insurance plan to create qualified trusts for the purpose of accepting contributions to pay for medical expenses. (MSAs were made available on a pilot basis with the number of accounts limited. The cut-off year for new accounts under the pilot program was 2003.)

   a. Withdrawals taken from an MSA for medical purposes are tax-free. If a withdrawal is not used to pay for medical costs, it is included in the participant's gross income and subject to a 15% penalty. After the participant reaches the age of Medicare eligibility (or becomes disabled or dies), the penalty tax is not applicable; however, any withdrawals not used exclusively to pay for medical expenses are still included in the participant's gross income.

5. The allowable deduction for health insurance costs of self-employed individuals and their spouses and dependents is now 100%.

6. Other key HIPAA provisions include:
   - limiting the period for which a group health plan can deny coverage for a preexisting medical condition to 12 months (18 months in the case of a late enrollee);
   - generally prohibiting a group health plan from establishing eligibility for enrollment based on an individual's health status, medical condition (physical or mental), claims experience, receipt of health care, medical history, genetic information, evidence of insurability, and disability;
   - guaranteeing availability of health coverage for small employers;
   - guaranteeing availability of health coverage in the individual market for all eligible individuals, which include those who:
     — have had at least 18 months of aggregate creditable coverage,
     — have been under a group health plan, a governmental plan, or church plan (or health insurance offered in connection with such plans) during the most recent period of creditable coverage,
     — are not eligible for coverage under a group health plan, Medicare, or Medicaid, and do not have other health insurance coverage,
     — have not had their most recent coverage cancelled for nonpayment of premiums or fraud; and
     — have elected and exhausted any option for continuation of coverage (COBRA coverage) that was available under the prior plan;
   - guaranteeing renewability of health coverage for all group health plans, unless the plan has failed to pay premiums, committed fraud, violated participation or contribution rules, terminated coverage, moved outside the service area, or ceased association membership; and
   - guaranteeing renewability of health coverage in the individual market for all individuals, unless the individual has failed to pay premiums, committed fraud, terminated the plan, moved outside the service area, or ceased association membership.

7. **Disclosures at point of sale** The Health Insurance Portability and Accountability Act (HIPAA) imposes specific requirements on health care providers with respect to the disclosure of insureds' health and medical information, or protected health information. Health care providers must preserve patient confidentiality and protect this information. If this information is inadvertently disclosed, providers must mitigate the harm to their patients. Insurers and producers are under similar requirements when dealing with the protected health information of applicants and insureds.

   a. Producers who work directly for insurers must receive training on the insurer's privacy practices within a certain time after they begin working for the insurer. Each insurer has guidelines that their employees must follow to maintain customer privacy. This will include methods of obtaining, using, protecting, and destroying information related to a particular client. Although the requirements are likely to vary from company to company, producers should strive to adhere to those requirements for which their client has insurance coverage.

   b. When examining an applicant for underwriting purposes, all medical information is to remain confidential and the insurer must protect the applicant's privacy. If the insurer wishes to share this information (such as in communications with medical professionals), including information related to HIV infection, the applicant must be given full notice of the insurer's practices with respect to the treatment of this information, his rights to maintain his privacy, and an opportunity to refuse the dissemination of the information.

   c. In responding to a request to disclose protected health information, the insured must be given the opportunity to:

      1.) specify the party to whom authority is being granted;

      2.) specify the type of information to be disclosed;

      3.) acknowledge that he may inspect or copy the protected health information;

      4.) revoke the authorization in writing (with no effect on the insured's health care or payment for health care);

      5.) acknowledge that the information disclosed in accordance with the authorization may be subject to redisclosure with no further legal assurances of confidentiality; and

      6.) set a date on which the authorization will expire.

H. **LONG-TERM CARE (LTC) INSURANCE** As individuals age, they are likely to suffer from acute and chronic illnesses or conditions. An acute illness, such as pneumonia, is a serious condition from which the body can fully recover with proper medical attention. A chronic condition, such as arthritis, is a treatable but not curable illness. Typically, the need for long-term care (LTC) arises when physical or mental conditions, whether acute or chronic, impair a person's ability to perform the basic activities of everyday life: feeding, toileting, bathing, dressing, and walking. This is the risk that long-term care insurance is designed to address.

1. **Three levels of categories of long-term care** Long-term care is rendered in three levels, depending on the patient's need.

   a. **Skilled nursing care** is continuous, around-the-clock care provided by licensed medical professionals under the direct supervision of a physician. Skilled nursing care is usually administered in nursing homes.

   b. **Intermediate nursing care** is provided by registered nurses, licensed practical nurses, and nurses' aides under the supervision of a physician. Intermediate care is provided in nursing homes for stable medical conditions that require daily, but not 24-hour, supervision.

   c. **Custodial care** provides assistance in meeting daily living requirements, such as bathing, dressing, getting out of bed, toileting, and so on. Such care does not require specialized medical training, but it must be given under a doctor's order. Custodial care is usually provided by nursing homes but can also be given in adult day-care centers, respite centers, or at home.

2. **Services and support** Services and support associated with long-term care are provided at three levels: institutional care, home-based care, and community care. Within each of these broad levels are many types of care, any or all of which may be covered by a long-term care insurance policy.

   a. **Home and community-based services** Home health care is provided in the insured's home, usually on a part-time basis. It can include skilled care (such as nursing, rehabilitative, or physical therapy care ordered by a doctor) or unskilled care (such as help with cooking or cleaning).

   b. **Adult day care** Adult day care is designed for those who require assistance with various activities of daily living, while their primary caregivers are absent. These day care centers offer skilled medical care in conjunction with social and personal services, but custodial care is usually their primary focus.

   c. **Respite care** Respite care is designed to provide a short rest period for a family caregiver. There are two options: either the insured is moved to a full-time care facility or a substitute care provider moves into the insured's home for a temporary period, giving the family member a rest from the caregiving duties.

   d. **Continuing care** Continuing care coverage is designed to provide a benefit for elderly individuals who live in a continuing care retirement community. It provides independent and congregate living and personal, intermediate, and skilled nursing care and attempts to create an environment that allows each resident to participate in the community's life to whatever degree is desired.

3. **LTC policy provisions and limits** As a result of passage of the Health Insurance Portability and Accountability Act (HIPAA) of 1996, all LTC policies must contain certain provisions so that their benefits qualify for tax-exempt treatment.

a. **LTC services** Qualified LTC services are defined as diagnostic, preventive, therapeutic, curing, treating, mitigating, and rehabilitative services, and maintenance or personal care services that are required by a chronically ill individual and are provided under a plan of care established by a licensed health care practitioner.

b. **Qualifying for benefits** A benefit trigger is an event or condition that must occur before benefits become payable. As a result of HIPAA, prior hospitalization can no longer be used as a benefit trigger. Instead, the individual must be diagnosed as chronically ill. Diagnosis of chronic illness can be made on two levels: physical or cognitive.

   1.) **Physical diagnosis of chronic illness** Physical diagnosis of a chronically ill individual is one who has been certified as being unable to perform at least two activities of daily living (ADL): eating, toileting, transferring (getting out of bed), bathing, dressing, and continence. An LTC policy must take into account at least five of these ADLs.

   2.) **Cognitive diagnosis of chronic illness** An individual would be considered chronically ill if he needs substantial supervision to protect his health or safety owing to severe cognitive impairment, and this condition was certified within the previous 12 months.

4. **Benefit limits** Almost all LTC policies set benefit limits, in terms of how long the benefits are paid or how much the dollar benefit will be for any one covered care service or a combination of services.

5. **Age limits** LTC policies typically set age limits for issue, the average age being about 79 years. Many policies also set a minimum purchase age, the average being 50 years.

6. **Renewability** As a result of HIPAA, all LTC policies sold today must be guaranteed renewable. The insurer cannot cancel the policy and must renew coverage each year, as long as premiums are paid. A guaranteed renewable policy allows the insurer to raise premiums, but only for entire classes of individuals.

7. **Elimination periods** LTC policy elimination periods can range from 0 to 365 calendar days, and many insurers give the insured the option of selecting the period that best serves his needs. The longer the deductible or probationary period, the lower the premium will be. Insurers may require that insureds provide proof of having received care and paying for it during the probationary period (service days) before the insurer will pay any benefits.

8. **Specified exclusions** Organic cognitive disorders, such as Alzheimer's disease, senile dementia, and Parkinson's disease, are almost always included in LTC insurance policies. However, the following are excluded from most LTC insurance policies: drug and alcohol dependency, acts of war, self-inflicted injuries, and nonorganic mental conditions.

9. Taxation of benefits Qualified LTC insurance policies are treated in the same manner as accident and health insurance contracts. Therefore, amounts received under an LTC policy are excluded from income because they are considered amounts received for personal injuries and sickness. Benefits payable under LTC policies are not taxable to the extent that they cover incurred costs. If an LTC policy pays a benefit that exceeds costs by a certain amount (adjusted annually for inflation), the excess is taxable to the insured.

I. SPECIFIED DISEASE (CANCER) INSURANCE Individuals may buy insurance coverage that pays benefits for only a single specified disease, such as cancer, or for a group of diseases. However, individuals cannot rely on specified disease insurance as a type of Medicare supplement coverage.

J. CRITICAL ILLNESS INSURANCE Critical illness policies pay a lump sum in the event the insured is diagnosed with a critical illness during the term of the policy. Like term life insurance, a critical illness policy can offer level coverage or decreasing coverage over the term of the policy. Also like term life, a critical illness policy does not build cash value. The funds can be used to pay for medical care, daily living expenses, and other costs associated with the illness.

K. WORKSITE INSURANCE Worksite insurance plans are made available to employees on a voluntary basis, allowing them to choose the benefits they need. Employees pay for the coverage through payroll deductions.

1. Worksite insurance plans are available as term, universal life, accident and disability, short-term disability, long-term disability, critical illness, long-term care, retirement, vision, and dental insurance. Plans can cover one or more of these.

2. These plans can be purchased by individuals or groups.

UNIT QUIZ

1. With regard to disability income insurance, the determination of whether an individual is disabled is based on
   A. the insured's condition matching those specifically set forth in his policy
   B. the diagnosis of the insured's primary physician
   C. the inability of the insured to perform duties of his job
   D. all of the above criteria must be met

2. A benefit of 50% of the monthly total disability benefit for up to 6 months is typical of a
   A. residual disability
   B. recurrent disability
   C. partial disability
   D. total disability

3. With regard to health insurance, which of the following best describes the elimination period?
   A. The period following the issue of a disability income policy during which no benefits will be paid
   B. The period following the onset of a disability during which no benefits from a disability income policy will be paid
   C. The period following the effective date of a group health insurance policy during which no benefits will be paid for preexisting conditions
   D. The underwriting period for a group health insurance policy during which all those with preexisting conditions are eliminated from coverage

4. All of the following statements concerning major medical insurance are true EXCEPT
   A. benefits have high maximum limits
   B. benefits are expressed as a percentage of eligible expenses
   C. it is characterized by percentage participation
   D. deductibles are usually of a variable nature

5. John owns a major medical policy with an 80/20 coinsurance provision. The policy also has a $500 deductible. If John incurs medical expenses of $3,700, how much will he be responsible for?
   A. $1,140
   B. $1,850
   C. $2,560
   D. $2,960

6. Amy is the insured under an accidental death and dismemberment policy, which provides for a principal sum of $50,000 and a capital sum of $25,000. She suffers the loss of her right arm in a car accident. Which of the following statements is TRUE?
   A. She will be paid an amount equal to half the capital sum.
   B. She will be paid $50,000.
   C. She will be paid $25,000.
   D. She will be paid an amount equal to twice the capital sum.

7. Bill has a disability income policy paying him $4,000 per month. The contract also has a 30-day waiting period. Bill was disabled for 75 days. How much will his policy pay?
   A. $4,000
   B. $6,000
   C. $8,000
   D. $10,000

8. A disability income contract that pays the expenses of a firm if the owner becomes disabled best describes
   A. key-employee disability
   B. business overhead expense
   C. residual disability
   D. business health expense

9. Deductibles found in a major medical policy are typically expressed as a
   A. variable amount
   B. fixed-dollar amount
   C. deferred amount
   D. percentage of expenses incurred

10. Intentionally self-inflicted injuries are generally excluded from coverage under

    A. disability income policies
    B. major medical policies
    C. basic hospital expense policies
    D. all of the above

11. An HMO is a form of health care coverage that emphasizes

    A. preventive medicine
    B. traditional medical care system
    C. an indemnity benefit structure
    D. a fee-for-service system

12. Which of the following is a nonprofit organization providing health care benefits?

    A. HMO
    B. MET
    C. Blue Cross/Blue Shield
    D. Business Overhead Expense Association

ANSWERS

1. C   2. C   3. B   4. D   5. A   6. C
7. B   8. B   9. B   10. D   11. A   12. C

DISCUSSION QUESTIONS

1. Define total disability.

2. Contrast partial and residual disability.

3. Describe disability income insurance.

4. Briefly describe the coverage provided by a business overhead expense contract.

5. Discuss the purpose of credit disability insurance.

6. Compare the coverage provided by an accidental death contract and those of a dismemberment policy.

7. What coverages are provided by a basic hospital expense plan?

8. Identify four main characteristics of a major medical policy.

9. Discuss the purpose of a Multiple Employer Trust (MET).

10. Briefly describe the coverage and other characteristics of Blue Cross/Blue Shield plans.

11. Briefly describe the purpose of a Medicare Supplement policy.

12. What are the basic differences between group health and individual health policies?

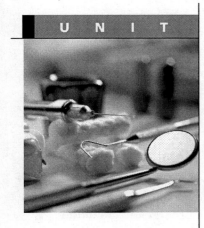

8

Health Insurance Policy Provisions, Clauses, and Riders

KEY TERMS

Mandatory Provisions	Optional Provisions	Insuring Clause
Probationary Period	Elimination Period	Preexisting Conditions
Recurrent Disability	Coinsurance	Impairment
Guaranteed Insurability	Multiple Indemnity	Noncancellable
Cancellable	Guaranteed Renewable	Conditionally Renewable
Optionally Renewable	Period of Time	

I. POLICY PROVISIONS, CLAUSES, AND RIDERS

Health insurance is characterized in part by the diversity of contract forms: medical expense, disability, long-term care, etc. However, all are subject to certain minimum policy provision requirements. These provisions were prescribed in the NAIC's Uniform Individual Accident and Sickness Provisions Law developed in 1950 and subsequently adopted by all 50 states and jurisdictions.

A. MANDATORY PROVISIONS There are 12 mandatory uniform policy provisions that must be included in every accident and health contract issued. The mandatory provision laws were developed to achieve a standardization of general provisions for the protection of the public. In addition, mandatory provisions were adopted to prevent insurers from including restrictive provisions in accident and health contracts which result in legitimate claims being denied. The 12 mandatory provisions are as follows.

1. **Entire contract** The application, all endorsements or riders, waivers, and any attached documents make up the entire contract.

2. **Time limit on certain defenses** This is the accident and health insurance equivalent to the incontestability clause found in a life insurance contract. It states that after a policy has been in effect for more than two years, claims may not be denied by the insurer due to any misinformation or misstatements made on the application. The time period for this provision may vary by state. Fraudulent representations by the insured may be contested at any time.

3. **Grace period** As in life insurance, a specific grace period is allowed under accident and health contracts for premium payments. If a premium is not paid on the due date, coverage will remain in effect during the grace period. If the premium is not paid by the end of the grace period, the policy will lapse. The grace period in most accident and health contracts is 31 days (seven days for policies paid weekly and 10 days for policies paid monthly).

4. **Reinstatement** This provision outlines the procedures involved regarding reinstatement of coverage following the lapse of a policy. The insurer will usually require the completion of a reinstatement application to ensure that the insured has not become disabled nor contracted any illness during the lapse period. The insurer may also require that evidence of insurability be provided. Once a policy has been reinstated, coverage for any accidents sustained is effective immediately and coverage for sickness begins following a 10-day waiting period. Applicants are automatically reinstated if the insurer has not informed them one way or the other within 45 days after they submitted the reinstatement application.

5. **Notice of claim** This provision specifies the amount of time an insured has to notify the insurer concerning a claim. An insured is required to send written notice to the insurer within 20 days of sustaining a loss.

6. **Claim forms** This provision specifies the procedures that an insured must follow to obtain claim forms from the insurer. An insurer must provide claim forms within 15 days of an insured's request. If it fails to do so, the insured is allowed to submit a claim (or proof of loss) in another manner.

TEST TOPIC ALERT

With health insurance policies, there is some uniformity in that all states require the same 12 provisions be included in all accident and health policies. Additional provisions are also available to insurers to include in their policies as they desire or as required by state law.

---

7. **Proof of loss** Written proof of loss must be supplied to an insurer within 90 days of the date of loss. If an insured fails to provide written proof within the time required, the claim will be honored if it was not reasonably possible to provide proof within the time limit allowed.

8. **Time of payment of claims** This provision requires an insurer to pay benefits immediately upon receipt of an acceptable written proof of loss submitted by an insured. Periodic payments are usually made at least once a month, such as with a disability income contract.

9. **Payment of claims** This mandatory provision states that all indemnities will be paid to a named insured by the insurance company. It also specifies any other benefits to be paid to an insured or a named beneficiary such as an accidental death benefit or a dismemberment claim.

10. **Physical examination and autopsy** The insurer has the right to request a physical examination and/or autopsy of the insured before paying any benefits. This provision is most commonly utilized when an insurer requires that a disabled submit to a physical examination to prove continued disability.

11. **Legal actions** The insured may not bring any action at law or equity to recover on the policy prior to the expiration of 60 days after written proof of loss has been furnished. Any legal actions available to an insured against the insurer, and vice versa, will be stipulated in the contract.

12. **Change of beneficiary** This provision states that an insured has the right to change a beneficiary unless the beneficiary is irrevocable.

B. **OPTIONAL UNIFORM POLICY PROVISIONS** There are several optional uniform policy provisions available to insurers. Insurers may include any or all of these optional provisions as they deem appropriate or as required by state regulations. Some of the more common optional provisions include the following.

1. **Change of occupation** This provides for a change in benefits or premiums if an insured changes his occupation. For example, if the insured changes from a more hazardous to a less hazardous occupation, he will experience a premium reduction. However, if the insured changes from a less hazardous to a more hazardous occupation, he will experience a benefit reduction.

2. **Misstatement of age** This is similar to the misstatement of age provision found in life insurance contracts. All amounts or benefits payable under the contract will be such as the premium paid would have purchased if the correct age had been stated originally.

3. **Illegal occupation** An insurer will not be liable for any loss if a contributing cause to the illness or injury was as a result of the insured being involved in any illegal activity or occupation. For example, an insurer will not be liable for any loss experienced by an insured if he is injured while committing a felony.

4. **Relation of earnings to insurance** This provision refers to disability income and restricts the amount of insurance that may be issued to an insured based upon that individual's average earnings. Insurers wish to prevent an insured from obtaining an amount of disability income insurance that is equal to or greater than their salary. This provision helps decrease the chance for malingering.

5. **Conformity with state statutes** This provision amends any policy provision to conform with state laws.

6. **Intoxicants and narcotics** No coverage is provided by an insurer while an insured is intoxicated or under the influence of any narcotic unless the substances have been administered by or taken on the advice of a physician.

7. **Unpaid premiums** Upon payment of a claim, any premium due and unpaid may be deducted from the benefits. This provision is usually utilized by an insurer when an insured experiences a loss during the grace period.

8. **Cancellation** An insurer may cancel the contract at any time by providing written notice to an insured stating the reasons for cancellation. Any claims pending at the time of cancellation will not be affected by an insurer's action.

9. Other optional uniform policy provisions included in some contracts, but rarely used today, include other insurance with this insurer and insurance with other insurers.

C. OTHER PROVISIONS AND CLAUSES

1. **Insuring clause** This clause is generally located on the first page of an accident and health contract. It defines the exposure or risk as "loss as a result of accident or sickness." It also stipulates that any covered loss must occur in a manner specified in the policy. For example, the insuring clause of an accident and health contract may stipulate that injuries sustained must be due to accidental bodily injury suffered following a probationary period and occurring within the policy period.

2. **Free look** This provision is included in many accident and health contracts and permits an insured to review a policy once it has been delivered. If the insured wishes to return the contract to the insurer to receive a full refund of the premium paid, it must occur within the stipulated time frame. The free look period must be printed on the first page of the policy. In addition, the free look period begins when the insured receives the policy. This provision provides the policyowner with an opportunity to review the policy at no cost. The duration of most free look periods is 10 days (though in some states, by law, it is 20 days).

3. **Consideration clause** The premium paid and the statements made on the application are the insured's **consideration**. If an application is submitted to the underwrit-

TEST TOPIC ALERT

The probationary period in a health insurance contract applies only to sickness or illness. It does not apply to injuries or illness sustained as a result of an accident that might occur during the probationary period.

ing department and the first premium has not been paid, a necessary consideration is missing.

4. **Probationary period** This is a stipulated period of time that may apply to a disability income or medical expense contract following the issuance of a policy during which no benefits will be paid or coverage provided. The purpose of the probationary period is to enable the insurer to avoid providing benefits for illnesses that an insured may have contracted before the date of policy issuance.

   a. The length of the probationary period may vary by policy and is usually stated in the insuring clause.

   b. A probationary period is a one-time occurrence that applies only to sickness or illness. Any injuries sustained as a result of an accident are covered immediately.

5. **Elimination (waiting) period** This is the period of time that must elapse before monthly benefits will begin under a disability income contract. It may also be described as a **waiting period**. Where a probationary period is a one-time event, an elimination period must be satisfied for each new disability incurred.

   a. The most common elimination or waiting period found in disability income contracts is 30 days. If an insured chooses a longer waiting period, he will save premium dollars.

   b. An elimination or waiting period is the equivalent of a deductible under other forms of health insurance.

6. **Waiver of premium** This provision functions in much the same way as the waiver of premium provision in a life insurance contract. It provides for premiums to be waived if an insured is totally disabled for 90 days or longer. Following 90 consecutive days, all future premiums will be waived as long as the disability continues; any premiums paid during the first 90 days of disability will be refunded to the insured. In a life insurance contract, an additional premium must be paid for this benefit; however, with an accident and health policy, there is no additional charge.

7. **Exclusions** Several exclusions are listed in accident and health contracts. Some of the more common exclusions are the following:

   ■ injury or illness due to war, whether declared or undeclared;

   ■ injuries sustained while an insured is a member of the armed services (the same types of clauses are found in life insurance contracts including the status clause and the results clause);

   ■ intentionally self-inflicted injuries;

■ illness as a result of preexisting conditions;

■ injuries sustained while an insured is serving as a pilot, co-pilot, or crew member of an aircraft; and

■ other exclusions including losses resulting from suicide, riots, use of drugs or narcotics, injuries sustained while committing a crime, or hernia. Note that hernia is covered as a sickness and not as an accidental injury.

8. **Preexisting conditions** Preexisting conditions are health conditions that have already manifested themselves before the insured's application for health insurance coverage. They are frequently excluded from coverage. Probationary periods have helped to reduce claims for preexisting conditions.

   a. Some insurers will issue a policy to an insured knowing that there is a preexisting condition. However, the policy may be issued with a rider excluding coverage for the condition for a specified period of time such as one or two years.

   b. This provision helps to protect an insurer when an applicant for coverage knows or suspects that he may be in need of medical treatment.

9. **Recurrent disability** This provision is utilized when an individual suffering from a total disability apparently recovers, and in subsequent weeks or months the disability reoccurs. This provision will determine how and when benefits are payable under certain circumstances.

   a. For example, if a previously disabled individual returns to work and within six months of returning, becomes disabled again due to the original cause of the disability, the insurer will view this as a recurrent disability. If this is the case, a new elimination period is not needed and the original benefit period will continue as if the disabled insured had not returned to work. However, if the insurer determines that a new disability has occurred, the insured must satisfy a new elimination period before benefits begin.

10. **Coinsurance** Most medical expense, major medical, and comprehensive medical expense contracts include coinsurance provisions. This provision states that an insured will be responsible for a certain percentage of the medical bills incurred after a deductible amount is satisfied. Though some health insurance contracts pay 100% of all eligible expenses up to a high maximum limit, most provide coverage on a 80/20 basis. For example, after a deductible has been satisfied, the insurer will pay 80% of the remaining covered expenses; the insured will pay 20%. Coinsurance provisions—that which the insurer covers—do not usually fall below 75%.

    a. Coinsurance computations Assume that Mr. Brown owns a comprehensive medical expense policy with a $100 deductible. The contract also includes a co-insurance provision of 80/20. Mr. Brown is hospitalized for injuries sustained in an automobile accident. Mr. Brown incurs a bill during his hospital stay of $6,000. To determine how much of this amount the insurer will be responsible for, subtract the deductible ($100) from the total bill ($6,000). Multiply the remaining $5,900 by 80%, which equals $4,720 paid by the insurer. The insured, Mr. Brown, is responsible for $1,280 (the $100 deductible and 20% of $5,900).

TAKE NOTE

Amount of medical bill – (Deductible) – (Insured's coinsurance portion) = Amount insurer pays

11. **Deductibles** Deductible provisions are clauses found in medical expense, major medical, or comprehensive medical expense policies, and state that all initial medical expenses incurred up to a specified limit are the responsibility of an insured. To determine the amount an insurer will pay or the amount an insured is responsible for, subtract the deductible from the total bill and then apply the coinsurance amount.

12. **Preauthorization and prior approval requirements** Insurers further control costs by requiring preauthorization and prior approval of medical treatment. These are two forms of utilization management that are used before health services are provided.

    a. **Prior approval** Many insurers require policyholders to obtain the insurer's approval before entering a hospital on a nonemergency basis. Even if the admission is for an emergency, most policies with this type of provision require the insured to notify the insurer within a short period of time (usually 24 hours) after admission. The insurer will then determine how much of the hospital stay it will cover, depending on the reason for the admission. If the insured wants to stay longer, the additional expense is his responsibility.

    b. **Preauthorization** An insured in a managed care organization that is not a point of service plan is expected to see a primary care physician before receiving any medical care. This physician acts as a gatekeeper to medical care, providing the medical care needed or refers the insured to a medical specialist, a hospital, or an ancillary health professional. This referral is a prerequisite if the insurer is to cover the costs of the specialist, hospitalization, or other health professional. Through the gatekeeper, the insurer is able to better control medical care costs by avoiding inappropriate, unnecessary, or unreasonably expensive treatment.

13. **Lifetime, annual, and per cause benefit limits** Benefits in general may be limited by the circumstances under which they may be exercised or the number or value of the services that are covered. Insurers may limit benefits for medical claims on a lifetime, annual, or per cause basis.

D. **RIDERS** Several types of riders are available which may be added to various accident and health contracts.

    1. **Impairment rider** When an impairment rider is added to an accident and health contract (whether it is a medical expense or disability income contract), it may be an indication that the underwriting department has not been able to adequately determine the degree of risk involved and elects to exclude coverage for the particular impairment involved. For example, with a disability income contract, an exclusion rider is the most traditional way to treat disability impaired risks.

    a. These riders may be attached to accident and health contracts to exclude coverage for the life of the contract. Other riders are attached which exclude coverage for specific periods of time, such as one year, two years, or five years.

    b. Insurers also handle impairments by only agreeing to issue a disability income insurance policy if the applicant accepts a longer elimination period, a reduced benefit period, or reduced benefit amount.

    c. Some insurers handle impairment situations by adding additional premiums (referred to as "rating-up" the risk).

2. Guaranteed insurability rider This is an optional benefit that permits an insured to add coverage at specified periods in specified amounts without providing evidence of insurability. This is similar in nature to the guaranteed insurability option provided with life insurance contracts.

    a. This option is provided to applicants for disability income contracts.

    b. The guarantee offered may be contingent upon an insured meeting an earnings test before purchasing additional amounts.

    c. In most cases, this option must be exercised by an insured before age 50.

3. Multiple indemnity rider (double, triple) This rider may be added to accident and health contracts to provide double or triple indemnity in the event of an insured's accidental death or disability. These riders may also be added to life insurance policies.

E. RIGHTS OF RENEWABILITY Accident and health policies may be classified according to their renewability provisions. There are several classifications including noncancellable, cancellable, guaranteed renewable, conditionally renewable, and optionally renewable.

1. Noncancellable A noncancellable contract may also be referred to as noncancellable and guaranteed renewable. This type of contract provides an insured with the right to renew the policy up to a specified age (such as age 65), as long as premiums are paid before the expiration of the grace period. In addition, the insurer may not cancel, alter the policy terms, or increase the premium charged.

2. Cancellable A cancellable contract is one that may be terminated or cancelled by an insurer at anytime. This type of contract is not advantageous to an insured since the company may cancel at any time, for any reason.

3. Guaranteed renewable This type of policy permits an insured to renew their coverage up to a specified age (such as age 65). An insurer may not cancel a contract nor alter any of its provisions as long as the insured pays the premium within the grace period. However, the insurer does reserve the right to increase the premium at policy renewal on a class basis. This means that the insurer may not increase an individual's premium, but can increase premiums for classes of insured.

4. **Conditionally renewable** An insured has the conditional right to renew the policy up to a given age, date, or for his lifetime. With conditionally renewable contracts, the insurer may choose not to renew the contract for specific circumstances such as the insured's retirement, but it may not nonrenew the contract due to a covered individual's deteriorating health. In addition, the insurer also has the right to increase premiums and modify benefits.

5. **Optionally renewable** With this type of contract, the insurer reserves the right to terminate or cancel coverage at any policy anniversary or premium due date. The insurer is prevented from cancelling the contract at any other time. In addition, premiums and benefits provided may be altered or modified by the insurer.

6. **Specified period of time** Policies that have no provision for continuation are simply single-term policies. They provide coverage for the stated period only.

UNIT QUIZ

1. Which of the following is a mandatory uniform provision?
   A. Conformity with state statutes
   B. Change of occupation
   C. Relation of earnings to insurance
   D. Entire contract

2. How many days is the grace period in most accident and health contracts?
   A. 5
   B. 20
   C. 28
   D. 31

3. Within how many days of sustaining a loss must an insured send written notice of claim to the insurer?
   A. 5
   B. 10
   C. 20
   D. 30

4. An insurer must send out claim forms when requested by a claimant within how many days?
   A. 5
   B. 10
   C. 15
   D. 20

5. Written proof of loss must be sent to an insurer within how many days of the date of loss?
   A. 30
   B. 60
   C. 90
   D. 180

6. Which of the following provisions involves a benefit or premium reduction?
   A. Change of beneficiary
   B. Relation of earnings to insurance
   C. Cancellation
   D. Change of occupation

7. The free look period under a health insurance policy begins upon completion of
   A. an application
   B. the underwriting process
   C. the delivery of the policy
   D. the statement of continued good health

8. A period of time that is satisfied for each new disability incurred best describes the
   A. probationary period
   B. elimination period
   C. recurrent period
   D. residential period

9. Which of the following statements concerning a guaranteed renewable policy is CORRECT?
   A. Premiums may not be increased.
   B. The policy may not be cancelled as long as the premium is paid.
   C. Policy provisions may be altered only for a class of insureds.
   D. The policy may be nonrenewed only on a class basis.

10. The waiver of premium benefit in a disability income policy waives premiums after how many months of disability?
    A. 2
    B. 3
    C. 6
    D. 12

ANSWERS

1. D	2. D	3. C	4. C	5. C
6. D	7. C	8. B	9. B	10. B

DISCUSSION QUESTIONS

1. Identify the 12 uniform policy provisions.

2. What will occur when a person changes from a more hazardous to a less hazardous occupation and vice versa?

3. Identify several optional provisions that may appear in A&H policies.

4. Briefly describe the importance of the free look period and when it begins.

5. Discuss the difference between a probationary and elimination period.

6. How does the waiver of premium provision under a disability income policy differ from the same provision found in a life insurance policy?

7. Identify several common exclusions that appear in A&H contracts.

8. How do noncancellable and guaranteed renewable contracts differ from guaranteed renewable policies?

9. Briefly describe each of the following:
   A. Noncancellable policy
   B. Guaranteed renewable policy
   C. Conditionally renewable policy
   D. Optionally renewable policy

10. Briefly discuss the importance of the concept of recurrent disability.

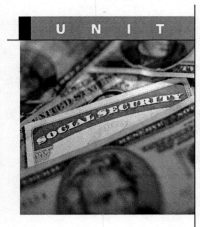

9

Government Programs and Social Health Insurance

KEY TERMS

Medicare	Hospital Insurance	Supplementary Medical
Medicare+Choice	Medicaid	Disability
Fully Insured	Currently Insured	HMO and Medicare
Waiting Period	Disability Offset	

I. SOCIAL HEALTH INSURANCE

Through a number of programs, federal and state governments provide health insurance and health care to select segments of our society: generally, those who are elderly, poor, or disabled. Significant among these programs are Medicare, Medicaid, and the disability benefits portion of Social Security.

A. MEDICARE This is a two-part federal health insurance program. It provides medical benefits for the aged and for qualified persons who are disabled. It comprises Part A (basic hospital insurance) and Part B (supplementary medical insurance).

1. Part A—hospital insurance All persons age 65 or older who are entitled to federal Social Security or railroad retirement benefits are automatically eligible for Medicare (on the first day of the month the individual turns 65). In addition, individuals under age 65 who have qualified for Social Security disability payments for at least two years and those who have end-stage renal disease are eligible. Eligible insureds do not have to pay any premiums for this coverage.

a. Other elderly persons not covered by Social Security may elect to participate voluntarily by paying a monthly premium.

b. Part A covers **inpatient hospital services** (subject to a deductible of $952 in 2006) for up to 90 days in each benefit period. All charges are paid (over the deductible) during the first 60 days; from the 61st through the 90th days, Part A pays for all covered services except for a coinsurance amount. The benefit period begins on the day of admittance to a hospital or extended-care facility and ends after the insured has been released for 60 consecutive days. Benefits include payment for prescription drugs only while in the hospital. No coverage is provided for the first three pints of blood.

c. Skilled nursing care This is provided for up to 100 days. All covered services for the first 20 days are fully paid after the insured pays the annual deductible ($952 in 2006); the next 80 days are subject to a daily coinsurance amount.

d. Home health services Home health services cover medically necessary home health visits including part-time skilled nursing services.

e. Hospice care Hospice care benefits are designed for the terminally ill, with emphasis on pain reduction and quality of life. Medicare recipients who elect hospice benefits must forego all other Medicare benefits except for physician services and treatment for conditions not related to the terminal illness.

f. Psychiatric hospital care This is covered for up to 190 days during the individual's lifetime.

g. Payment by Medicare for charges under Part A is made directly to the hospital or provider of the service on a reasonable cost basis.

h. Medicare Part A is financed primarily by employment-related tax funds provided through the Social Security (FICA) program. It is financed on a contributory basis, shared equally by employer and employee.

i. If an individual is covered by both private insurance, such as an HMO, and Medicare, the private insurance is considered primary and will pay benefits first. Medicare would then pay the balance of eligible expenses.

j. Part A has a lifetime reserve of 60 days. Reserve days may be used when more than 90 days of inpatient hospital care in a benefit period are needed (a daily coinsurance amount applies). Once used, reserve days are not renewed.

2. **Part B—supplementary medical insurance (SMI)** This aspect of Medicare is a voluntary medical insurance plan available to all who are entitled to, or have purchased, Part A which pays benefits for physician and surgeon fees, related medical services and supplies, medically necessary outpatient hospital services, x-rays and laboratory tests, and other health services such as ambulance services and durable medical equipment, such as hospital beds and wheelchairs.

   a. The individual pays a monthly premium ($88.50 in 2006), an annual deductible ($124 in 2006), and coinsurance of 20% of all remaining covered expenses. After the deductible is satisfied, Part B pays 80% of approved charges.

   b. The Medicare-approved amount for physician services is based upon a national fee schedule; physicians who accept assignment on a Medicare claim agree to take the Medicare-approved amount as payment in full. The patient is responsible for amounts in excess of the Medicare-approved amount for unassigned claims.

   c. Limitations include 50% of approved charges for outpatient mental health treatment and no coverage for the first three pints of blood.

   d. Part B is financed by monthly contributions (premiums) of those who choose to participate, as well as tax revenues. In other words, the cost for SMI is paid by the enrollee and the federal government. The latter pays approximately 75%.

   e. **Exclusions** Medical services not covered under Part B include eye and hearing examinations, routine physical exams, foot care, immunizations, and private nurses.

   f. Individuals are automatically enrolled in Part B following Medicare eligibility. This may be delayed for individuals who are covered under an employer's group health plan. Once the individual leaves the group, they then must enroll within seven months of that date.

Medicare Part A   Hospital expenses

Medicare Part B   Physician, surgeon, and other medical expenses

Medicare Part C   Optional coordinated care plan, fee-for-service plans, or MSA

Medicare Part D   Prescription drug benefit program (PDP)

3. **Part C—Medicare Advantage plans** Federal law allows Medicare-eligible participants to opt out of the traditional program (Parts A and B) and enroll in one of the plans described below. These plans comprise the Medicare Advantage option (previously called Medicare+Choice).

   a. **Coordinated-care plans** These include the following:

   ■ health maintenance organizations of various types, but all requiring services to be rendered by its own providers, except in an emergency;

   ■ preferred provider organizations which allow beneficiaries to receive services from providers outside the plan, but with higher cost-sharing; and

   ■ provider-sponsored organizations which are similar to PPOs except that they are operated by a group of physicians and hospitals.

   b. **Private-fee-for-service plans** These are similar to PSOs, except that they may pay providers more than Medicare recognizes and can charge beneficiaries additional premiums and cost-sharing payments.

   c. **Medical Savings Accounts (MSAs)** This is a pilot program that enables senior citizens to establish a special medical savings account. As with regular MSAs, individuals with Medicare Advantage (or Medicare+Choice) can apply their contributions to their MSAs for health care expenses. However, this kind of MSA must be used in conjunction with a high-deductible (up to $6,000 per year) MSA health plan.

      1.) Annual contributions are limited to 75% of the individual's deductible under the required MSA health plan. For example, if the deductible was $5,000, contributions cannot exceed $3,750.

      2.) All earnings on MSA accounts are excluded from taxable income for the current year.

      3.) Distributions to pay for qualified medical expenses are not included in the participant's income. However, distributions for purposes other than medical expenses must be included in taxable income.

4. **Part D—Prescription Drugs** The Medicare Prescription Drug, Improvement, and Modernization Act of 2003 (MMA) created a new Medicare Part D as an optional outpatient prescription drug benefit for individuals who are currently enrolled in Medicare benefits under Part A, Part B, or both.

a. The new Medicare Prescription Drug Benefit Program went into effect on January 1, 2006.

b. Because of the addition of a prescription drug benefit to Medicare, the MMA also prescribes changes to the law applicable to Medigap policies (discussed below). The most significant changes are the prohibition against selling Medigap policies with prescription drug coverage after 2005 and the establishment of two new standardized Medigap benefit packages.

5. Employer group health plans   Individuals who are participating in an employer group health plan and are Medicare participants are subject to the following.

a. Special rules apply to working people age 65 and over. Medicare may be the secondary payor to any employer group health plan (employer's plan pays hospital and medical bills first). If the employer plan does not cover all expenses, Medicare becomes the secondary payor for eligible expenses.

b. Special rules apply to certain disabled Medicare beneficiaries who have group coverage provided by an employer with 100 or more employees. Medicare would be the secondary payor of benefits (with the exception of those with permanent kidney failure).

c. Medicare is the secondary payor for up to 21 months for beneficiaries with permanent kidney failure. Following this period, the employer group health plan becomes the secondary payor and Medicare becomes primary.

B. MEDICARE SUPPLEMENT (MEDIGAP) POLICIES   Medigap policies are issued by insurance companies and are designed to provide benefits for specific expenses not covered under Medicare that result from deductibles, exclusions, limitations, or coinsurance.

1. In late 1990, Congress mandated that Medigap coverages and policies be standardized to reduce the number of supplement policies that were being marketed and to help consumers better understand and compare coverages and premiums. The result was 10 standard Medigap plans: A, B, C, D, E, F, G, H, I, and J. (In 2006, Plans H, I, and J will be discontinued and Plans K and L will be introduced. More on this below.)

a. Plan A is the most basic policy.

b. Plan J is the most comprehensive in coverage.

c. Those in between offer various combinations of benefits. These benefit combinations cannot be altered by insurers and all insurers must use the same format, language, and definitions in describing the benefits and limitations of each plan.

2. The Balanced Budget Act of 1997 authorized new high deductible versions of Plans F and J. These versions begin paying benefits after the high deductible is paid. Expenses that can be applied to the deductible are expenses that would usually be paid by the policy, such as Medicare coinsurance and deductibles for Parts A and B. However, they do not include the plan's separate foreign travel emergency deductible. A separate deductible must be met before these expenses can be applied to the overall plan deductible.

3. As of January 1, 2006, insurers may not sell Medigap Plans H, I, and J.

    a. If these policies were purchased before 2006, they can be renewed as long as the policyholder has not enrolled in Medicare Part D.

    b. When the policyholder enrolls in Medicare Part D, the drug coverage must be eliminated from the Medigap policy and the premium must be adjusted accordingly.

4. As noted, two new Medigap benefit packages became available on January 1, 2006. These Plans (K and L) have higher copayments and coinsurance requirements and impose a limit on annual out-of-pocket expenditures incurred by a policyholder.

    a. Once the out-of-pocket limit on annual expenditures is reached, the policy covers 100% of all cost-sharing under Medicare Parts A and B for the balance of the calendar year.

    b. For 2006, the out-of-pocket limit for Plan K is $4,000 and $2,000 for Plan L.

    c. A Medigap policy does not pay cost-sharing for expenses incurred under Medicare Parts C and D.

    The table on page 140 outlines the provisions of the standard Medicare supplement plans.

5. All Medigap policies must include a free look period. In most states, this period is 30 days, though it may be longer.

C. MEDICAID Created in 1965, **Medicaid** substantially expanded the role of the federal government in healthcare financing by permitting states to receive matching federal funds to expand their public assistance programs to individuals with insufficient income to pay for medical care. Each state administers its own Medicaid program.

1. Medicaid is a form of welfare that provides assistance to the needy. It is not funded by Medicare.

2. The extent of covered costs varies among states.

3. It provides supplemental medical care for low income and needy individuals who are aged, blind, disabled, or under 21 years of age.

D. SOCIAL SECURITY DISABILITY BENEFITS In addition to retirement and survivor benefits, Social Security provides benefits for disabilities.

1. Social Security disability income coverage extends to any employment where an individual works for salary or wages as well as most self-employed persons.

2. **Benefits** The amount of disability benefits paid by Social Security depends upon the insured status of the individual worker and the primary insurance amount (PIA). The worker must be fully insured in order to receive this benefit.

    a. **Fully insured** A person becomes fully insured by acquiring a sufficient number of quarters of coverage to meet either of the following two tests.

        1.) A person is fully insured if he has 40 quarters of coverage (10 years of covered employment). Once a person has acquired 40 quarters of coverage, he is fully insured for life, even if he spends no further time in covered employment (or covered self-employment).

        2.) A person is fully insured if: (1) he has at least six quarters of coverage; and (2) he has acquired at least as many quarters of coverage as there are years elapsing after 1950 (or, if later, after the year in which he reaches age 21) and before the year in which he dies, becomes disabled, reaches, or will reach age 62, whichever occurs first.

    b. **Currently insured** A person is currently insured if he has acquired at least six quarters of coverage during the full 13-quarter period ending with the calendar quarter in which he (1) died, or (2) most recently became entitled to disability benefits, or (3) became entitled to retirement benefits.

        1.) The six quarters of coverage need not be consecutive, but they must be acquired during the 13-quarter period.

3. **Definition of total disability** The definition of disability under Social Security is much more restrictive than that found in individual or group plans. It states that a person is totally disabled if he "cannot perform the duties of any gainful employment and that the disability is expected to last at least one year or result in death."

4. **Waiting period** There is a five-month waiting period for disability income benefits; payments start in the sixth month.

5. **Disability benefits offset** In many cases, group disability (LTD) income benefits are reduced or offset by any amount received from Social Security (or other social insurance such as workers' compensation). However, if a person owns and pays the premium on an individual disability income policy, any benefits received are not reduced by amounts collected from social insurance plans.

E. **MEDICARE AND HMOs** Health maintenance organizations may be sponsored by the government to provide benefits for those persons eligible for Medicare. There are two basic ways for an HMO to cover Medicare members.

    1. **Risk contracts** In this situation, an HMO enters into a contract with the federal government to be liable (at risk) for all medical expenses incurred by a Medicare

12 Standard Medigap Plans

A	B	C	D	E	F**	G	H	I	J**	K	L
Basic Benefits*	Basic Benefits*	Basic Benefits*	Basic Benefits*	Basic Benefits*	Basic Benefits*	Basic Benefits*	Basic Benefits*	Basic Benefits*	Basic Benefits*	Basic Benefits***	Basic Benefit***
	Part A Deductible	Part A Deductible	Part A Deductible	Part A Deductible	Part A Deductible	Part A Deductible	Part A Deductible	Part A Deductible	Part A Deductible	50% Part A Deductible	50% Part A Deductible
		Skilled Nursing Coinsurance	Skilled Nursing Coinsurance	Skilled Nursing Coinsurance	Skilled Nursing Coinsurance	Skilled Nursing Coinsurance	Skilled Nursing Coinsurance	Skilled Nursing Coinsurance	Skilled Nursing Coinsurance	50% Skilled Nursing Coinsurance	50% Skilled Nursing Coinsurance
		Part B Deductible			Part B Deductible				Part B Deductible		
					Part B Excess (100%)	Part B Excess (80%)		Part B Excess (100%)	Part B Excess (100%)		
		Foreign Travel Emergency	Foreign Travel Emergency	Foreign Travel Emergency	Foreign Travel Emergency	Foreign Travel Emergency	Foreign Travel Emergency	Foreign Travel Emergency	Foreign Travel Emergency		
			At-Home Recovery			At-Home Recovery		At-Home Recovery	At-Home Recovery		
							Basic Drugs ($1,250 Limit) ***	Basic Drugs ($1,250 Limit) ***			
				Preventive Care Not Covered by Medicare					Preventive Care Not Covered by Medicare		
					Annual Deductible **				Annual Deductible **	Annual Deductible *****	Annual Deductible *****

*The Basic Benefits policy covers 100% of the Part A hospital coinsurance amount for each day used from the 61st through the 90th day in any Medicare benefit period and 100% of the Part A hospital coinsurance amount for each Medicare lifetime inpatient reserve day used from the 91st through the 150th day in any Medicare benefit period; 100% of the Part A-eligible hospital expenses for 365 additional days after all hospital benefits are exhausted; Part B coinsurance amount (generally 20% of Medicare-approved expenses) after the annual deductible is met, and the cost of the first three pints of blood each year.

**Plans F and J have a high deductible plan option that pays the same benefits as Plans F and J after one has paid a calendar year deductible. Benefits from high deductible Plans F and J will not begin until out-of-pocket expenses exceed the deductible. Out-of-pocket expenses for this deductible are expenses that would ordinarily be paid by the policy. These expenses include the Medicare deductible for Part A and Part B, but do not include the plan's separate foreign travel emergency deductible.

***The basic benefits under Plans K and L provide for different costsharing for items and services than Plans A through J. Plan K pays 100% of Part A hospitalization coinsurance plus coverage for 365 days after Medicare benefits end, 50% of hospice cost-sharing, 50% of Medicare-eligible expenses for the first three pints of blood, and 50% of Part B coinsurance, except 100% coinsurance for Part B preventive services. Plan L pays 100% of Part A hospitalization coinsurance plus coverage for 365 days after Medicare benefits end, 75% of hospice costsharing, 75% of Medicare-eligible expenses for the first three pints of blood, and 75% of Part B coinsurance, except 100% coinsurance for Part B preventive services.

Once a person reaches the annual limit, the plan pays 100% of the Medicare copayments, coinsurance, and deductibles for the rest of the calendar years. The out-of-pocket annual limit does not include charges from a provider and that exceed Medicare-approved amounts. Such charges are called "excess charges," and the policyowner is responsible for paying them.

****These out-of-pocket annual limits increase each year for inflation.

enrollee for covered services. As a result of this exchange of coverage, the government pays the HMO a monthly sum per covered person. Therefore, Medicare is no longer liable to provide coverage for that person. Enrollment in an HMO by a recipient of Medicare is voluntary.

2. **Wrap coverage**   Here an HMO is not required to enter into a contract with the government. Medicare continues to pay for all of the member's Medicare eligible expenses (costs). The HMO, however, provides excess (additional) services in comparison to Medicare and is responsible for the cost. Therefore, the HMO coordinates benefits with Medicare and sends it a bill for the amount Medicare should cover. The HMO pays the balance. An HMO's risk is less under wrap coverage which means it costs less.

3. HMO options for Medicare recipients include the following.

   a. Medicare risk plans are paid a per capita premium set at approximately 95% of the projected average expenses for fee-for-service beneficiaries in a given county. Risk plans assume full financial risk for all care provided to Medicare beneficiaries. Risk plans must provide all Medicare-covered services, and most plans offer additional services, such as prescription drugs and eyeglasses. With the exception of emergency and out-of-area urgent care, members of risk plans must receive all of their care through the plan. However, as of January 1, 1996, risk plans can provide an out-of-network option that, subject to certain conditions, allows beneficiaries to go to providers who are not part of the plan.

   b. Medicare cost plans are paid a predetermined monthly amount per beneficiary based on a total estimated budget. Adjustments to that payment are made at the end of the year for any variations from the budget. Cost plans must provide all Medicare-covered services but do not provide the additional services that some risk plans offer. Beneficiaries can also obtain Medicare-covered services outside the plan without limitation. When a beneficiary seeks care or services outside the plan, Medicare pays its traditional share of those costs and the beneficiary pays Medicare's coinsurance and deductibles.

   c. Medicare health care prepayment plans (HCPPs) are paid in a similar manner as cost plans but only cover part of the Medicare benefit package. HCPPs do not cover Medicare Part A services (inpatient hospital care, skilled nursing, hospice, and some home health care), but some do arrange for services and may file Part A claims for their members.

UNIT QUIZ

1. All of the following statements are correct regarding Medicare EXCEPT

   A. benefits may continue beyond the hospitalization period
   B. payments are made directly to the provider of services
   C. Part A is financed by tax funds
   D. Part B covers prescription drugs only after hospitalization

2. All of the following statements are correct regarding Part B of Medicare EXCEPT

   A. a coinsurance percentage of 75/25 applies after the deductible is satisfied
   B. a deductible is required
   C. Part B is financed in part by the participants
   D. coverage is provided for physician's expenses

3. Social Security disability benefits will begin following a waiting period of how many months?

   A. 2
   B. 5
   C. 6
   D. 12

4. Disability benefits will be paid by Social Security to a party who is

   A. partially insured
   B. primarily insured
   C. fully insured
   D. none of the above

5. Disability benefits paid under Social Security begin in the

   A. 1st month
   B. 3rd month
   C. 5th month
   D. 6th month

6. All of the following statements are correct concerning Medicaid EXCEPT

   A. the program provides benefits for needy and low-income individuals
   B. the extent of covered costs varies by state
   C. Medicaid is partially funded by Medicare recipients' premiums
   D. Medicaid is administered at the state level

ANSWERS

1. D   2. A   3. B
4. C   5. D   6. C

DISCUSSION QUESTIONS

1. Briefly describe the benefits provided by Parts A and B of Medicare.

2. To what party are payment of bills made under basic hospital insurance?

3. Briefly describe the purpose of Medicaid and how is the program financed.

4. Discuss the difference between fully insured and currently insured status.

5. What two factors determine the amount of disability benefits paid by Social Security?

6. How will benefits be affected if a person owns an individual disability income policy and is eligible for Social Security benefits?

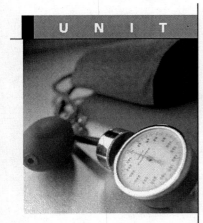

10

Other Health Insurance Concepts

KEY TERMS

Dependent Children

Beneficiaries

Nonduplication/
  Coordination

Occupational

Nonoccupational

Managed Care

Utilization Review

I. OTHER HEALTH INSURANCE CONCEPTS

The field of health insurance is broad. Other important concepts as they relate to beneficiaries and taxation are briefly reviewed in this section.

A. POLICYOWNERS' RIGHTS Accident and health policyowners have a variety of contractual rights. These include:

- the right of renewal;
- incontestable provision;
- the right to change beneficiaries;
- the right to cancel a policy;
- reinstatement provisions; and
- the grace period.

B. DEPENDENT CHILDREN BENEFITS Under an individual health policy, dependent children may also be covered. For this purpose, children must be <u>unmarried and under 19 years of age.</u> Stepchildren and legally adopted children are included in this group.

1. Coverage ends on the policy renewal date following the attainment of age 19 or marriage, unless the child is handicapped.

2. Coverage continues for a handicapped child as long as he remains unmarried and the incapacity continues.

C. PRIMARY AND CONTINGENT BENEFICIARIES The benefits provided by health insurance contracts are usually payable to an insured, hospital, physician, or dentist for services rendered. However, there are situations where beneficiaries must be named in the event of accidental death. Beneficiary designations in a health insurance contract are expressed as follows.

1. **Primary beneficiary** This is the individual who is first in line to receive the policy's death benefit.

2. **Contingent beneficiary** This is the individual who will receive benefits if the primary beneficiary dies before the insured. The most common contingent beneficiaries are the children of an insured. For example, a husband will name his wife as primary beneficiary and list his children as contingent beneficiaries.

3. **Tertiary beneficiary** This is the beneficiary who will receive death benefits if the primary beneficiary and no contingent beneficiaries survive the insured.

D. MODES OF PREMIUM PAYMENTS Applicants for health insurance have a choice as to how they wish to pay their health insurance premiums. As in life insurance, health insurance premiums may be paid annually, semiannually, quarterly, monthly (check-o-matic), or weekly.

1. Premiums that are not paid on an annual basis are subject to a small additional charge due to the added expense of collecting premiums two, four, or twelve times a year instead

of only once. In situations where premiums are paid other than annually, the insurer experiences a loss of interest since less money is collected at the beginning of the policy term.

E.   NONDUPLICATION AND COORDINATION OF BENEFITS One of the primary concerns of health insurers centers on avoiding overinsurance and providing duplicate benefits to insureds. Duplicate benefits would enable an insured to profit from the purchase of health insurance. Insurers providing duplicate coverage or protection that is too liberal find that it is not in the best interest of the public. This would not only contribute to higher premiums charged but also increased healthcare costs.

1. Methods an insurer employs to control overinsurance include the use of **deductibles** and **percentage participation (coinsurance)**. In addition, insurers also use disability income insurance to help control overinsurance or duplication of benefits by restricting coverage to a percentage of an insured's average earnings.

2. Group health insurance policies also include a **coordination of benefits provision** to avoid duplicate coverage. This provision limits total benefits payable to 100% of covered expenses, regardless of the number of group policies involved. Under this provision, each insurer, following the **primary carrier**, pays in a specified order so that the combined benefits paid will not be greater than the total allowable expenses. For example, an individual's primary insurer would be the company providing group health insurance benefits through their employer. The secondary insurer might be his spouse's group insurer.

F.   OCCUPATIONAL VERSUS NONOCCUPATIONAL CONTRACTS

1. **Occupational** An **occupational** contract is one that provides coverage both on and off the job. Generally, only nonhazardous occupations qualify for coverage.

2. **Nonoccupational** Nonoccupational health insurance policies are those that cover off-the-job accidents or illnesses. These policies provide accident and sickness coverage which excludes employment related injuries or illness. An individual who works in a coal mine, for example, would only be eligible for a nonoccupational policy since the insurer would not want to provide coverage for this type of risk on the job.

G.   TAX TREATMENT OF PREMIUMS PAID AND PROCEEDS RECEIVED The tax treatment of health insurance premiums and proceeds will depend upon the type of policy in question.

1. **Individual health insurance premiums** Premiums paid on personal or individual health insurance policies are generally not tax deductible. The basic reason for this is that the Internal Revenue Service considers these premiums as a personal expense.

    a. Premiums paid on an individual disability income policy are not deductible.

    b. Premiums paid on an individual medical expense policy are not deductible.

2. **Taxation of medical expense insurance** Incurred medical expenses that are reimbursed by insurance may not be deducted from an individual's federal income tax. Furthermore, incurred medical expenses that are not reimbursed by insurance may only be deducted to the extent they exceed 7.5% of the insured's adjusted gross income. For example, an individual who has an adjusted gross income of $35,000 would be able to deduct only the amount of unreimbursed medical expenses over $2,625. Self-employed individuals may deduct all amounts paid for medical care, including insurance premiums.

3. **Proceeds received** The proceeds or benefits received from an individual disability income contract are income tax free. The proceeds received from medical expense insurance are also free of income taxation because they are considered a reimbursement for expenses incurred.

4. **Business health insurance premiums and proceeds**

    a. With a disability income policy, an employer paying the premium on a policy covering the life of a key employee will not be able to deduct the premium if the monthly benefit is payable to the employer or corporation. The benefits received from the policy are income tax free.

    b. With a disability income contract where the employer pays the premium and monthly benefits are paid to the key employee, the premiums will be deductible to the employer. However, the monthly income benefits received by the employee are taxable. If an employee contributes to any portion of the premium, the benefit will be tax free in proportion to the employee's contribution.

    c. With a medical expense insurance plan where a key employee is covered, the premiums paid by an employer are usually deductible since they are considered a customary and usual business expense (group insurance). Benefits received are usually not taxable since they are a reimbursement of incurred medical expenses.

H. **MANAGED CARE** Managed care attempts to place cost controls on the providers and receivers of medical care. It includes formal programs for monitoring the quality of the treatment and determination of what constitutes appropriate treatment in a particular case. Utilization review is the major tool of health care management.

1. Utilization review techniques include:
- hospital precertification;
- continued stay review;
- second surgical opinion programs; and
- medical care management programs.

2. Programs that monitor the quality of treatment and determination of appropriate treatment include:

■ preadmission testing provisions that encourage the performance of medical tests on an outpatient basis before hospitalization;

■ preadmission certification that makes nonemergency hospital admission subject to approval either by the insurer or by an independent review organization;

■ second surgical opinions that are designed to prevent unnecessary surgery;

■ concurrent review, which is the monitoring of the patient's inpatient stay on an ongoing basis, usually by the group that administers the precertification program; and

■ provider charges, which represent another major target in managed care; the emphasis is on controlling fees charged by the providers of services.

U N I T   Q U I Z

1. All of the following are examples of health insurance policyowner's rights EXCEPT
   A. the right of renewal
   B. reinstatement provisions
   C. the right to cancel a policy
   D. the right to change an irrevocable beneficiary without his permission

2. All of the following are common modes of paying health insurance premiums EXCEPT
   A. weekly
   B. monthly
   C. annually
   D. every 2 years

3. Which of the following is used by an insurer to prevent duplication of coverage?
   A. Deductible
   B. Coinsurance
   C. Coordination of earnings
   D. Coordination of benefits

4. Which of the following best describes the coverage provided to an insured under an occupational policy?
   A. Covers on the job only
   B. Covers on and off the job
   C. Covers off the job only
   D. Covers hazardous jobs only

5. Premiums paid on an individual disability income insurance policy are
   A. generally tax deductible
   B. generally not tax deductible
   C. deductible if they exceed 7% of the insured's gross income
   D. deductible if paid for by the insured's employer

ANSWERS

1. D   2. D   3. D   4. B   5. B

DISCUSSION QUESTIONS

1. Identify a health policyowner's rights under the contract.

2. Identify the various modes of premium paying available to an insured. Which method is the least expensive?

3. How does the coordination of benefits provision avoid duplicate coverage?

4. Compare the definitions of occupational and nonoccupational health policies.

5. Discuss the tax treatment of premiums and proceeds of a personal health insurance contract; of a business policy.

11

Accident and Health Insurance Practice Final Examination

Following your thorough study of Units 1, 2, and 7 through 10, take this 50-question practice final on accident and health insurance. Grade your performance using the answer key provided. Carefully review the information in this book regarding those questions answered incorrectly.

ACCIDENT AND HEALTH INSURANCE PRACTICE FINAL EXAMINATION

1. Social Security benefits may be payable to a disabled individual after a waiting period of how many months?

   A. 3
   B. 5
   C. 6
   D. 12

2. A health insurance contract that does not permit an increase in premiums, modifications to policy provisions, and is not cancellable, best describes a(n)

   A. noncancellable and guaranteed renewable policy
   B. guaranteed renewable policy
   C. optionally renewable policy
   D. conditionally renewable policy

3. Most Medicare Supplement (Medigap) policies have a _____ free look period.

   A. 60-day
   B. 45-day
   C. 30-day
   D. 10-day

4. Which of the following provides the option for an employee to continue to maintain his group health insurance coverage after he is no longer employed by the employer?

   A. ERISA
   B. HIPPA
   C. FICA
   D. COBRA

5. The mandatory physical exam and autopsy provision found in health insurance policies is most commonly applied by insurers

   A. to determine the cause and validity of a health insurance claim that exceeds $50,000
   B. to determine the cause of death when a claim is made under an AD&D policy
   C. to validate that an individual claiming disability benefit remains disabled
   D. whenever benefits are payable to a beneficiary due to the death of the insured

6. Roger has a major medical policy with a $500 deductible and an 80/20 coinsurance provision. If he incurs medical expenses of $4,000, the insurer would pay

   A. $800
   B. $2,700
   C. $2,800
   D. $3,200

7. All of the following statements concerning the coordination of benefits provision found in accident and health policies are true EXCEPT

   A. the provision guards against duplication of it benefits
   B. it prevents an insured from profiting from an if illness or injury
   C. it does not apply to group policies
   D. premiums would be higher without this provision

8. Assume Hal, the insured under a disability income policy, is severely injured in an accident. He is unable to work for a period of 8 months, during which he receives his policy's full benefit. After 8 months, he returns to work, but due to his injury, he can work only on a part-time basis. In order to continue to collect benefits under the policy, the policy must include what kind of provision?

   A. A total disability provision
   B. A partial disability provision
   C. A residual disability provision
   D. A fully insured disability provision

9. In a disability income policy, an elimination period provision refers to the period

   A. between the first day of disability and the actual receipt of payment for the disability incurred
   B. during which any specific accident or illness is excluded from coverage
   C. between the first day of disability and the day to which the disability must continue before it can result in the insured receiving any benefits
   D. between the effective date of the policy and the date on which payments under the policy become due

10. Which of the following is commonly and specifically excluded under a medical expense policy?
    A. Loss of income as a result of illness
    B. Self-inflicted injuries
    C. Hospitalization due to mental illness
    D. Injuries caused by accidents

11. The purpose of a grace period in an accident and health insurance contract is to
    A. allow the insurer to determine the deceased's cause of death
    B. permit the beneficiary to establish an insurable interest in the contract
    C. protect the insurer against the adverse selection of policyowners
    D. protect a policyowner against the unintentional lapse of a contract

12. A guaranteed renewable accident and health policy gives the insurer the right to
    A. increase premiums on a class basis
    B. alter policy provisions during the policy term
    C. reduce the amount of insurance after each claim
    D. cancel the policy due to the filing of numerous claims

13. Bob owns a disability income policy paying $1,500 per month in the event that he becomes totally disabled. The policy has a 30-day elimination period. Bob is involved in a traffic accident and is disabled for 105 days. How much will his disability income policy pay?
    A. $2,250
    B. $3,750
    C. $4,500
    D. $5,250

14. The preexisting condition exclusion found in an accident and health policy is designed to protect the insurer against
    A. adverse selection
    B. over insurance
    C. malingering
    D. compliance

15. Which of the following statements regarding surgical expense benefits is CORRECT?
    A. Benefits are typically subject to deductibles of $250 or more.
    B. The amount on the benefit schedule is typically expressed in terms of the maximum benefit payable.
    C. Coverage is usually provided for rehabilitation costs following surgery.
    D. A small amount, usually no more than $350, is provided for incidentals while hospitalized.

16. A comprehensive medical expense insurance policy combines which of the following coverages under one contract?
    A. Major medical coverage and accidental death
    B. Disability income and accidental death
    C. Basic hospital and surgical coverage with major medical coverage
    D. Disability income with basic hospital and surgical coverages

17. Which of the following is an eligibility requirement in order to receive full Social Security disability benefits?
    A. An individual must have obtained PIA insured status.
    B. An individual must have obtained fully insured status.
    C. An individual must be at least 65 years old.
    D. The recipient must be disabled for at least 12 months before benefits may be received.

18. Long-term care insurance provides all of the following coverages EXCEPT
    A. skilled nursing care
    B. surgical expense
    C. intermediate (rehabilitative) care
    D. custodial care

19. The contractual provision that specifies the time limit that an insured has to return accident and health claim forms to the insurer is known as
    A. payment of claims
    B. claim forms
    C. grace period
    D. proof of loss

20. Which of the following types of health insurance policies provides for a death benefit, payable to the insured's beneficiary?

   A. DI
   B. AD&D
   C. LTC
   D. COBRA

21. Which of the following statements regarding participation in Part A of Medicare is CORRECT?

   A. The insured must pay a deductible.
   B. The insured must pay an annual premium.
   C. Benefits are paid directly to the insured.
   D. To participate, an individual must be covered by Social Security.

22. All of the following statements concerning Part B of Medicare are correct EXCEPT

   A. a coinsurance feature of 80/20 is included to cover charges after a deductible is satisfied
   B. benefit payments are subject to an annual deductible
   C. annual physical exams are required to maintain coverage
   D. a premium is charged for Part B participation

23. Will owns an individual disability income policy paying $800 per month with a 60-day waiting period. If he becomes disabled for 45 days, how much will his contract pay?

   A. Nothing
   B. $200
   C. $400
   D. $800

24. The period of time that that elapse after the onset of a disability and before monthly disability income benefits begin is referred to as the

   A. probationary period
   B. conversion period
   C. elimination period
   D. holding period

25. An insured must provide written notice of a claim to the insurer within how many days of a loss?

   A. 5
   B. 10
   C. 15
   D. 20

26. After receiving notice of claim from an insured, the insurer must provide claim forms to that insured within how many days of the request?

   A. 5
   B. 10
   C. 15
   D. 20

27. Chris receives $50,000 from a $100,000 accidental death and dismemberment policy as a result of the loss of his left arm in an accident. He has received the

   A. primary amount
   B. principal amount
   C. capital amount
   D. contributory amount

28. Medicare Part A benefit periods end when a person has been released from a hospital or skilled nursing facility for a period of

   A. 60 days
   B. 90 days
   C. 6 months
   D. 12 months

29. Ann owns a major medical policy with a $1,000 deductible and a provision that provides for percentage participation of 80/20. Due to an illness, Ann incurs covered medical expenses of $3,000. How much of this amount will Ann be responsible for?

   A. $400
   B. $1,400
   C. $1,600
   D. $2,400

30. Responses to questions given by applicants on an accident and health insurance application are considered to be

    A. warranties
    B. mandated statements
    C. entitlements
    D. representations

31. Which of the following terms best defines the approach that Blue Cross and Blue Shield organizations use to provide for health care?

    A. Indemnity
    B. Valued
    C. Service
    D. Reimbursement

32. With regard to the reinstatement of a health insurance contract, all of the following statements are true EXCEPT

    A. evidence of insurability may be required
    B. upon reinstatement, coverage for illness is effective immediately
    C. upon reinstatement, coverage for accidents is effective immediately
    D. reinstatement is automatic unless the insurer informs the applicant within 45 days that he has been rejected

33. Which of the following is a typical benefit period for group short-term disability income coverage?

    A. 1 to 3 months
    B. 6 to 18 months
    C. 12 to 28 months
    D. 18 to 24 months

34. Which of the following statements is CORRECT regarding the change of occupation provision found in a disability income policy?

    A. It sets forth the rights and obligations of the insurer and the insured in the event that the insured engages in a more hazardous or less hazardous occupation.
    B. It voids the policy if the insured suffers an otherwise compensable loss while engaged in an illegal occupation.
    C. It requires that the insurer deny benefits if the insured changes his occupation following the policy effective date.
    D. It provides a formula by which adjustments are made to the elimination periods in the event that the insured changes to a higher risk occupation.

35. All of the following are optional uniform health insurance policy provisions EXCEPT

    A. reinstatement
    B. change of occupation
    C. conformity with state statutes
    D. misstatement of age

36. What advantage does the recurrent disability provision provide to the insured under a disability income policy?

    A. It eliminates the imposition of a second elimination period for the same disability.
    B. It provides the insured with lifetime disability benefits.
    C. It eliminates the imposition of an elimination period for a separate disability.
    D. All of the above.

37. The amount payable in the event of the insured's death under an accidental death policy is referred to as the

    A. capital sum
    B. principal sum
    C. accidental death sum
    D. dismemberment benefit

38. With regard to the taxation of disability income insurance provided by a business on a key employee, whereby the premium is paid by the employer and the benefits are paid to the employee, which of the following statements is TRUE?

    A. Premiums are not tax deductible; benefits are tax-free.
    B. Premium are tax deductible; benefits are tax-free.
    C. Premiums are not tax deductible; benefits are taxed.
    D. Premiums are tax deductible; benefits are taxed.

39. When added to a health insurance contract, an impairment rider

    A. provides for a discontinuance of premium payments if the policyowner becomes impaired as defined by the rider
    B. defines the criteria for a disability or impairment before benefits are payable
    C. excludes from coverage any loss associated with the defined impairment
    D. identifies specific impairments or disabilities that the contract will cover

40. A medical expense policy's coinsurance provision

    A. specifies the percentage of costs that will be paid each by the insurer and the insured
    B. defines the amount of costs the insured must cover before any benefits under the policy are payable
    C. identifies which provider has primary responsibility for benefit payments if the insured is covered by more than one policy
    D. provides that once an insured's costs exceed a specified limit, the insurer pays 100% of covered expenses

41. When Lupe suffered a broken hip, she notified her agent in writing within 12 days of the loss. However, her agent did not notify the insurance company until 60 days after the loss. Which of the following statements correctly explains how this claim would be handled?

    A. The insurer may deny the claim since it was not notified within the required 20-day time frame.
    B. The insurer is considered to be notified since the notification to its agent amounts to notification to the insurer; the claim will be paid in full.
    C. The insurer may delay the payment of this claim for up to 6 months.
    D. The insurer may settle this claim for less than it otherwise would had the notification been provided in a timely manner.

42. Which of the following statements concerning a Health Maintenance Organization (HMO) is CORRECT?

    A. It provides coverage for overhead expenses in the event that a businessowner becomes disabled.
    B. It is an organization stressing preventive health care and early diagnosis.
    C. Closed-panel plans account for approximately 10% of all HMOs.
    D. Routine physical exams are generally not covered.

43. What is the maximum number of months that group health coverage be continued for a terminated employee under the COBRA rules?

    A. 12
    B. 18
    C. 24
    D. 36

44. A stop-loss provision is common to what kind of health insurance policy?

    A. Major medical
    B. Basic medical
    C. Disability income
    D. All of the above

45. What kind of coverage does a business overhead expense policy provide?

    A. Monthly income payments to a businessowner in the event of a key employee's disability
    B. Monthly income payments to cover the operational costs of a business if the owner becomes disabled
    C. Disability income payments for a businessowner
    D. Medical expense insurance for a businessowner

46. Medicare Part A provides coverage for all of the following EXCEPT

    A. hospitalization
    B. home health care services
    C. hospice care
    D. surgeon fees

47. With regard to health insurance, the Fair Credit Reporting Act

    A. restricts an insurer's review of an applicant's credit history to only those sources the applicant approves
    B. requires the insurer to contact at least 1 source named by the applicant to gain information on the applicant
    C. requires applicants for health insurance to submit a credit report with the insurance application
    D. requires the disclosure of the third-party source if the applicant is denied coverage due to information provided by a third party

48. Jon's major medical policy contains an annual deductible of $1,000; 50/50 coinsurance; and a $5,000 stop-loss limit. If Jon incurs $21,000 in covered medical expenses, what will be his total out-of-pocket cost?

    A. $11,000
    B. $10,500
    C. $10,000
    D. $5,000

49. Carol's health insurance policy pays benefits according to a list which indicates the amount that is payable under each type of covered treatment or procedure. Carol's policy provides benefits on a

    A. scheduled basis
    B. reimbursement basis
    C. service basis
    D. cash basis

50. Company X receives a health insurance application from David with a prepaid premium. One week later, they receive the MIB report indicating a prior heart condition. Company X will most likely

    A. disregard the MIB report
    B. return David's premium and decline coverage
    C. cover the applicant
    D. cover the applicant excluding the preexisting condition

ANSWERS TO ACCIDENT AND HEALTH INSURANCE PRACTICE FINAL EXAMINATION

1. **B**   There is a 5-month waiting period for Social Security disability benefits. Payments begin in the 6th month.

2. **A**   A noncancellable policy may be referred to as noncancellable and guaranteed renewable. This type of contract provides an insured with the right to renew the policy up to a specified age, as long as premiums are paid before the end of the grace period. In addition, the insurer may not cancel, alter the policy term, or increase the premium charged.

3. **C**   Medicare supplement (Medigap) policies must provide a 30-day free look period.

4. **D**   Enacted in 1985, COBRA (the Consolidated Omnibus Budget Reconciliation Act) stipulates that employers must offer continuation of group health benefits for a specified period of time to qualified employees and their beneficiaries who would not otherwise be eligible for continued coverage due to certain events such as being laid off.

5. **C**   This provision is most commonly utilized when insurers require disabled claimants to submit to a physical exam to prove continued disability.

6. **C**   The $500 deductible is subtracted from the medical expenses first, leaving $3,500 that is subject to the 80/20 coinsurance provision. Therefore, the insurer will pay $2,800 of the total bill. Roger's total out-of-pocket expense will be $1,200 ($500 deductible plus 20% of the balance, or $700.)

7. **C**   Group health insurance policies also include a coordination of benefits provision to avoid duplicate coverage. This provision limits total benefit payable to 100% of covered expenses, regardless of the number of group policies involved.

8. **C**   In order to continue to collect benefits after returning to work, Hal's policy must have a residual benefit provision which provides for a reduced monthly benefit in proportion to the loss of income experienced after the insured returns to work, but at reduced earnings.

9. **C**   The elimination or waiting period is the time that must elapse before monthly benefits will begin under a disability income contract. An elimination period must be satisfied for each new disability incurred. The most common period is 30 days.

10. **B**   One of the most common exclusions under a health insurance policy is self-inflicted injuries.

11. **D**   The grace period follows the date each premium is due and permits the continuance of coverage even though the premium has not been paid.

12. **A**   An insurer may not cancel a guaranteed renewable policy or alter its provisions as long as the insured pays the premium within the grace period. However, the insurer reserves the right to increase the premium at policy renewal on a class basis.

13. **B**   After the elimination period is satisfied, the disability income policy will pay $1,500 per month while Bob remains totally disabled. Bob's disability continues for 2½ months after the elimination period, so he will receive $3,750 in benefits.

14. **A**   Exclusions for preexisting conditions are intended to protect the insurer from adverse selection. Preexisting conditions are usually excluded through the policy's standard provisions or by waiver.

15. **B**   Surgical expense coverage lists (or schedules) surgical procedures and the corresponding reimbursable amounts in the policy. The most common approach used by surgical expense coverage is to establish a maximum limit for coverage. The amount of the benefit schedule is typically expressed in terms of the maximum benefit payable.

16. **C**   Comprehensive major medical expense policies provide broader benefits than major medical insurance. They combine all of the basic medical

expenses benefits into a single package ranging from hospital and surgical expenses through major medical type coverage.

17. **B**   In order to receive disability benefits under Social Security, a person must be fully insured (i.e., 10 years of covered employment).

18. **B**   Long-term care insurance is designed to cover services for those who can't care for themselves (custodial care or skilled nursing care). It does not provide for surgical expense coverage.

19. **D**   Written proof of loss must be submitted to the insurer within 90 days of the date of loss. If an insured fails to provide written proof within the time required, the claim will still be honored if it was not reasonably possible to provide proof within the time limit allowed.

20. **B**   AD&D, or accidental death and dismemberment policies, protect against the accidental death of an insured in addition to paying a specific benefit if an insured suffers a dismemberment covered under the policy. Accidental death coverage may be purchased as a separate policy or as an added benefit to a health insurance policy.

21. **A**   Insureds do not need to pay a premium for Part A coverage, though insureds must satisfy a deductible each benefit period. Benefits are paid directly to the medical care provider.

22. **C**   Participation in Medicare Part B is subject to the payment of a monthly premium, 20% coinsurance payments, and an annual deductible. No physical exams are required.

23. **A**   Will's disability lasted 45 days, well within the 60-day waiting (elimination) period. Because his disability did not last beyond the elimination period, he will not receive any benefits from his disability income policy.

24. **C**   The elimination, or waiting period is the time that must elapse before monthly benefits will begin under a disability income policy. An elimination period must be satisfied for each new disability incurred. It is the equivalent of a deductible under other forms of health insurance.

25. **D**   An insured is required to submit written notice to the insurer within 20 days of sustaining a loss. Failure to do so within this period may result in the insurer reserving the right to deny coverage.

26. **C**   An insurer must provide claim forms to an insured within 15 days of the insured's request. If it fails to do so, the insured may submit a claim (or proof of loss) in another manner designed to give the insurer notice of the claim or loss.

27. **C**   The benefit amount payable for an accidental dismemberment is referred to as the capital sum. The capital sum is generally a percentage (i.e., 50%) of the principal sum.

28. **A**   The Medicare Part A (hospital insurance) benefit period begins on the day of admittance to a hospital or extended care facility and ends after the insured has been released for 60 consecutive days.

29. **B**   Ann first pays the $1,000 deductible before the 80/20 coinsurance provision is invoked. Then the insurer pays 80% of the $2,000 balance, or $1,600. Ann will be responsible for the remaining 20%, or $400. Therefore, Ann's total cost, including the deductible, will be $1,400.

30. **D**   Statements made by an applicant on an application for health insurance are generally considered to be representations. They are statements that are true to the best knowledge of the individual making them.

31. **C**   Blue Cross and Blue Shield organizations operate on a service approach whereby they actually deliver health care and services, as opposed to insurers that reimburse insureds or health care providers for the cost of care delivered.

32. **B**   Once a health policy has been reinstated, coverage for accidents is effective immediately. Coverage for sickness requires a short waiting period, usually 10 days.

33. **B**   The typical benefit period for group short-term disability policies is 6 to 18 months.

34. **A**   The change of occupation provision, an optional provision, allows for a change in benefits or premiums if an insured changes his occupation. If the insured changes from a more hazardous to

a less hazardous occupation, the premium will be reduced. If the insured changes from a less hazardous to a more hazardous occupation, the benefit will be reduced.

35. **A** Reinstatement is one of the 12 provisions required in health insurance policies, as prescribed in the NAIC's Uniform Individual Accident and Sickness Provisions Law.

36. **A** The recurrent disability provision is invoked when an individual suffering from a total disability apparently recovers and subsequently the disability recurs. This provision sets the time in which a recurrence will be treated as a continuation of the original disability or a new occurrence altogether. This is important to the insured because a new occurrence will require him to satisfy a new elimination period, but a continuation of the original disability will allow him to resume benefit payments.

37. **B** The benefit payable as a result of accidental death is the principal sum. The benefit amount payable for accidental dismemberment is the capital sum and is generally a percentage of the principal sum.

38. **A** Under a disability income policy purchased and paid for by an employer on a key employee, the latter being the recipient of the benefits, the premiums are not tax deductible, but the benefits are tax free.

39. **C** The purpose of an impairment waiver added to a health insurance policy is to exclude from coverage any loss associated with the specified impairment. Impairment waivers enable insurers to provide coverage that might otherwise be denied if the waiver were not included.

40. **A** A medical expense policy's coinsurance provision indicates the percentage of costs for which each the insurer and the insured will be responsible. Typically, an insurer's share of costs is 70% to 80%; the insured is responsible for 20 to 30%.

41. **B** The laws of agency dictate that knowledge of the agent is imputed to the principal. Therefore, Lupe's notice to the agent is deemed to be notice to the insurer.

42. **B** Health maintenance organizations (HMOs) emphasize preventive medicine with early treatment and diagnosis by way of prepaid routine physical examinations and diagnostic screening techniques.

43. **B** The Consolidated Omnibus Budget Reconciliation Act (COBRA) of 1985 stipulated that employers must offer continuation of group health coverage for a specified period of time to qualified employees and their beneficiaries who would otherwise be eligible for continued coverage because of particular qualifying events involving the covered employee. These events include death, divorce, or termination of employment. If an individual is laid off from a job or otherwise terminated from employment, COBRA mandates continued coverage for a period not to exceed 18 months.

44. **A** A stop-loss provision, common to major medical expense policies, provides for 100% payment of costs by the insurer once the insured's out-of-pocket payments for eligible expenses reach a certain specified level.

45. **B** Business overhead expense insurance is designed to provide monthly income to cover the overhead costs of a business's operation during a business-owner's disability.

46. **D** Medicare Part A covers the costs associated with hospitalization, as well as skilled nursing care, home health care, hospice benefits and limited psychiatric care. Surgeon fees are covered by Medicare Part B.

47. **D** The application of the Fair Credit Reporting Act to health insurance is the same as for life insurance: it requires that an insurance applicant be notified of the source of information if, based on that information, the insurer denies issuing the requested coverage.

48. **D** Jon must first satisfy the $1,000 deductible before the insurer will pay any benefit, subject to the coinsurance provision. Once he pays the deductible, the insurer will pay 50% of the balance ($20,000), or $10,000. Jon is responsible for the other 50% in accordance with the coinsurance provision. This would require him to pay $10,000 in addition to the $1,000 deductible, for a total of

$11,000. However, the stop-loss provision limits Jon's expenses to $5,000. The insurer becomes responsible, therefore, for the expenses beyond this limit ($16,000).

49. **A**   Carol's health insurance policy pays benefits according to a schedule for surgical procedures and the corresponding reimbursable amounts. The most common approach is to set a maximum limit for coverage. The amount of the benefit schedule is typically expressed in terms of the maximum benefit payable. In addition, many other surgical procedures are listed with a dollar amount or a percentage of the maximum limit. These listings are referred to as surgical schedules and provide payment for the usual and customary charges extended for various surgical procedures.

50. **D**   Preexisting conditions are health conditions that have already manifested themselves before the insured's application for health insurance coverage. They are frequently excluded from coverage. They do not necessarily cause the insurer to reject the application.

12

New Jersey Life, Accident, and Health Insurance Law

KEY TERMS

Commissioner	Consultant	Replacement
Domestic	Producer	Policy Summary
Foreign	Surplus Lines	Buyer's Guide
Alien	Controlled Business	Surplus
Stock	Rebating	Reserves
Mutual	Twisting	Home Health Care
Certificate of Authority	Defamation	Medicare Supplement
Agent	Guaranty Association	Temporary Disability
Broker	New Jersey Fraud Prevention Act	Health Care Quality Act

IMPORTANT: CHECK FOR UPDATES

Exam publishers sometimes change topics on the exam unexpectedly or on short notice. To see if we have issued an update for this product to accommodate a change in the exam, please go to **www.kaplanfinancial.com**, where you will see a heading for *TestAlerts!* Click on *View Insurance TestAlerts!* to see a list of updates we have issued for our License Exam Manuals. Then, click on your state to see a link to a portable document file (PDF) that you can download to study with your License Exam Manual. (If you do not see a *TestAlert!* listed for your state, we have not issued one.) We suggest you check now, sometime during your study period, when you've completed your study, and one last time just before you take your exam.

I. NEW JERSEY LAWS, RULES, AND REGULATIONS PERTINENT TO INSURANCE

A. **STATE REGULATORY JURISDICTION** The purpose of state insurance regulation is to protect the public against unfair acts of an insurer or its representatives. Regulation also protects the public against the insolvency of insurers as well. The area of insurance is subject to state and federal regulation because it is a business that is affected with a public interest. (Note that the producer licensing exams for life, accident, and health insurance devote more than half of the state law questions to topics found in Section I. New Jersey Laws, Rules, and Regulations Pertinent to Insurance. The life insurance exam will have three out of every four questions from this section. The accident and health insurance exam will have two out of every four questions from this section.)

1. **Legislation** This is one of the primary methods the government uses to regulate the insurance business. Legislation creates insurance law.

   a. **State laws** The insurance laws created by each state are combined with an insurance code which helps to regulate business. Each state has an **Insurance Commissioner**, usually appointed by the Governor, who possesses broad powers to enforce the insurance laws (code) of his particular state. A Commissioner has the authority to license insurers and producers, regulate rates, and conduct investigations.

   b. **Court action** The judicial process is of primary importance with regard to insurance regulation as well. Interpretations of state insurance and other laws are provided by the courts. Specifically, in the insurance business the Commissioner has the authority to provide notice of and conduct hearings in order to arrive at Department of Banking and Insurance rulings. These actions may be reviewed by state courts to ensure that the Commissioner is complying with state laws and regulations. The courts may be used in actions against the Commissioner and may also be petitioned by the Commissioner to enforce policy form compliance with state insurance law.

   c. **Related federal laws and court cases** Individual states have regulated the insurance industry for many years. However, some feel that federal government regulation of insurance would better serve the public. Many court cases have been heard regarding the question of federal versus state regulation. Some of the more famous court cases include but are not limited to the following.

      1.) *Paul v. Virginia* This court case heard in 1869 declared that an insurance policy was not an article of commerce and that it was actually a contract of indemnity. Therefore, because insurance was not commerce, it was also not interstate commerce and the federal government (i.e., Congress) had no authority to regulate it.

      2.) *US v. South-Eastern Underwriters Association* This court case found that although *Paul v. Virginia* affirmed the authority of each state to regulate insurance, Congress still had the authority to regulate the industry as a whole. After an appeal, a further ruling held that the insurance business was, in fact, interstate commerce and thus subject to federal antitrust laws.

3.) McCarran-Ferguson Act (Public Law 15) The McCarran-Ferguson Act, also known as **Public Law 15**, was passed in 1945. It stated that continued regulation of insurance by individual states was in the public interest. The act stated that no act of Congress was to be construed to invalidate, impair, or supersede any law enacted by any state for the purpose of regulating the business of insurance, or which imposes a fee or tax upon the business.

a.) States regulate insurance in accordance with this Act. The federal government will not intervene unless a state fails to regulate insurance, state regulation proves to be inadequate, or the federal government retains jurisdiction, as in the case of Medicare.

b.) This act also stipulated that after June 30, 1948, federal antitrust laws would apply to insurance but only to the extent that state regulation was not effective. The Sherman Anti-Trust Act would always apply to cases involving boycott, coercion, or other similar unfair trade practices.

B. COMMISSIONER OF INSURANCE

1. Department of Banking and Insurance [17:1-8.1; 17:1-15, 16; 17:22A-20] The Department of Banking and Insurance regulates the banking and insurance industries in New Jersey. The chief executive officer of the Department is the Commissioner, who is appointed by the governor. The Commissioner is appointed for the duration of the governor's term in office and until a successor is appointed and approved. The Commissioner may appoint deputy commissioners to act in his stead when necessary.

a. The Insurance Commissioner is required to provide a surety bond in the amount of $25,000; Deputy Commissioners provide a bond in the amount of $10,000.

b. The Department of Banking and Insurance has two divisions: the Division of Banking and the Division of Insurance. Each division has its own director. Each director reports directly to the Commissioner.

2. Broad powers [17:22A-45; 17:1-8.1; 17:1C-3, 6] The Commissioner of Insurance has the power to conduct investigations, to administer oaths, to interrogate licensees and others, and to issue subpoenas to any licensees or other persons with regard to any investigations, hearings, or other proceedings. Subpoenas are issued in the name of the Commissioner (or the Deputy Commissioner or other designated employees). Any person failing to comply with a subpoena may be penalized for contempt by the state Superior Court.

a. Rules and regulations to effectuate purposes of Title 17 The Commissioner shall make and enforce and may alter, modify, amend or repeal rules and regulations to effectuate the purposes of Title 17. These rules shall be altered or modified only after the publication of notice and public hearing and shall be effective not less than five days after the same have been filed with the Secretary of State. The notice shall be published at least 10 days prior to any hearing required by New Jersey law. This hearing shall be conducted by the Commissioner, his deputy, or by any employee authorized by the Commissioner.

b. The Commissioner of Insurance is the head and chief executive officer of the department. The Commissioner is appointed by the Governor (with the advice and consent of the Senate) and shall serve during the governor's term of office. Additional powers and duties of the Commissioner include but are not limited to the following.

1.) Administer the work of the department

2.) Appoint and remove department personnel

3.) Report illegalities committed by insurers, agents, brokers, or other insurance persons to the attorney general

4.) Regulate insurers for insolvency

5.) Regulate most insurance rates

6.) Issue insurance licenses and collect the appropriate fees

7.) Suspend and revoke licenses for just cause

8.) Issue cease and desist orders for just cause

9.) Make a report each year concerning the department's operations and submit it to the Governor

10.) Perform any function which he deems necessary regarding the insurance business in his state

3. **Notice and hearing [17:22A-45; 17:29B-6 through 13; 17:1-16]** Any public hearing required shall be held by the Commissioner (or a deputy or designated employee). Whenever a hearing is required, the Commissioner shall give notice to any person, firm, corporation, or association, or other legal entity affected of the: time, place, and nature of the hearing; the authority under which the hearing is to be held; and other information necessary to appraise the party of the nature of the hearing.

a. Notice may be made by delivering it to the party by registered or certified mail. The notice shall refer to the matter in question (but lack of the reference will not render the notice invalid). The hearing must be scheduled at least 10 days after the notice is delivered.

b. Any person asked to produce books, records, or accounts at a hearing must do so.

c. A report of the hearing shall be made to the Commissioner. Every hearing shall be open to the public unless the Commissioner feels that a private hearing is in the public interest. Any interested party will be allowed to inspect all evidence or examine or cross-examine witnesses, and present proof in his interest.

d. The Commissioner (and any deputy or employee) will have the power to subpoena witnesses, compel witness attendance, administer oaths, examine any person under oath, and to compel any person to subscribe to his testimony after it has been correctly reduced to writing.

e. Whoever conducts a hearing shall admit all testimony (and not be bound by common law or statutory rules of evidence), but also be able to exclude immaterial testimony.

f. If a person fails to comply with a subpoena, the Superior Court may issue an order requiring the attendance of the person. Anyone failing to obey the court's order may be charged with contempt.

g. If after a hearing the Commissioner issues a cease and desist order, he may also assess a fine not to exceed $1,000 for every violation of New Jersey law committed unknowingly.

> **1.)** If the violation was done knowingly, or if the violator should have known the act was illegal, a fine not to exceed $5,000 may result for each violation. Any person violating a cease and desist order may be fined up to $5,000 for each violation.

h. Immunity from prosecution is available for some individuals provided perjury is not involved.

i. The Commissioner may compel testimony with due notice. The Fifth amendment guarantees against self-incrimination when a witness's testimony is offered in exchange for immunity from prosecution while making statements made before the Commissioner during a hearing.

j. **Allowance for intervention** An intervenor is any party with a material interest in a proceeding before the Commissioner. Such a party may appeal a decision of the Commissioner with proper notice to the Superior Court within 30 days of the Commissioner's final order.

4. Penalties [17:22A-40, 45] The Commissioner may place on probation, suspend, revoke or refuse to issue or renew an insurance producer's license or may levy a civil penalty. In addition to, or as an alternative to any other penalty, the Commissioner may impose a fine of up to $5,000 for the first violation and up to $10,000 for each subsequent violation. The Commissioner may also order restitution of monies owed any person and reimbursement of the costs of investigation and prosecution.

a. Since the Commissioner also has the power to subpoena, any person failing or refusing to comply with a subpoena may be charged with contempt (by a judge of the Superior Court).

C. DEFINITIONS

1. Domestic, foreign, and alien insurers [17B:17-7]

a. **Domestic insurance company** A company incorporated, chartered, organized, and formed under the laws of New Jersey is referred to as a domestic company. A domestic insurer generally has its home or principal office located in the state where it is chartered.

   1.) For instance, the ABC Casualty Company is formed under and has its principal office in Wayne, New Jersey. Therefore, in the state of New Jersey, the ABC Company is referred to as a domestic company.

b. **Foreign company** A foreign company incorporated, chartered, organized, or formed under the laws of another state, but is licensed and permitted to conduct the business of insurance in the state of New Jersey.

   1.) For instance, Travelers Insurance Company of Hartford, Connecticut is formed under the laws of Connecticut but is licensed to conduct insurance business in the state of New Jersey. Therefore, in the state of New Jersey, the Travelers Insurance Company is viewed as a foreign company.

c. **Alien company** An alien company incorporated, chartered, organized, or formed outside the United States but licensed in the state of New Jersey.

   1.) For instance, Sun Life of Canada is incorporated and formed under the laws of another country (Canada). However, it is licensed to conduct the business of insurance in this state.

   2.) Although Lloyds of London is not a true insurance company, the Department of Banking and Insurance considers it to be an alien "insurer."

2. Stock insurer [17B:18-2]
A domestic stock insurer is an insurer incorporated in accordance with the laws of the state of New Jersey with its capital divided into shares and owned by its stockholders. A stock insurer is mostly concerned with gaining profits. Policyholders of the stock company are not entitled to dividends nor are they liable for any assessments.

3. Mutual insurer [17B:18-3]
A domestic mutual insurer is an insurer incorporated in accordance with the laws of this state without permanent capital stock, the governing body of which is elected by its policyholders. Again, a mutual insurer is owned by its policyholders. These policyholders may share in the company's profits in the form of dividends. Some mutual companies issue assessable policies and others issue non-assessable policies.

4. Certificate of authority and license [17B:17-12]
A certificate of authority is a certificate issued by the Commissioner of Insurance demonstrating the authority of an insurer to transact insurance business in this state. A license is authority granted to an individual, partnership, or corporation authorizing the licensee to engage in a business or operation of insurance in this state as an agent, broker, or consultant to sell insurance.

   a. Certificates of authority and licenses are written evidences of authority to transact insurance business in the state of New Jersey.

   b. Principal office [17B: 17-10, 12] The principal office of an insurer is generally the office from which the insurer directs or manages its affairs. With respect to alien insurers who are authorized to transact insurance in the US, it is the US office from which the insurer directs or manages its affairs.

5. Reinsurance [17B:18-62] Reinsurance is a contract under which an originating insurer, called the **ceding insurer** procures insurance for itself from another insurer called the **assuming insurer,** with respect to part or all of the insurance of the originating (ceding) insurer. An assuming insurer that sells reinsurance in New Jersey must have a specific license to do so.

   a. Reinsurance is the transfer of insurance business from one insurer to another. Its basic purpose is to shift risks from an insurance company whose financial safety may be threatened by retaining too large an amount of risk to other reinsurers which will share in the risk of large losses. In addition, reinsurance aids in stabilizing profits and losses of insurance companies.

6. Extended reinsurance An insurer authorized to conduct insurance business in the state may reinsure any risks provided they involve the line of insurance in which the insurer is licensed. In addition, a company may retrocede any risks provided it has the approval of the Commissioner. **Retroceding** or **retrocession** occurs when a reinsurer accepts too many risks and has to reinsure some of those with another reinsurance company.

   a. Extended reinsurance is also called secondary reinsurance. An extended reinsurance transaction may be executed only with written permission from the Commissioner.

7. Producers [11:17B-1.3; 17:22-28]

   a. Insurance producer Insurance producer is a term commonly applied to an agent, broker, personal producing agent, general agent, solicitor, or other person who sells insurance, producing business for the insurer.

   b. Insurance agent An insurance agent is an insurance producer acting as though authorized, in writing, by any insurance company to act as its agent to solicit, negotiate, or sell insurance contracts on its behalf or to collect insurance premiums and who may be authorized to countersign insurance policies on its behalf.

      1.) Solicitation, sale, and negotiation of insurance The insurance code defines solicitation of insurance as the attempt to sell insurance to a person from a particular insurer. The sale of insurance is the exchange of an insurance contract or policy on behalf of an insurer for any valuable consideration. The negotiation of insurance involves any act that provides a buyer or prospective buyer of insurance with information about the benefits, terms, or conditions of a policy, if the party giving the information sells or obtains insurance for buyers.

c. **Insurance broker** An insurance producer acting as an insurance broker who, for a commission, brokerage fee, or other consideration, acts or aids in any manner concerning negotiation, solicitation, or sale of insurance contracts as the representative of an insured or prospective insured; or a person who places insurance in an insurance company that he does not represent as an agent.

d. **Insurance consultant** This is a person who, for a fee, acts or holds himself out to the public or any licensee as offering any advice, counsel, opinion, or service with respect to the benefits, advantages, or disadvantages under any policy issued in this state. A consultant shall not include bank trust officers, attorneys at law, and certified public accountants.

D. LICENSING INFORMATION

1. Types of licenses, authorities, and requirements

a. **Producer (individual) [17:22A-29, 32, 33; 11:17-1.2, 2.2 through 2.4, 2.6]** No person shall act as an insurance producer or maintain or operate any office in New Jersey for the transaction of the business of an insurance producer, or receive any commission, brokerage fee, compensation, or other consideration without obtaining a license from the Commissioner. The Producer Licensing Model Act, drafted by the National Association of Insurance Commissioners (NAIC), defines agents as producers. Agents who are residents of or have their offices in New Jersey fall within the jurisdiction of the Department of Banking and Insurance.

1.) Licensed producers shall be authorized to write the kinds of insurance designated, if qualified by each authority described below.

a.) **Life authority** All coverages defined as life insurance and all coverages defined as an annuity.

b.) **Accident and health or sickness authority** All coverages defined as health insurance.

c.) **Property authority** All coverages written by authorized insurers for direct and consequential loss or damage to property of any kind including fire and allied lines; earthquake; growing crops; ocean marine; inland marine; boiler and machinery; credit property; burglary and theft; glass, sprinkler leakage, and water damage; livestock; smoke or smudge; physical loss to buildings; radioactive contamination; mechanical breakdown or power failure; and other property losses.

d.) **Casualty authority** All coverages written by authorized insurers for coverage against legal liability from death, disability, injury or damage to real or personal property including employers' liability, automobile liability bodily injury, automobile liability property damage, other liability, credit casualty, other casualty loss, fidelity and surety, workers' compensation, mortgage guaranty insurance, and municipal bond insurance.

e.) Surplus lines authority All coverages written by unauthorized insurers and defined as surplus lines.

f.) Title insurance authority All policies of insurance guaranteeing or indemnifying owners of real property or others interested therein against loss or damage suffered by reason of liens, encumbrances upon, defects in, or the unmarketability of the title to said property, guaranteeing, warranting, or otherwise insuring by a title insurance company the correctness of searches relating to the title to real property, or doing any real business in substance equivalent to any of the foregoing.

g.) Variable life and variable annuity authority All coverages defined as a contract on a variable basis. In addition to their state license to sell life insurance, agents need a Series 6 or Series 7 NASD license to transact variable life insurance.

h.) Personal lines authority All property and casualty insurance coverage sold to individuals and families for primarily noncommercial purposes.

i.) Limited lines authority This includes bail bonds; credit insurance; ticket insurance; group mortgage cancellation; legal insurance; self-storage and personal property insurance; and special nonresident limited lines; title insurance; and surplus lines insurance.

2.) Requirements for a first time applicant for an individual license are as follows. A **first-time applicant** is a person who has not been licensed as a producer for the previous 12 months.

a.) A properly completed application, in a form approved by the Department or the current version of the NAIC uniform application for individual nonresident producers in effect at the time of application, requesting issuance of an insurance producer license with one or more authorities, which shall contain the applicant's legal name, home address, date of birth, Social Security number, business mailing and location address, business trade name (if any), and response to questions concerning applicant's character and fitness for licensing. The application must be signed, dated, and certified to be correct by the applicant. In lieu of the NAIC uniform application, a nonresident applicant may submit a copy of the application for licensure submitted to the home state.

b.) If a resident, when required, a certificate evidencing completion of an approved course of prelicensing education or a certificate evidencing waiver of that requirement; and a certificate evidencing that the applicant has passed the state licensing examination for the authority or authorities requested, or a certificate evidencing waiver of the examination requirement. Such certificates must have been issued within the preceding two years.

The time requirements for prelicensing education courses are the following:

- Life insurance class: 25 hours
- Accident and health insurance class: 25 hours
- Common content law class: 15 hours

Persons holding the following designations or educational credentials may qualify for exemption from the following prelicensing education requirements:

- CLU (life insurance)
- CPCU (property and casualty insurance)
- CIC (life and health, property and casualty insurance)
- College degrees in insurance
- Attorneys (title insurance)

c.) If a nonresident, the applicant shall certify, within the previous years that s/he has held a currently valid license authorizing transaction of insurance business in the applicant's home state for the kinds of insurance for which application is made.

d.) Any documents or statements required to explain responses to questions concerning the applicant's character, fitness, or financial responsibility.

e.) Payment of the required fees. Fees for insurance license applicants are as follows:

License application, major lines: $300

License application, limited lines: $150

Finger print fee: $48

Initial application fee: $20

Late renewal fee, major lines: $100

Late renewal fee, limited lines: $50.

f.) A producer licensed in another state who moves to New Jersey is exempt from New Jersey's prelicensing education requirements if the person's license is in good standing in his home state within 90 days before he moves to New Jersey. Any producer with his principal residence or principal office in another state may choose to be a resident producer in that state or in New Jersey.

Under the Producer Licensing Model Act, a producer is allowed to choose his home state regardless of his residence. Therefore, even though a producer may have an address in New Jersey, he can choose New York as his home state and be licensed as a nonresident in New Jersey.

3.) A currently licensed individual producer may obtain additional authorities by submitting the following.

a.) His current original license, marked to request the additional authority or authorities, dated, signed, and certified to be correct by the applicant.

b.) If a resident, a certificate evidencing completion of an approved course of prelicensing education, if required, or a certificate evidencing waiver of this requirement, and a certificate evidencing that the applicant has passed the state licensing examination for the authority or authorities requested or a certificate evidencing waiver of this requirement.

c.) If a nonresident, certification from the applicant that he holds a current license with comparable authority in the home state.

d.) Payment of the required processing fee.

4.) An individual applying for a resident insurance producer license shall make application to the Commissioner on the uniform application and declare under penalty of refusal, suspension, or revocation of the license that the statements made in the application are true, correct, and complete to the best of the individual's knowledge and belief. Before approving the application, the Commissioner must comfirm that the individual:

- is at least 18 years of age;
- has not committed any act that is a ground for denial, suspension, or revocation;
- has completed a prelicensing course of study for the lines of authority for which the individual has applied as prescribed by the Commissioner by regulation; this course must be completed no more than two years before the application is filed;
- has paid the required fees; and
- has successfully passed the examinations for the lines of authority for which the individual has applied, and no later than one year after the application is filed.

a.) **Exemptions** Persons who hold professional designations such as CLU, ChFC, CIC, and lawyers seeking authority to sell title insurance may be exempt from the insurance license exam. A person serving in the armed forces of the United States may also apply for an exemption.

b. Business entity producer [17:22A-32; 11:17-22 through 2.4, 2.6]

1.) A first-time applicant for a business entity license shall submit the following.

a.) A properly completed application in a form approved by the Department or the current version of the NAIC uniform application for business entities, which shall contain the business entity's legal name; business mailing and location address; other business names, if any; names, license reference numbers, if any, and license authorities of each licensed officer or partner; names, addresses, and license reference numbers, if any, of all persons owning 5% or more of the business entity; and responses to questions concerning the applicant's character, fitness, and financial responsibility.

b.) If the applicant is a corporation, limited liability company, limited partnership, or limited liability partnership applying for a resident license, a copy of the original business certificate stamped "filed" by the Department of Treasury, Division of Revenue Business Services, County Clerk, or other authority as applicable or a certificate filed by the Department of Treasury, Division of Business Services authorizing the applicant to transact business in New Jersey.

- Foreign organizations must obtain a certificate of authority from the Secretary of State.
- Domestic organizations must file their partnership documents or certificate of incorporation with the county clerk in which they reside.

c.) If the applicant is a business entity applying for a nonresident license, a certification evidencing that the applicant is authorized in the home state to transact insurance business with comparable authorities.

d.) For resident business entities, properly completed fingerprint forms in a format prescribed by the Department for each officer, director, partner, or owner of 5% or more of the applicant business entity. This requirement applies to all principals of the business, whether or not they are individually licensed.

e.) Any documentation required to explain responses to questions and concerning the applicant's character, fitness, and financial responsibility.

f.) Payment of the required fees.

2.) A business entity may add an additional authority by submitting the following.

a.) Its current original license, marked to request the additional authority or authorities, dated, signed, and certified to be correct by a licensed officer or partner who holds or has applied for that authority.

b.) If a nonresident applicant, certification from the applicant that it holds a currently valid license with the comparable authority in its home state.

c.) Payment of the processing fee.

3.) A business entity insurance producer may receive qualification for a license in one or more of the following lines of authority.

a.) Life-insurance coverage on human lives, including benefits of endowment and annuities, and which may include benefits in the event of death or dismemberment by accident and benefits for disability income.

b.) Accident and health or sickness-insurance coverage for sickness, bodily injury, or accidental death, and which may include benefits for disability income.

c.) Property-insurance coverage for the direct or consequential loss or damage to property of every kind.

d.) Casualty-insurance coverage against legal liability, including that for death, injury, or disability or damage to real or personal property.

e.) Variable life and variable annuity products-insurance coverage provided under variable life insurance contracts, variable annuities, or any other life insurance or annuity product that reflects the investment experience of a separate account.

f.) Credit-limited line credit insurance.

g.) Personal lines—property and casualty insurance coverage sold to individuals and families for primarily noncommercial purposes.

h.) Any other line of insurance permitted under any law or regulation of this state.

c. Nonresident [17:22A-34; 11:17-1.2, 2.2b]

1.) Producer The Commissioner may (often by reciprocal agreement with another state's insurance department) issue a nonresident license to a person who holds comparable license authority in a state (other than New Jersey), who meets all other license requirements (e.g., is 18 years of age, is competent and trustworthy, etc.), and who:

- is currently licensed as a resident insurance producer in good standing in his home state;
- has submitted the proper request for licensure and has paid the fees required;
- has submitted or transmitted to the Commissioner the application for licensure that the person submitted to his home state, or in lieu of the same, a completed uniform application; and
- the person's home state awards nonresident insurance producer licenses to residents of this state on the same basis.

a.) The Commissioner may verify the nonresident insurance producer's licensing status through the Producer Database maintained by the NAIC. The Commissioner will also accept a letter of certification from the insurance department of the producer's home state.

b.) A nonresident insurance producer who moves from one state to another state or a resident insurance producer who moves from this State to another state shall file a change of address and provide certification from the new resident state within 30 days of the change of legal residence. No fee or license application shall be required.

c.) A person licensed as a surplus lines insurance producer in his home state shall receive a nonresident surplus lines insurance producer license.

■ Under the Producer Licensing Model Act, a producer can choose his home state. Therefore, even though a producer may have an address in New Jersey, he can choose New York as his home state and be licensed as a nonresident in New Jersey.

d.) A person licensed as a limited line credit insurance or other type of limited lines insurance producer in his home state shall receive a nonresident limited lines insurance producer license, pursuant to subsection a. of this section, granting the same scope of authority as granted under the license issued by the producer's home state.

e.) The Commissioner acts as the agent to receive notice of legal action for any nonresident producer.

2.) Organization The Commissioner may issue a nonresident organization a license if it meets all the requirements of New Jersey law and provided the organization holds a comparable license in another state. A certificate verifying licensure with the other state must be submitted to the state.

d. Prelicensing requirement [11:17-3.5, 3.7, 4] In general, resident applicants for insurance licenses in New Jersey must pass a state licensing examination administered by the Department of Banking and Insurance or a vendor under contract with the Department, within one year of application.

1.) Exemptions Applicants for certain limited lines of insurance (ticket insurance, group mortgage cancellation insurance, legal insurance, credit insurance, and self-storage personal property insurance) do not need to pass a state licensing exam. Persons with certain professional designations are also exempt from the exam requirement. For life and health insurance, persons holding a Chartered Life Underwriter (CLU) or a Chartered Financial Consultant (ChFC) designation are exempt. Applicants who were previously licensed as nonresidents and apply for licensure as residents are also exempt.

a.) Order to retake exam The Commissioner may, for good cause, order a licensee to retake the state examination within a specified period of time. If the licensee fails to retake the exam within this period, the Commissioner will order the licensee to show why the license should not be revoked and offer a hearing on the matter. Similarly, the Commissioner may refuse to issue a license to a license applicant and order the applicant to retake the exam within a specified period. If the applicant fails to do so, the Commissioner may refuse to issue the license and advise the applicant of his right to a hearing on the matter.

2.) The application must also be:

- signed and dated and certified as correct by the applicant;
- if a resident, a certificate evidencing completion of an approved course of prelicensing education (or a waiver of that requirement), and a certificate proving the applicant passed the written state exam;
- if a nonresident, a recent certification from the insurance licensing agency of the applicant's home state that he holds a currently valid license authorizing the ability to sell the kinds of insurance that the applicant is applying for;
- any documents or statements required to explain responses to questions concerning the applicants's character and trustworthiness;
- a fingerprint of the applicant to be filed with the Department of Banking and Insurance; and
- the appropriate license fee (check or money order).

3.) A first-time applicant for an organization license shall submit:

- a properly completed application with the name of the organization, its address and trade name, and the names of anyone owning 5% or more of the organization;
- a copy of the organization's articles of incorporation;
- if a foreign organization, a copy of a certificate of authorization issued by the Secretary of State;
- a properly completed criminal history form;
- evidence of a bond if a surplus lines applicant; and
- the appropriate fee.

4.) No license shall be issued to any individual who has last passed the state licensing examination more than one year before the date of application. The date of application shall be deemed to be the date the application was received by the Department. In addition, no license shall be issued to any individual who has last completed the course of prelicensing education more than two years before the date of application (the date of application is the date the application was received by the Department).

e. Surplus lines [Title 17:22A-38] No license granting surplus lines authority shall be issued or renewed unless the applicant holds or will hold property and casualty authorities.

1.) No surplus lines producer shall charge any fee to an originating broker in connection with the negotiation or procurement of any contract of surplus lines insurance that shall exceed $50 plus the actual costs incurred for any services performed by a person that is not associated with the surplus lines producer, such as inspection services.

2. **Temporary work authority [11:17-2.1, 2.4]** The Commissioner may issue a temporary certificate evidencing that the applicant may begin work when the applicant has submitted a proper application for a license that does not disclose any information that would disqualify the individual. A temporary certificate expires no more than 60 days after issuance.

   a. Nonresident licensees shall notify the Department within 30 days of their change of address and intent to qualify as a resident insurance producer; the Commissioner will issue a temporary certificate that is valid for 90 days.

3. **Contractual relationships**

   a. **Company and producer [17:22A-42; 11:17-2.9]** Any insurance company authorized to transact business in New Jersey may, by written contract, appoint as its agent, a person that holds a valid insurance producer license issued in accordance with the provisions of state law. The contract shall authorize the producer to act as an agent for the appointing company for all lines of insurance for which the company is authorized in this state. The contract shall contain the duties, responsibilities, and limitations of authority between the agent and the appointing company. The agent must abide by the contract's terms. The agency appointment shall continue in effect until it is terminated. Both parties shall maintain a copy of the agreement in their office and make it available for inspection by the Commissioner upon request. The Commissioner does not have the authority to determine contractual disputes between an appointing company and an appointed agent.

      1.) **The Law of Agency** Though the law of agency cannot be properly treated in a brief paragraph or two, the following will summarize the concepts most pertinent to insurers and their producers.

      - An insurer (the principal) can appoint a producer (the agent) to act on its behalf. Both parties must consent to the appointment.

      - The acts of a properly-appointed producer are considered the acts of the principal.

      - Principals can empower agents to act on their behalf through express, implied, or apparent authority.

      - Express authority is plainly set forth in the agency agreement between the principal and the agent.

      - Implied authority is the authority that an agent can reasonably expect to have from an agency agreement, though the agreement does not specifically grant it. This authority is necessary for the agent to carry out his daily or routine responsibilities under the agency agreement. For instance, it arises when the agent uses the principal's letterhead, application forms, or business cards.

      - Apparent authority is the power that the public can logically assume an agent possesses, whether he has actually been granted that power by the principal. It is the authority that the agent appears to have by his words or actions, whether or not the principal actually granted such authority. It arises from the way the agent holds himself out to the public and the public's reasonable expectations from it.

2.) Upon the cancellation of an agency contract, the insurer shall within 15 days file written notice of cancellation with the Commissioner. The notice shall also include the reason for the cancellation. Agency appointment shall not terminate until the notice of cancellation has been filed with the Commissioner.

3.) Any insurer appointing an agent shall file with the Commissioner, on a form prescribed by the Commissioner, a notice of appointment providing the names and business addresses of its agents, including notice of any limitations on the agent's authority. The filing of a single notice of appointment by each insurer represented by a licensed business entity shall cover all of its licensed producers.

4.) The filing of a notice of appointment shall constitute notice that the named insurance producer has been appointed an agent for any subsidiary or affiliate company of the insurer if certified copies of any resolution duly adopted by the board of directors of each insurer requesting that authority are filed with the Commissioner.

b. Producer employing another producer [Title 11:17-2.9 (b)] The employment of another producer by a producer is subject to the following requirements. (This situation primarily arises among property and casualty brokers when individual producers contract with a brokerage rather than an insurer's home office.)

1.) Licensed producers may enter into employment contracts by which the employed producer (employee) conducts business under the supervision of and in the name of an employing producer (employer). The contract may stipulate that it does not include all license authorities of the parties. The contract shall be in writing. Both parties shall retain copies and shall make them available to the Department upon request.

2.) An employer who has entered into such an employment contract shall notify the Department of the agreement by submitting a document signed by the employer, or licensed officer or partner if an organization containing the employee's name, license reference number, and the date of employment. The employer shall examine the credentials of the employee to determine that he is licensed to conduct the kinds of business described in the contract. Notice of a producer's appointment must be given to the Department of Banking and Insurance within 15 days of the appointment.

3.) If authorized by an employer, an employee may execute the employer's name to contracts of insurance in accordance with a written agency contract. An employer shall oversee the insurance related conduct of an employee. In any disciplinary proceeding, the existence of the employment contract shall be prime evidence that the employer knew of the employee's activities. Upon the termination of any contract, the employer shall notify the Department of the termination. Notice of a producer's termination must be given to the Department of Banking and Insurance within 15 days of the termination.

4.) Existence of a business relationship between two licensed producers by which each acts as an independent contractor shall not require the filing of any notice in accordance with New Jersey law, nor create any responsibility for the acts of the other in the absence of knowledge or concerted action.

c. Producer substituting for or taking over the business of a deceased or disabled person [Title 17:22A-37; 11:17-2.10(c)] The Commissioner may issue a temporary insurance producer license (note that this is different from the Temporary Certification addressed earlier in item 2) for a period not to exceed 180 days without requiring an examination if the Commissioner determines that the temporary license is necessary for the servicing of an insurance business in the following cases:

■ to the surviving spouse or court-appointed personal representative of a licensed insurance producer, upon the death or disability of that producer, to allow adequate time for the sale of the insurance business owned by the producer or for the recovery or return of the producer to the business or to provide for the training and licensing of new personnel to operate the producer's business;

■ to a member or employee of a business entity licensed as an insurance producer, upon the death or disability of an individual designated in the business entity application or the license as responsible for the business entity's compliance with the insurance laws, rules and regulations of this state;

■ to the designee of a licensed insurance producer entering active service in the armed forces of the United States; or

■ in any other circumstance in which the Commissioner determines that the public interest will best be served by the issuance of a temporary insurance producer license.

1.) The Commissioner may, by order, limit the authority of any temporary licensee in any way necessary to protect insureds and the public. The Commissioner may require the temporary licensee to have a suitable sponsor who is a licensed insurance producer or insurer and who, by contract, assumes responsibility for all acts of the temporary licensee. The Commissioner may impose other similar requirements designed to protect insureds and the public, and may by order revoke a temporary license if the interest of insureds or the public is endangered.

a.) Sharing commissions with temporary licensees A temporary licensee would share commissions with a producer who the insurer appoints to oversee the licensee's actions.

2.) A temporary license shall not continue after the owner or the personal representative disposes of the insurance producer's business.

4. Maintenance and duration of license

a. Renewal [11:17-2.1, 2.5] The Commissioner shall prescribe the terms of all insurance producer licenses.

1.) A **renewal license** shall be issued only after a renewal application has been submitted to the Commissioner by the licensee along with the payment of any required license renewal fee. No license shall be renewed unless the producer has satisfied the requirements for continuing education required by the Commissioner.

   a.) License termination Failure to satisfy continuing education requirements results in the termination of the license.

   b.) License reinstatement within one year of termination A producer can reinstate a license within one year of termination by satisfying the requirement for continuing education, filing the application for renewal, and paying the license renewal fee.

   c.) License reinstatement beyond one year of termination If more than one year has passed since the license was terminated, the producer must meet all of the standard prelicensing requirements again, including successful completion of prelicensing education and passing the state licensing exam.

2.) The standard term of an insurance producer license shall be 16 licensing quarters. Licensing quarters begin on the first day of February, May, August, and November of each year. Licenses shall expire in the fourth year on the last day of the quarter before the quarter in which the license was effective. Each license issued shall contain an expiration date. An initial license shall be deemed effective as of the date of issuance of any temporary certificate issued according to New Jersey law.

   a.) Renewal versus expiration dates A license's renewal date is not the same as its expiration date. For instance, if a license expires on October 31, its renewal date is November 1.

   b.) Continuing education requirements Producers must complete 48 continuing education credits within a four-year period to maintain their licenses. Of the 48 required credits, 24 must be on topics within the producer's own line of authority. Of those 24 credits, 6 must be on the subject of ethics.

   c.) Courses approved for continuing education The Department approves certain courses for continuing education credit. It also approves national designation programs including those for Certified Life Underwriter (CLU), Certified Financial Planner (CFP), Chartered Financial Counselor (ChFC), Certified Property and Casualty Underwriter (CPCU), and Certified Insurance Counselor (CIC). The Department will not approve the following courses for continuing education: insurance prelicensing courses, sales courses, motivational courses, and courses that teach general business skills, such as a course in automated office systems.

d.) Major lines versus limited lines of authority; continuing education Producers transacting major lines of insurance are required to fulfill CE requirements. Producers transacting limited lines of insurance do not need to fulfill CE requirements.

e.) License as state property A producer's license is considered the property of the State of New Jersey.

f.) Commissioner as agent for producers The granting of a license to a nonresident producer also appoints the Commissioner as that producer's registered agent for the purpose of receiving legal process in New Jersey.

3.) A current licensee shall renew a license in the following manner: at least 10 days before the license expiration date, each licensee must submit a completed application and the appropriate fee. The renewal application must be signed and dated. Failure to submit the renewal application for receipt by the date of the expiration shall be deemed to have expired (on the date shown). If a licensee does not wish to renew a license, he must inform the Department of that fact.

b. Lapsed license [11:17-2.5] If a license lapsed less than one year before an application for renewal, the applicant can apply for late renewal by attaching the following items to the application:

- Proof that the applicant met all continuing education requirements to date
- Certification that the applicant has or has not transacted any insurance business as a producer during the unlicensed period and, if so, information about the number of policies transacted
- The late renewal fee

1.) Certification of status is now accomplished by electronic means through the Department's Website. Information provided by the state is considered public information.

c. Certification of license status [11:17-2.15(c)] Upon request by any person, the Department shall issue a certification of the license status of any currently licensed producer or producer licensed within the preceding four years. Such certification shall contain the licensee's name, date of birth, license reference number, whether currently licensed or expired, kinds of insurance for which authorized whether qualified by examination or the equivalent, and whether any formal disciplinary action was taken during the last four years.

d. Military service [17:22A-32] A producer who cannot comply with license renewal procedures due to military service or other extenuating circumstances may ask the Commissioner to waive the procedures, or to waive a fine or other sanction for failing to comply with the renewal procedures.

e. Change of address [17:22A-32] A producer who changes an address must notify the Commissioner within 30 days of the change.

5. License refusal and termination

a. Denial [11:17-2.13; 17:22A-40] Whenever it appears from an application, renewals form, attached documents or Department records that an applicant has not demonstrated the qualifications prescribed, the Department shall advise the applicant in writing that the license requested is denied; shall specify the reason for denial; and shall further advise the applicant of the right to request a hearing in accordance with the Administrative Procedure Act and the Uniform Administrative Procedure and the procedure for doing so.

1.) Upon receipt of a request for a hearing on a license denial, the Department shall review the application and attachments, its records and any additional information submitted and determine whether the license may be issued. If after this review the Department determines that the applicant is not qualified, the Department shall find that the matter is a contested case and transmit it to the office of Administrative Law for hearing within 30 days.

b. Cancellation and reinstatement [11:17-2.14] A licensee may terminate a current producer license by returning it to the Department for cancellation at any time before expiration. The Department may refuse to accept a request for cancellation of an organization license unless all current licensed officers or partners consent to the request.

1.) A producer license may be reinstated after termination during the same license period by completing an application according to state law. No additional license fee for that period shall be required but the processing fee shall be paid. Submitting a license for cancellation shall not void or terminate any disciplinary action against the licensee, nor prevent disposition of any penalty, ordered restitution, or costs. If a license is lost or destroyed, the licensee may request a duplicate by submitting a certified statement attesting to the loss.

c. Revocation and suspension [17:22A-40; 11:17-2.11(c)] The Commissioner may place on probation, suspend, revoke, or refuse to issue or renew an insurance producer's license or may levy a civil penalty or any combination of actions, for any one or more of the following causes:

- providing incorrect, misleading, incomplete or materially untrue information in the license application;
- violating any insurance laws, or violating any regulation, subpoena or order of the Commissioner or of another state's insurance regulator;
- obtaining or attempting to obtain a license through misrepresentation or fraud;
- improperly withholding, misappropriating, or converting any monies or properties received in the course of doing insurance business;
- intentionally misrepresenting the terms of an actual or proposed insurance contract, policy or application for insurance;
- engaging in controlled business (writing business on oneself, one's family, or business associates) that accounts for more than 50% of commissions earned within the preceding 12 months;

- having been convicted of a felony or crime of the fourth degree or higher;
- having admitted or been found to have committed any insurance unfair trade practice or fraud;
- using fraudulent, coercive, or dishonest practices, or demonstrating incompetence, untrustworthiness, or financial irresponsibility in the conduct of insurance business in this state or elsewhere;
- having an insurance producer license, or its equivalent, denied, suspended, or revoked in any other state, province, district, or territory;
- forging another's name to an application for insurance or to any document related to an insurance transaction;
- improperly using notes or any other reference material to complete an examination for an insurance producer license;
- knowingly accepting insurance business from an unlicensed insurance producer;
- failing to comply with an administrative or court order imposing a child support obligation;
- failing to pay income tax or comply with any administrative or court order directing payment of income tax pursuant to New Jersey Statutes;
- intentionally withholding material information or making a material misstatement in an application for a license;
- committing any fraudulent act;
- knowingly facilitating or assisting another person in violating any insurance laws; or
- failing to notify the Commissioner within 30 days of his conviction of any crime, indictment or the filing of any formal criminal charges, or the suspension or revocation of any insurance license or authority by a state, other than this state, or the initiation of formal disciplinary proceedings in a state, other than this state, affecting the producer's insurance license; or failing to obtain the written consent pursuant to or failing to supply any documentation that the Commissioner may request in connection therewith.

  1.) Revocation of license If a producer's license is revoked, he must wait five years before applying for reinstatement. He must wait 10 years before he may own a share of an insurance organization. If a producer's license is suspended, he may apply for reinstatement immediately after the period of suspension.

E. TRADE PRACTICES

1. **Prohibited practices [17:29B-1 through 14; 11:2-17]** The purpose of this law is to regulate trade practices in order to identify those which are unfair or deceptive. There are several types of unfair trade practices which are prohibited including but not limited to the following.

   a. **Rebating [17:29B-4 (8)]** No company, officer, agent, or broker, shall pay or allow, or offer to pay or allow, in connection with placing or negotiating any policy of insurance, any valuable consideration or inducement not specified in the policy or contract, or any special favor or advantage in the dividends accrued on these policies. Any item or consideration given under these circumstances will be considered a rebate if its value exceeds $25.

1.) Insurance personnel shall not give, sell, or purchase or offer to give, sell, or purchase as inducement to the insurance any stocks, bonds, or other securities of an insurance company or other corporation, association, or partnership, or any dividends or profits accrued thereon, or anything of value not specified in the contract. The **offeror** is the party offering the rebate (agent). The **offeree** is the party accepting the rebate (insured). New Jersey law with regard to rebating shall not apply to the following:

a.) Any contract or policy paying bonuses to policyholders or otherwise abating their premiums in whole or in part out of surplus accumulated from nonparticipating insurance.

b.) Readjustment of the rate of premium for a group policy based on the loss or expense experience.

b. Misrepresentation [17:29B-4 (1)] No company, officer, agent, broker, or insurance person shall make, issue, circulate, or use, or cause or permit to be made, any written or oral statement misrepresenting the terms of any policy or contract of insurance, or the benefits or privileges promised under these contracts. In addition, none of the aforementioned parties may make any misleading statements as to the dividends or share of surplus previously paid on insurance policies, or make any misleading misrepresentation or any misrepresentation as to the financial condition of any insurer.

1.) Twisting Any person making any misrepresentation to any policyholder/insured in any company for the purpose of inducing or tending to induce a policyholder to lapse, forfeit, or surrender his insurance in order to sell a new policy is guilty of **twisting**, which is a form of misrepresentation.

2.) An insured induced to lapse or surrender his current insurance policy may recover from the company or parties involved, all premiums paid on the new policy or contract less any indebtedness to the company. This action may be brought against the company or parties involved within a reasonable time as determined by the Commissioner of Insurance.

c. Defamation [17:29B-4 (3)] Making, publishing, disseminating, or circulating, directly or indirectly, or aiding, abetting, or encouraging the making, publishing, disseminating, or circulating, of any oral or written statement, or any pamphlet, circular, article, or literature which is false, or maliciously critical of or derogatory to the financial condition of an insurer, and which is calculated to injure any person engaged in the business of insurance is considered to be defamation and is illegal.

d. Unfair discrimination [17:29B-4 (7)] Making or permitting any unfair discrimination between individuals of the same class and equal expectation of life in the rates charge for any contract of insurance (including life insurance or annuities) or in the dividends or other benefits payable thereon, or in any other of the terms and conditions of the contract is considered to be unfair discrimination.

1.) Making or permitting any unfair discrimination between individuals of the same class and of essentially the same hazard in the amount of premium, policy fees, or rates charged for any policy or contract of insurance or in the benefits payable thereunder, or in any of the terms or conditions of any contract, is also considered to be unfair discrimination.

2.) Making or permitting any discrimination against any person or groups of persons because of race, creed, color, national origin, or ancestry is prohibited.

3.) Making or permitting any unfair discrimination solely because of age in the issuance, withholding, extension, or renewal of any policy or contract of automobile liability insurance or in the fixing of the rates, terms, or conditions therefore, or in the issuance or acceptance of any application therefore, is also prohibited.

4.) Making or permitting any discrimination against any person on the basis of DNA or genetic screening.

5.) Legitimate (fair) discrimination Note that differences in premiums or product offerings to applicants due to legitimate actuarial distinctions are legal. For example, it is legal to charge a male insured a higher premium for a life insurance policy than the premium charged a female insured for the same policy due to the difference in their average life expectancy. Similarly, a female annuitant must invest more than a male annuitant of the same age in order to receive the same lifetime annuity benefit.

e. False advertising [17:29B-4 (2)] Making, publishing, circulating, disseminating, or placing before the public, or causing, directly or indirectly, to be made, published, circulated, disseminated, or placed before the public, in a newspaper, magazine, or other publication, or in the form of a notice, circular, pamphlet, letter, or poster, or over any radio station, or in any other way, an advertisement, announcement, or statement containing any assertion, representation, or statement with respect to the business of insurance or with respect to any person in the conduct of his insurance business, which is untrue, deceptive, or misleading, is considered to involve false information and advertising.

f. Boycott and coercion [17:29B-4 (4)] Entering into any agreement to commit any act of boycott, coercion, or intimidation resulting in unreasonable restraint or monopoly in the business of insurance is prohibited. For example, a bank loan officer who informs a borrower that a home loan will only be approved if the borrower purchases homeowners insurance from the bank officer's brother (who is an agent) would be viewed as coercion.

g. False financial statements [17:29B-4 (5)] It is illegal to file or publish any false financial statements with the intention of deceiving the public or a Department examiner. For example, an insurer which alters its financial statements to mask how poorly it is doing would violate this law.

h. Stock operations and advisory board contracts [17:29B-4 (6)] Issuing or delivering agency company stock, securities, or advisory board contracts as an inducement to purchasing insurance is prohibited.

i. Unfair claim practices [17:29B-4 (9); 11:2-17.1ff] Any unfair acts such as settling a claim for less than the benefits provided by a policy is prohibited. All insurers must act in good faith and effectuate prompt and fair settlements of claims.

   1.) All claims must be reported to the insurer by a broker within five working days following receipt of notification of claim by the broker. An insurer must investigate any claim before it can deny it. Any denial of a claim shall be confirmed in writing and be kept on file by the insurer.

   2.) No insurer shall coerce a claimant to settle a disability income claim on a lump-sum basis. Settlement of claims for a fraction of an indemnity period shall be on a pro rata basis. No insurer may terminate disability benefits based solely on lack of medical attention.

   3.) If the Commissioner finds that a person or insurer has violated state unfair claim practice law, a cease and desist order will be issued.

   ■ Any individual who engages in unfair methods of competition or deceptive acts or practices may have his license suspended, revoked, or non-renewed by the Commissioner. If any licensee is or has been engaged in these activities, the Commissioner will issue a cease and desist order which requires that person to discontinue all operations or activities involving insurance.

2. Cease and desist orders [17:29B-7, 11] If the Commissioner determines that an insurer or producer has engaged in an unfair trade practice, a cease and desist order will be issued. In addition, a penalty not to exceed $1,000 will be assessed for every violation unless the violater knew, or should have known, that the act was illegal. In the latter case, the penalty shall not exceed $5,000 for every violation. Violation of a cease and desist order will result in a penalty not to exceed $5,000.

3. Licensee responsibilities and reporting information to the Department of Banking and Insurance [17:22A-36; 11:17-1.2, 2.7; 11:17-2.7 (f and g), 2.8; 11:17A-2.1 through 17D]

a. Public and nonpublic records Licensees must make available to the Commissioner any records and accounts whenever requested. Whether these records are classified as public or nonpublic will be left to the discretion of the Commissioner and the Department of Banking and Insurance. Note, however, that the state will not disclose criminal or financial details without a proper court order. For instance, it may disclose that a license was revoked because of a criminal act, but it will not provide details or records relating to the act.

b. Business names An insurance producer doing business under any name other than the producer's legal name shall notify the Commissioner prior to using the assumed name. Any licensee who advertises using a fictitious trade or firm name shall file with the Commissioner a copy of the name. The Commissioner will not accept the filing of a name that is similar to another already on file because it may be misleading to the public. No producer may file a name using the words *insurance company*, *guaranty company*, or similar words unless the word *agent*, *agency*, *broker*, or *brokerage* (or words of similar import) are used to distinguish the business from an insurance company.

   1.) Legal name versus fictitious name The legal name of an entity may be a registered fictitious name—a name that does not refer to an individual—yet be perfectly legal. For example, ABC Insurance Company would be a fictitious yet legal name.

      a.) Registration of fictitious names To register a fictitious name, one must do the following.

      ■ Request permission from the Department of Banking and Insurance to use the name

      ■ Obtain a 90-day authorization from the DOBI following approval of the name

      ■ Register the name with either the county in which the organization is domiciled or, in the case of foreign corporations, with the Secretary of the State of New Jersey

      ■ File the "Change of Name" with the DOBI

      These steps must be completed within 90 days of receiving the initial 90-day authorization from the DOBI.

c. Branch offices [11:17-1.2, 2.8] These offices are an extension of an insurer's home office. They conduct the regional business of an insurer in specific areas. All branch offices carry on the business of licensed insurers and shall also comply with the laws and regulations of New Jersey. The Commissioner, at his discretion, may examine, or have a deputy examine, the solicitation, negotiation, of effectuation procedures and practices utilized by these entities at any time.

   1.) Licensees shall file with the Department a branch office registration form within 30 days before business is first conducted there. This form shall be accompanied by a processing fee. A branch office certificate shall be issued when the form and fee are received by the Department. This certificate will authorize the transaction of business at the named location. If a branch office is closed down, the licensee must provide 20 days notice to the Department and return the certificate for cancellation. The hours and days of business operation must be posted in order to inform the public.

   2.) Failure to notify the Department of the opening or closing of a branch location is subject to a $500 fine.

d. Change of address [11:17-2.7(f), (g)] The requirements for business addresses and notification of change of mailing or location address and residence address are as follows: all licensees shall provide their current business mailing address and residence address; all licensees shall provide the Department notification of change of business or residence address within 30 days of the change. Any legal process (i.e., subpoenas) may be served by being delivered to the licensee's business or residence address. The licensee must also inform the Department of any business or legal name change by using a Change of Name or Address form, with evidence of such a change accompanying the notice.

> **1.)** Failure to report a change of name to the Department is subject to a fine of $250. If the name change has not been reported for more than 60 days, the fine could reach a maximum of $5,000.

4. Standards of conduct [11:17A through 17D] No person may act as a producer, collect commissions, or other considerations without a license. Selling insurance without a license is a misdemeanor. Salaried officers or employees of insurers authorized to do business in this state who solicit insurance for compensation of any type shall be licensed as a producer or a limited representative. Other standards of conduct to be met by licensees include but are not limited to the following.

a. All of the following are considered to be insurance transactions for which a person must be licensed:

- discussing the effect of age, health, or other risk related conditions of a prospective policyholder;
- initiating sales over the telephone;
- making (or proposing) an insurance contract;
- completing applications for insurance covering any person;
- signing binders, endorsements, riders, and policies;
- adding or deleting coverage;
- interpreting or explaining policies in response to policyholder questions; and
- quoting premiums.

b. Persons who do not require licenses include: office employees performing clerical duties (i.e., filing, typing, billing, mailing, scheduling appointments for producers, general communications with policyholders, etc.).

c. Premiums collected by a producer shall be deemed to be received by the insurer the producer represents. A producer is also required to witness an applicant's signing of an insurance application. All funds must be remitted to the insurer within five business days of receipt (seven business days for accident and health policies). Any return premiums due shall be paid to the insured within five business days (seven business days for accident and health policies). A nonlicensed person may only accept a premium at a producer's office.

d. Policies, certificates, or other evidences of insurance which are received by a producer or limited representative from an insurer must be delivered to the insured within 10 calendar days of their receipt from the insurer (unless the insured agrees to a later date).

e. Any policies or materials an insured gives to a producer to review must be itemized and a list (receipt) provided to the insured. This list or receipt must be signed by the producer or limited representative and the insured.

f. An individual may be paid a commission if he is not licensed only if he held a license at the time of the original sales transaction.

g. Only a producer acting as a broker or consultant may charge a fee to a policyholder for services rendered. If the producer is acting as an agent he may not charge such a fee. If acting as a broker or consultant and charging a fee, all parties must sign a written agreement including the fee to be charged, any additional commissions to be received, and the execution date of the agreement.

> **1.)** The maximum service fee on a personal lines policy is $20 per year.

h. Insurance producers and brokers must maintain a (premium) trust account. Premiums collected may be deposited there. Nonpremium monies received by an insurance producer for soliciting, negotiating, effecting, renewing, or binding policies may be deposited into this account. These type of monies include service or policy fees, late charges, inspection fees, or surplus lines premium taxes.

i. A producer or broker may place trust account funds in interest-bearing or income-producing assets (and retain the interest earned) provided the nature of the account has been disclosed to the principal (insurer) and it has issued written authorization (permission).

> **1.)** If accounts receivables exist, they must be cleared within 120 days. After that, any unpaid receivables may not be carried forward as assets, but must be written off.

> **2.)** If a brokerage has a premium trust account that yields interest, or any account with a minimum balance requirement, the brokerage may deposit funds to maintain the required minimum balance.

j. Legal disbursements from trust accounts include: nonpremium monies; net or gross premiums due insurers or producers; claim payments; premiums due insureds; commissions due the producer; voluntary deposits; interest that can be retained by the producer; and funds for permitted investments.

k. A producer must issue a receipt for each premium received from an insured at the time payment is tendered. Premium receipts must be kept for five years.

l. All receipts must: be sequentially numbered; be clearly signed by the producer (or authorized employee); indicate the name of the insured, insurer, the name and address of the agency, the date and type of coverage, and the date of the transaction; indicate the purpose of the payment (i.e., premium); and indicate the amount paid.

m. All producers shall maintain adequate records of transactions. All records of any fees or monies collected must be maintained and a written explanation of any discrepancies must also be maintained. All transactions must indicate the amount, policy number, date of transaction, and so forth. Net commissions shall not be greater than the amount of the disbursements recorded.

   1.) The producer must also maintain: a monthly reconciliation of the trust account; a copy of all applications; and all correspondence received or sent.

   2.) Maintenance of records All records must be maintained for a period of five years after termination of coverage. If these records are kept electronically, at least once every 30 days they must be printed out in hardcopy.

n. Administrative penalties If a producer violates New Jersey law regarding procedures or standards of conduct he will be advised by certified mail (or personal delivery) of any administrative penalty. The notice shall include: a reference to the violated statute; a concise statement of facts regarding the violation; a statement describing the administrative penalty; and a statement advising the violator the right to a hearing.

o. If a violator fails to respond to such a notice, it will be considered as an admission to the allegations. This could result in a license suspension or revocation and a monetary penalty. The Department could also ask for: the return of the producer's license; the payment of a fine; reimbursement for investigative expenses; or restitution of monies owed to any person. The violator will have 20 days from receipt of the notice in which to file a written request for a hearing. The Department will notify the violator of action (hearing) to be taken within 60 days of receiving the written request.

   1.) A producer who does not request a hearing must pay the fine within the 20 days following receipt of the notice advising her of her right to request a hearing.

5. Penalties for producer licensing violations Several penalties may be assessed for various violations including the following.

a. $250 for failure to maintain on file with the state a complete and accurate business or home address or failure to notify of a change of address (within 30 days of the change).

   1.) If the producer fails to notify the Commissioner of a change of address after 60 days, the producer may be fined the maximum amount of $5,000.

b. $500 for failing to notify the state (i.e., Department of Banking and Insurance) of the opening of a branch office within 30 days, or of a branch office closing within 20 days.

c. $500 for payment of a license fee with a check that is returned for insufficient funds.

d. $250 for failure to notify the state of a change of business name within 30 days.

e. $250 for failure to notify the state of the addition or deletion of owners of more than 5% or officers, directors, or partners.

f. $100 (per contract) for failure to maintain all copies of employment or agency contracts.

g. $500 for failure by an employing producer, insurer, or other custodian to return a license to the possession of another (named) insurance producer.

1.) No person whose license has been suspended or revoked will be refunded any license fees for an unexpired term of a license. No producer whose license is suspended or revoked shall become or act as a limited representative during the suspension or revocation period. A person whose license has been revoked or suspended must wait five years from the effective date of the action to reapply. He must then reapply like a new applicant, provide a statement of employment history, and inform the state whether restitution has been made to any aggrieved parties.

2.) Selling insurance without a license to do so is a misdemeanor.

F. NEW JERSEY LIFE AND HEALTH INSURANCE GUARANTY ASSOCIATION ACT [17B:32A] The purpose of this act is to protect the public from hardship because of the impairment or insolvency of any member insurer which issues life, health, or annuity contracts.

1. The act, which created the Life and Health Guaranty Association, provides protection for direct, non group life, health, annuity, and supplemental policies or contracts, for certificates under the same, and for individual and group long-term care insurance policies and contracts, and for unallocated annuity contracts issued by member insurers. Protection is also provided for policies issued by medical service corporations which are declared insolvent.

2. This act does not provide coverage for: any portion of a policy or contract not guaranteed by the insurer, or under which the risk is borne by the policyholder; any policy of reinsurance; any plan which is self funded or uninsured; any policy issued by a member insurer when it was not licensed (i.e., no valid certificate of authority); or any unallocated annuity contract issued to an employee benefit plan covered by the Pension Benefit Guaranty Corporation (PBGC).

3. The benefits for which the Association may become liable shall in no event exceed the lesser of: the contractual obligations for which the insurer would have become liable if it were not impaired or insolvent; $500,000 in life insurance death benefits but not more than $100,000 in net cash surrender and net cash withdrawal values for life insurance; $100,000 in health insurance benefits; or $500,000 in present value annuity benefits but not more than $100,000 in net cash surrender or withdrawal values. In no event shall the Association be liable to expend more than $500,000 in the aggregate with respect to any one individual.

4. The Association is a nonprofit legal entity. All insurers writing life and health insurance in this state must participate in the Association as a condition of their authority to transact business in New Jersey. An insurer who is a member of the Association shall remain a member for four years after it ceases to hold a certificate of authority or license in New Jersey. The Association is under the immediate supervision of the Commissioner of Insurance.

5. For purposes of administration and assessment the Association shall maintain two accounts.

    a. The life insurance and annuity account which shall include the following subaccounts; life insurance; annuities; unallocated annuity subaccount.

    b. The health insurance account.

6. Funding When an insurer is deemed to be insolvent and the Guaranty Fund assumes management and administration of the insurer's assets, the following will occur.

    a. The insolvent insurer's assets are liquidated and the balance is transferred to the Guaranty Fund.

    b. Any funds needed to pay claims (up to the fund's statutory limit) are collected from assessments against other insurers authorized to do business in New Jersey.

    c. The other insurers may pass on the cost of these assessments to their policyowners in the form of a premium surcharge, the amount of which the Commissioner determines.

7. Prohibited advertising Insurers may not use the Fund's existence to market insurance. When delivering a policy, insurers must inform the policyowner of the limits of coverage allowed under the Act.

G. NEW JERSEY INSURANCE FRAUD PREVENTION ACT [17:33A] The New Jersey Insurance Fraud Prevention Act is intended to address insurance fraud in the state by securing the means to detect it, eliminating it through fraud prevention programs, requiring restitution of insurance benefits obtained through fraud, and reducing the amount of premium dollars used to pay fraudulent claims.

The state attorney general and the director of the Division of Anti-Fraud Compliance in the Department of Banking and Insurance share enforcement authority.

1. Violations of act [17:33A-4] A person or entity violates the act by doing any of the following:

■ Knowingly making a false or misleading statement concerning a material fact or information on a claim for payment or benefit under an insurance policy or the Unsatisfied Claim and Judgment Fund Law

■ Knowingly concealing or failing to disclose a fact that affects a person's right or entitlement to an insurance benefit or payment or the amount of a benefit or payment

■ Preparing a written or oral statement intended to be given to an insurer or producer for the purpose of obtaining an insurance policy, knowing that the statement contains false or misleading information about a material fact concerning the insurance application or policy

■ Knowingly concealing or failing to disclose evidence that may be relevant in showing that a material fact about an application or policy for insurance was knowingly concealed or misrepresented, or that such material fact was not knowingly concealed or misrepresented

■ Knowingly assisting, conspiring with, or encouraging anyone to violate the act

■ Knowingly benefiting from the proceeds resulting from a violation of the act

■ Knowingly benefiting from the proceeds that result from the assistance, conspiracy, or encouragement of any person in violating the act

2. **Penalties for violations [17:33A-5]** If the Commissioner finds that a person has violated the act, he may:

   a. bring a civil suit against the offender; or

   b. assess a civil penalty and order the offender to pay restitution to the victim of the fraud.

      1.) A fine may be assessed against the offender as follows:
         ■ $5,000 for the first offense
         ■ $10,000 for the second offense
         ■ $15,000 for subsequent offenses

   c. The Commissioner may, in addition to or as an alternative to these penalties, ask the Attorney General to charge the offender with a criminal offense. Furthermore, the Commissioner may refer the matter to the state licensing authorities, who may suspend or revoke the offender's license.

3. **Surcharge [17:33A-5.1]** In addition to any penalty, fine, or charge, a person who is found to have committed insurance fraud is subject to a surcharge of $1,000. If the person charged settles the case with a money payment, he is subject to a surcharge equal to 5% of the settlement payment. This money is paid to the state treasurer. The Department of Banking and Insurance uses the money to fund its efforts to fight insurance fraud.

4. **Actions by insurance companies [17:33A-7]** An insurance company that is a victim of insurance fraud may sue to recover money it spent on investigating the claim, filing the lawsuit, and attorneys' fees. If the defendant is found to be liable and to have engaged in a pattern of insurance fraud, the insurance company is entitled to three times that amount of money. The Commissioner may join in the insurance company's suit and recover civil penalties from the defendant.

   a. An insurance company cannot sue a party for insurance fraud more than six years after it knew or should have known that it was a victim of insurance fraud.

5. Reporting and investigating suspicions of fraud [17:33A-9] Anyone who believes that insurance fraud is being or will be committed must notify the Division of Anti-Fraud Compliance. The division will examine the facts of the alleged violation to determine whether fraud, deceit, or intentional misrepresentation exists.

   a. No one is liable for libel, violation of privacy, or simply filing a report or giving information related to good-faith suspicions of insurance fraud.

6. Fraud prevention and detection plan [17:33A-15] Every insurance company writing health insurance in New Jersey must file with the Commissioner a plan for prevention and detection of fraudulent insurance applications and claims. The Commissioner will either approve or reject the plan within 90 days of filing. If the Commissioner fails to act within this period, the plan will be deemed to have been approved. The Commissioner may impose a penalty of up to $25,000 per violation on any insurer who fails to submit, implement, or report on this plan.

II.   NEW JERSEY LAWS, RULES, AND REGULATIONS PERTINENT TO LIFE, ACCIDENT, AND HEALTH INSURANCE

A. CREDIT LIFE, ACCIDENT, AND HEALTH INSURANCE [11:2-3.1 THROUGH 3.19]

All life, accident and health insurance sold in connection with loans or other credit transactions shall be subject to New Jersey law except insurance sold in connection with first mortgage loans made to individual borrowers for the purpose of purchasing residential real estate. The creditor—not the insured—is the beneficiary of a credit insurance policy. The maximum term is the length of the loan or five years, whichever is shortest.

Credit life insurance is a form of decreasing term insurance. Credit accident and health insurance is another name for credit disability insurance. In general, premiums for group credit insurance are less expensive than individual credit insurance.

1. Credit life, accident, and health insurance shall be issued only in the following forms:
   - individual policies of life insurance issued to debtors on a term plan;
   - group policies of life insurance issued to creditors providing insurance upon the lives of debtors on the term plan;
   - group policies of accident and health insurance issued to debtors on a term plan, or disability provisions in individual policies of credit life insurance; and
   - individual policies of accident and health insurance issued to debtors on a term plan, or disability provisions in individual policies of credit life insurance.

2. Amount The amount of credit life insurance issued in connection with a specific loan shall not exceed the amount of indebtedness. The amount of indemnity payable in connection with a specific loan by credit accident and health insurance in the event of disability, shall not exceed the aggregate of the periodic scheduled unpaid installments of indebtedness.

   a. Debtor groups must have at least 100 members to qualify for credit insurance.

3. **Term of coverage** Coverage begins when the borrower becomes obligated to the creditor (the effective date of the policy). The term of the insurance shall not extend more than 15 days beyond the scheduled maturity date (pay-off date of the indebtedness). The maximum term is 5 years.

4. **Policy provisions** All insurance coverage shall be evidenced by an individual policy or a certificate (in the case of a group). Each policy or certificate must include: the name and home office address of the insurer; the identity of the person insured; the amount and term of coverage; the premium rate; a description of the coverage; and the circumstances under which refunds are payable.

5. **Delivery** The policy or group certificate shall be delivered to the insured at the time of the effective date or no later than 30 days from the date the indebtedness is incurred.

6. The Commissioner may disapprove any policy form filed with the state if he feels the benefits are not reasonable in relation to the premium charged. He may require the insurer to increase or decrease the premium and refile the policy for approval.

7. **Refunds** Each policy of credit life, accident, and health insurance for which a payment is collected from the debtor must provide that in the event of termination prior to the scheduled maturity date of the indebtedness any refund due shall be paid to the insured debtor within a reasonable time.

8. **Maintenance of statistics** Each insurer writing credit life, accident, and health shall maintain annual records of policies sold including: gross premiums received; refunds of terminated insurance; increase in unearned premium reserve; earned premiums; claims paid; increase in claim reserve; claims incurred; commissions; fees and other allowances; dividends and experience rating refunds; mean amount of life insurance in force; and the mean number of individual policies in force.

9. All policies issued and delivered must be done so by an authorized insurer in the state of New Jersey.

10. **Claims** All claims must be reported promptly to the insurer and the insurer must maintain adequate claim files.

11. **Choice of insurer** A debtor does not have to purchase credit insurance through the lender when it is required in certain instances. A debtor has the option of furnishing the required amount through existing policies owned or controlled by him.
    The debtor may purchase a new policy that he owns or controls. If the debtor chooses the insurer, he may be required to provide proof of insurance when the debt is incurred.

B. GROUP COVERAGE DISCONTINUANCE AND REPLACEMENT [11:2-13.1 THROUGH 13.9]

This regulation is applicable to all life and accident and health policies (and subscriber contracts) issued on a group (or group type) basis. This regulation does not apply to contracts issued in connection with temporary disability benefits or workers' compensation laws. It also does not apply to individual policies purchased at the worksite where premiums are paid by payroll deductions.

1. Group (or group type) basis means a benefit plan, other than "salary savings" or "salary budget" plans utilizing individual insurance policies or subscriber contracts. Coverage may be provided through insurance policies to classes of employees. Coverage is not available to the general public (must be part of a group). There must also be sponsorship of plan by an employer, union, association (i.e., credit union), or creditor.

2. **Discontinuance** If a policy provides for automatic discontinuance after a premium has been unpaid (through the grace period), the carrier shall be liable for valid claims for covered losses incurred prior to the end of the grace period. If the actions of the carrier after the end of the grace period indicate that it considers the policy as continuing in force beyond the end of the grace period (i.e., continuing to recognize claims subsequently incurred), the carrier shall be liable for valid claims beginning prior to the effective date of the written notice of discontinuance. This date shall not be prior to midnight at the end of the third work day after the date upon which the notice is delivered.

3. **Requirements for notice** Any notice of discontinuance shall include a request to the group policyholder (e.g., employer) to notify all covered members of the date on which the policy will discontinue and that the carrier shall not be liable for claims for losses incurred after that date. Discontinuance of the group policy will not serve to reduce the specified time limit which must be satisfied for the furnishing of notice of claim or proof of loss.

4. **Extension of benefits** Every group policy must provide a reasonable provision for extension of benefits in the event of total disability at the date of discontinuance of the group policy. Any applicable extension of benefits shall be described in the policy as well as in the group certificates.

5. **Replacement** When replacement of coverage occurs, the prior carrier remains liable only to the extent of its accrued liabilities and extensions of benefits. The position of the prior carrier shall be the same whether the group policyholder secures replacement from a new carrier, self-insures, or forgoes the provision of coverage.

   a. Each person who is eligible for coverage in accordance with the succeeding carrier's plan of benefits shall be covered by that carrier's plan of benefits.

   b. Each person not covered under the succeeding carrier's plan of benefits in accordance with New Jersey law must nevertheless be covered by the succeeding carrier in accordance with the law if the individual was validly covered under the prior plan on the date of discontinuance and if the individual is a member of the class or classes of individuals eligible for coverage under the succeeding carrier's plan.

   c. In the case of a preexisting conditions limitation included in the succeeding carrier's plan, the level of benefits applicable to preexisting conditions of person's becoming covered by the succeeding carrier's plan during the period of time this limitation applies under the new plan shall be the lesser of:
   - the benefits of the new plan determined without application of the preexisting conditions limitation; and
   - the benefits of the prior plan.

  d. The succeeding carrier shall give credit for the satisfaction or partial satisfaction of the same or similar provisions under a prior plan providing similar benefits. For example, the insured will get credit for the number of days he spent under the prior plan satisfying the probationary period and the amount of money he spent satisfying the deductible under the prior policy within the previous 90 days.

  e. In any situation where a determination of the prior carrier's benefit is required by the succeeding carrier, at the succeeding carrier's request the prior carrier shall furnish a statement of the benefits available of permanent information, sufficient to permit verification of the benefit determination or the determination itself by the succeeding carrier.

6. Provisions as favorable No policy of group insurance shall be issued or delivered in this state if the policy contains any provision inconsistent with any provisions of New Jersey law.

III. NEW JERSEY LAWS, RULES, AND REGULATIONS PERTINENT TO LIFE INSURANCE ONLY

A. MARKETING METHODS AND PRACTICES [17B:30-1 THROUGH 22] No person may engage in any trade practices which are deemed to be unfair acts or practices. There are several types of unfair marketing practices which have been reviewed previously.

1. Misrepresentations and false advertising of policies or annuity contracts No person shall make, issue, circulate, or cause to be made, issued, or circulated any estimate, illustration, circular, or statement misrepresenting the terms of any policy, or annuity contract issued or to be issued, or make any false or misleading statements as to the dividends or share of surplus previously paid on similar policies or annuity contracts. In addition, no person shall make any misleading representation or any misrepresentation as to the financial condition of any insurer, or as to the legal reserve system upon which any life insurance company operates, or use any name or title of any policy or annuity contract or class of policies or annuity contracts misrepresenting the true nature thereof.

2. Defamation No person shall make, publish, or disseminate, directly or indirectly, the making, publishing, or dissemination of any oral or written statement or any pamphlet, circular, article, or literature which is false or maliciously critical of or derogatory to the financial condition of an insurer and which is calculated to injure any person engaged in the business of insurance or annuities.

3. False advertising This involves the making or publishing of any advertisements (on radio or TV, in a newspaper, etc.) which are untrue, deceptive, or misleading. For example, an individual who runs an advertisement in a newspaper stating that a rival agent or company does not pay his or its claims promptly, when in fact they do, would be guilty of false information in advertising.

4. **False financial statements** No person shall file with any supervisory or other public official, or make, publish, or circulate to any person any false statement of financial condition of an insurer with intent to deceive. No person may make any false entry in any book, report, or statement of any insurer with the intent to deceive any agent or examiner lawfully appointed to examine into its conditions or affairs.

5. **Twisting [17B:30-6]** No person shall make any misleading misrepresentations or incomplete or fraudulent comparison of any insurance policies or annuity contracts or insurers for the purpose of inducing, or tending to induce, any person to lapse, forfeit, surrender, terminate, retain, or convert any insurance policy or annuity contract, or to take out a policy of insurance or annuity contract in another insurer. This inducement to buy a new insurance policy is **twisting**, a form of misrepresentation.

   a. Twisting is illegal. It is a common form of misrepresentation. For example, if an agent misrepresents or unfairly compares the policy terms and benefits of a prospective client's current policy in order to persuade that individual to lapse or surrender that plan and purchase a new one with the agent, twisting has occurred.

6. **Boycott, coercion, and intimidation** No person shall enter into any agreement to commit any act of boycott, coercion, or intimidation resulting in or tending to result in unreasonable restraint of or monopoly in the business of insurance or annuities.

7. **Rebates and special inducements** No person shall knowingly make, permit to be made or offer to make any contract of life insurance, annuity, or health insurance, or agreement as to the contract other than as plainly expressed in the contract issued thereon, or pay or allow, or give or offer to pay, allow, or give, directly or indirectly, as an inducement to the insurance, or annuity, any rebate of premiums or considerations payable on the contract or of any agents, solicitors, or brokers commission relating thereto, or any special favor or advantage in the dividends or other benefits thereon, on any valuable consideration or inducement whatever not specified in the contract. Any item or consideration given under these circumstances will be considered a rebate if its value exceeds $25.

   a. No person shall give, sell, or purchase, or offer to give, sell, or purchase as an inducement to the insurance or annuity, any stocks, bonds, or other securities of any insurance company or other corporation, association, or partnership, or any dividends or profits accrued thereon, or anything of value not specified in the contract.

   b. Generally, rebating involves the offering or giving of anything of value not listed in the policy. An individual who offers a rebate is guilty of rebating. In addition, an individual (the insured) who accepts such an offer is also guilty of rebating. The most common form of rebating occurs when an agent or broker shares his commissions with an insured in return for the purchase of a policy by that insured.

      1.) The offeror is the party making the offer.

      2.) The offeree is the party who accepts or receives the rebate.

8. **Unfair discrimination** No person shall discriminate against any person or group of persons because of race, creed, color, or ancestry with regard to the issuance, renewal, or premium rates charged on any life or health policy or annuity.

9. **Record of complaints** Insurers must maintain a complete file and written record of all complaints received for at least 5 years, or until the next departmental inspection, whichever is later. Failure of any person to maintain a complete and written record of all complaints which it has received since its last examination will be deemed a prohibited practice. The records shall indicate the total number of complaints, the classification by line of insurance, the nature of each complaint, the disposition of the complaints, and the time it took to process each complaint. A complaint is a written communication primarily expressing a grievance.

10. **Unfair claim settlement practices** Committing any of the following acts, if done without just cause and if performed with the frequency indicating a general business practice will be deemed to be an unfair claim settlement practice:

   - knowingly misrepresenting to claimants pertinent facts or policy provisions relating to coverage at issue;
   - failing to acknowledge within a reasonable promptness pertinent communications with respect to claims arising under insurance policies;
   - failing to adopt and implement reasonable standards for the prompt investigation of claims arising under insurance policies;
   - not attempting in good faith to effectuate prompt, fair, and equitable settlements of claims submitted in which liability has become reasonably clear;
   - compelling insureds to institute suits to recover amounts due under its policies by offering substantially less than the amounts ultimately recovered in suits brought by them when the insureds have made claims for amounts ultimately recovered;
   - making known to insureds or claimants a policy of appealing from arbitration awards in favor of insureds or claimants for the purpose of compelling them to accept settlements or compromises less than the amount awarded in arbitration;
   - attempting settlement or compromise of claims on the basis of applications which were altered without notice to, or knowledge or consent of insureds;
   - attempting to settle a claim for less than the amount to which a reasonable person would have believed one was entitled by reference to written or printed advertising material accompanying or made a part of an application;
   - attempting to delay the investigation or payment of claims by requiring an insured and the insured's physician to submit a preliminary claim report and then requiring the subsequent submission of formal proof of loss forms, both of which submissions contain substantially the same information;
   - failing to affirm or deny coverage of claims within a reasonable time after a proof of loss has been completed;
   - refusing payment of claim solely on the basis of the insured's request to do so without making an independent evaluation of the insured's liability based upon all available information;
   - refusing to pay claims without conducting a reasonable investigation; and
   - making claims payments without specifying the portion of the coverage under which the payment is being made.

11. **Cease and desist orders for prohibited practices** If the Commissioner has reason to believe that any person or individual has been engaged in or is engaging in this state in any unfair method of competition or any unfair or deceptive act or practice expressly prohibited by New Jersey law, he shall issue and serve upon the person or individual a statement of the charges in that respect and a notice of hearing thereon as provided by New Jersey law. The hearing date must be set at least 10 days after delivery of the notice.

   a. If, after the hearing, the Commissioner shall determine that the method of competition or act or practice in question is defined under New Jersey law as an unfair trade act or practice in violation of the law, he shall make his findings in writing and shall issue and cause to be served upon the person or individual charged with the violation an order requiring these persons to cease and desist from engaging in this method of competition, act, or practice. In addition, the Commissioner may order payment of a penalty not to exceed $1,000 for each and every act or violation unless the person knew or reasonably should have known he was in violation of New Jersey law. In cases where the individual knowingly committed these acts, he shall be fined not more than $5,000 for every act or violation. All penalties shall be collected by the Commissioner in the name of the state of New Jersey in a summary proceeding in accordance with the penalty enforcement law of this state.

12. **Violation of cease and desist order** Any person who violates a cease and desist order of the Commissioner according to New Jersey law shall be assessed a penalty not exceeding $5,000 for each violation, to be collected by the Commissioner in the name of this state in a summary proceeding in accordance with the penalty enforcement law. In addition, the Commissioner, in his discretion, may revoke or suspend the license or certificate of authority of any person or entity.

13. **Immunity from prosecution** If any person shall ask to be excused from providing records or accounts on the grounds that the evidence will incriminate him, he must produce the information but will be immune from prosecution and not be subject to any penalty, provided that perjury is not involved (in which case action may be taken against him).

14. **Discharge of insurer's liability [17B:24-5]** If an insurer pays the proceeds of a life or health insurance policy or makes a final payment under an annuity contract, the insurer is discharged of all claims on the policy or contract.

15. **Proceeds exempt from creditors' claims [17B:24-6, 7, 8]** If proceeds are paid to a beneficiary of a life insurance policy (other than to the insured himself or paid with the intent to defraud creditors), they are exempt from creditors' claims. Similarly, proceeds paid under an annuity contract are protected from creditors if they total less than $500 per month for the installment payment period. Creditors may garnish payments that exceed this monthly limit. Furthermore, if the payments due to an annuitant exceed $500 per month, a court may order the annuitant to pay a creditor the portion of the excess benefits that is reasonable in light of the debtor's financial circumstances.

   If proceeds are paid under a health insurance policy or an accidental death and dismemberment policy, they are exempt from creditors' claims. However, creditors may sue to collect amounts due on contracts the insured entered into for necessities after the benefit period began.

16. Separate premiums for separate risks [17B:24-12] If a policy gives coverage for more than one hazard or peril, the insurance against a particular hazard or peril cannot be canceled separately unless a separate premium is charged for that coverage. A life insurance policy or annuity contract cannot cover anything other than bodily injury or accidental death and the health of the insured.

B. REPLACEMENT [TITLE 11:4-2.1 THROUGH 2.8] The definition of **replacement** according to New Jersey law means any transaction where new life insurance or annuity is to be purchased, and it is known or should be known to the proposing agent, or to the proposing insurer if there is no agent, that by reason of the transaction, existing life insurance or an annuity has been or is to be lapsed, forfeited, surrendered, or otherwise terminated; converted to reduced paid up insurance; continued as extended term insurance; or otherwise reduced in value by the use of nonforfeiture benefits or other policy values; amended so as to effect either a reduction in benefits or in the term for which coverage would otherwise remain in force or which benefits would be paid; reissued with any reduction in cash value; or pledged as collateral or subjected to borrowing, whether in a single loan or under scheduled borrowing over 13 months.

1. The purpose of a replacement regulation is to regulate the activities of insurance companies and agents with respect to the replacement of existing life insurance and annuities; and to protect the interests of life insurance policyowners and annuities by establishing minimum standards of conduct to be observed in the replacement or proposed replacement of existing life insurance and annuities by:

   ■ assuring that the policyowner receives information with which a decision can be made in his own best interest;

   ■ reducing the opportunity for misrepresentation and incomplete disclosures; and

   ■ establishing penalties for failure to comply with the requirements of replacement regulation.

2. **Duties of agents** Each agent shall submit to the replacing insurance company with or as part of each application for life insurance or an annuity a statement signed by the applicant as to whether or not the insurance or annuity will replace existing life insurance or an annuity; and a signed statement as to whether or not the agent knows replacement is or may be involved in the transaction. Where a replacement is involved, the agent shall do the following.

   a. Present (and read aloud, or at least offer to do so) to the applicant, no later than at the time of taking the application, a *Notice Regarding Replacement of Life Insurance and Annuities* in the form as described by New Jersey law or other substantially similar form approved by the Commissioner. The notice must be signed by and left with the applicant.

   b. Leave with the applicant the original or a copy of all sales proposals used for presentation to the applicant.

   c. Submit to the replacing insurer with the application, a copy of the *Notice Regarding Replacement of Life Insurance* signed by the applicant and a copy of all sales proposals used for presentations to the applicant.

■ Each agent who uses a sales proposal when conserving existing life insurance shall leave with the applicant the original or a copy of all sales proposals used in the conservation effort and submit to the existing insurer a copy of all sales proposals used in the conservation effort.

3. **Duties of replacing insurers** Each replacing insurance company shall inform its field representatives of the requirements of New Jersey law regarding replacement and require with or as part of each completed application for life insurance or annuity: a statement signed by the applicant as to whether or not the insurance or annuity will replace existing life insurance or annuity; and a statement signed by the agent as to whether or not he knows replacement is or may be involved in the transaction. In addition, each replacing insurer, where a replacement is involved, must do the following:

■ requires from the agent, with the application for life insurance, a copy of the *Notice Regarding Replacement of Life Insurance* signed by the applicant and a copy of all sales proposals used for presentation to the applicant;

■ must furnish to the applicant a policy summary in accordance with the provisions of the New Jersey Life Insurance Solicitation Regulations;

■ must provide, if it is also the existing insurer, the policyowner a policy summary for the new policy prior to accepting the applicant's initial premium or premium deposit (unless the replacing insurer provides in its *Notice Regarding Replacement* or on a separate written notice that is delivered with the policy that the applicant has a right to an unconditional refund of all premiums paid which may be exercised within a period of 30 days from the date the policy is delivered); and

■ must maintain copies (records) of the *Notice Regarding Replacement*, the Policy Summary, and all sales proposals used by the replacing agent and existing insurer to be replaced for at least five years or until the conclusion of the next succeeding regular examination by the Department of Banking and Insurance, whichever is later. These requirements also apply to situations in which a producer is soliciting the replacement of a group insurance policy.

4. **Violations of laws regarding replacement [11:4-2.9]** An agent or insurer violates the laws regarding replacement by:

■ using deceptive or misleading information in sales material;

■ failing to ask an applicant pertinent and required questions about the possibility of financing or replacement;

■ knowingly recording an applicant's answer incorrectly;

■ advising an applicant to respond negatively to a question regarding replacement to prevent giving notice to the existing insurer; or

■ advising a policyholder to write directly to the insurance company in a way that attempts to obscure the identity of the replacing producer or insurer.

   a. **Penalties** A producer or insurer that violates the rules of replacement will be subject to revocation or suspension of a license or certificate of authority, monetary fines, and the forfeiture of any commissions or compensation paid to the producer for the transaction. If the Commissioner finds that the violation was material to the sale, the insurer or producer may be ordered to pay restitution to the insured, restore policy or contract values, and pay interest on the amounts paid back.

C. LIFE INSURANCE SOLICITATION [11:4-11.1 THROUGH 11.8]

1. **Policy Summary** A policy summary is to be provided to all purchasers of life insurance which: identifies the life or annuity contract; provides the name and address of the insurance agent; provides the full name, address and home office location of the insurer; and a prominent statement that the contract does not provide cash surrender values if that is the case.

   a. A policy summary which includes dividends shall also include a statement that dividends are based on the company's current dividend scale and are not guaranteed, in addition to a statement in close proximity to the equivalent level annual dividend. A policy summary must also include the date on which the summary was prepared.

2. **Buyer's guide** A buyer's guide is a document which contains information regarding life insurance or annuity contracts. This guide provides specific information in order to aid the purchaser in understanding the contract. Insurers are required under New Jersey law to provide a buyer's guide to each prospective purchaser.

3. **Disclosure requirements** The insurer shall provide, to all prospective purchasers, a buyer's guide and a policy summary at least seven days prior to accepting the applicant's initial premium or premium deposit, unless the policy for which application is made contains an unconditional refund (free look) provision of at least 10 days or unless the policy summary contains an unconditional refund offer, in which event the buyer's guide and policy summary must be delivered with the policy or before delivery of the policy, and the initial premium may be accepted with the application.

   a. The insurer shall provide a buyer's guide and a policy summary to any prospective purchaser upon request, and without charge.

   b. In the case of a policy whose equivalent level death benefit does not exceed $5,000, the requirement for providing a policy summary will be satisfied by delivery of a written statement containing information required by New Jersey law.

   c. In the case of a policy whose equivalent level death benefit is less than $2,000, the provision of a policy summary and a buyer's guide will be optional for the insurer.

   d. For in-force-premium paying policies, policyholders shall have the right to obtain a policy summary at cost. The company may charge a reasonable fee for preparing this summary, not to exceed $5, and may utilize reasonable assumptions in providing the cost disclosure information, provided they are clearly disclosed.

   e. **Contracts with minors [17B:24-2]** A minor who is at least 15 years old may enter into contracts for annuities or insurance, or affirm such contracts, on his own life and health or on the life and health of another person in whom the minor has an insurable interest.

1.) Capacity to accept payment A minor can accept an insurer's payment (and discharge the insurer's duty to pay it) under an annuity or insurance policy in which the minor has an insurable interest or is a beneficiary as follows.

- Minors who are at least 15 years old may accept payments of up to $2,000 in a single calendar year.
- Minors who are at least 18 years old may accept payments of up to $5,000 in a single calendar year.
- Payment may be made to the minor's legal guardian if one has been appointed.

   f. A minor cannot use his minority to break or void an insurance contract; however, he may not be held to an agreement to pay, by promissory note or otherwise, any premium on an annuity or insurance policy. (In such a case, the insurer may terminate coverage.)

D. ADVERTISING [11:2-23.1 THROUGH 23.10] New Jersey law includes the regulation of advertising with regard to insurance practices. The purpose of this regulation is to implement, through guidelines, a full and truthful disclosure to the public of all material and relevant information with regard to the advertisement of life insurance and annuities.

   1. Applicability These regulations shall apply to any life insurance or annuity advertisement distributed in this state. Every insurer shall establish and maintain a system of control over the content, form, and method of dissemination of advertisements of its policies. All advertisements are the responsibility of the insurer (the regulations also apply to agents and brokers as well).

   2. Advertisement means material designed to create public interest in life insurance or annuities or in an insurer; or to induce the public to purchase, increase, modify, reinstate or retain a policy. Note that the Life and Health Insurance Buyers' Guide is not considered an advertisement. An advertisement includes:

- printed and published material, audio visual material, and descriptive literature of an insurer used in direct mail, newspapers, magazines, radio and television scripts, billboards, and similar displays;
- literature and sales aids of all kinds issued by an insurer or agent including circulars, leaflets, booklets, depictions, illustrations, and form letters;
- material used for the recruitment, training, and education of an insurer's sales personnel, agents, solicitors, and brokers which is designed to be used or is used to induce the public to purchase, increase, modify, reinstate, or retain a policy; or
- prepared sales talks, presentations, and material for use by sales personnel, agents, solicitors, and brokers.

   3. Advertisements may also include: communications used within an insurer's own organization and not intended for dissemination to the public; communications with policyholders other than material urging policyholders to purchase, increase, modify, reinstate, or return a policy; a general announcement from a group or blanket policyholder to eligible individuals who are currently employees that a policy has been written or arranged (to cover them); or any disclosure required by New Jersey law regarding replacement, cost comparison indices, or rules regarding annuities.

4. Advertisements shall be truthful and not misleading. The form and content of an advertisement shall be sufficiently complete and clear so as to avoid deception. Whether an advertisement has the tendency to mislead or deceive shall be determined by the Commissioner.

   a.) No advertisement shall use the terms *investment, investment plan, founder's plan, charter plan, savings, savings plan,* or other similar terms in connection with a policy which misleads a purchaser or prospective purchaser into believing that he will receive some benefit which is actually not available.

5. **Disclosure requirements** All pertinent information must be disclosed to the purchaser. Any advertisement for a policy containing graded or modified benefits shall prominently display any limitation of benefits. If the premium is level and coverage decreases or increases with age, the information shall be prominently disclosed. Additional information that must be disclosed includes but is not limited to:

   ■ advertisements of policies with nonlevel premiums shall prominently describe the changes;

   ■ dividend information must be disclosed to the policyholder;

   ■ any policy information or advertisement shall not state that the purchaser of a policy will share in the earnings or general assets of a company;

   ■ the type of policy being advertised must be stipulated such as group, term, or whole life insurance;

   ■ advertisements stating that cost savings are involved in the purchase of a policy (i.e., purchasing a policy through direct mail) may not be stipulated unless such is the case;

   ■ testimonials or endorsements made by third parties must be genuine and represent the current opinion of the author (they must also be applicable to the policy advertised and if the person making the testimonial has a financial interest in the company, this fact must be disclosed);

   ■ an advertisement shall not describe an enrollment period as *special* or *limited* when the insurer uses successive enrollment periods as its usual method of marketing its policies;

   ■ advertisement shall not state or imply that prospective insureds shall be members of a special class or group; and

   ■ advertisements shall not make unfair or incomplete comparisons of policies.

6. **Identification of insurer** The name of the insurer shall be clearly identified in any advertisement. An advertisement shall not use a trade name, an insurance group designation, name of a parent company of an insurer, service mark, slogan, or other symbol without disclosing the name of the insurer. No advertisement may use colors, words, or physical materials which are similar to a government program or agency and intended to deceive the public.

   a. Advertisements that may be seen or heard in states where the insurer is not authorized or licensed to transact insurance must disclose such limitations on the insurer's ability. For example, a radio advertisement may state that the offer is not available to residents of a particular state, or that the offer is valid only in a particular state.

b. Advertisements must be documented and kept by insurers for at least five years following their first use.

7. **Status of insurer** Advertisements may state that an insurer is licensed in the state where the advertisement appears providing it does not imply that competing insurers may not be so licensed.

   a. Advertisements shall not create the impression that the insurer, its financial condition or status, the payment of its claims, or the merits, desirability, or advisability of its policy forms or kinds of plan of insurance are recommended or endorsed by any government entity.

8. **Insurer responsibility** All advertisements, regardless of by whom written (e.g., agents, brokers, company personnel) shall be the responsibility of the insurer sponsoring the same. Every insurer shall maintain complete control of all advertisements and the methods of their distribution.

   a. Insurers must maintain a file and record of all published and printed advertisements.

   b. All advertisements shall be maintained in the file for a period of not less than five years after the last use of the material.

   c. An annual statement must be supplied to the Commissioner which states that all advertisements used during the preceding year complied with New Jersey law.

9. Failure to comply with New Jersey law regarding advertisements shall subject the offender to a fine not to exceed $1,000 for every violation unless the violation was done knowingly, in which case the penalty shall not exceed $5,000 for every violation.

E. **VARIABLE CONTRACTS [11:4-1.1 THROUGH 1.5; 17B:28]** Prior to the issuance of any individual contract on a variable basis, the company must reasonably satisfy itself that the total amounts being applied to provide the prospective annuitant with income on a variable basis will not exceed the amount which would be required to purchase the income in predetermined dollar amounts which the annuitant could reasonably expect to receive.

   1. In determining the reasonably expectable fixed dollar income, the company may consider, alone or in combination, any direct source such as a pension, annuity, Social Security benefit, or trust fund as well as any indirect source, such as an asset having a principal amount expressed in fixed dollars and capable of being used to produce a fixed dollar income, as for example, bonds, mortgages, or life insurance policies.

   2. All application forms for individual variable contracts shall contain a specific question as to any provision previously made by the prospective annuitant for income on a variable basis.

3. Semiannually, each company organized under the laws of this state and authorized to issue contracts on a variable basis shall determine whether the investments held in its variable contract account meet the applicable statutory standards for new investments. Written notification shall be given immediately to the Commissioner of any investment which fails to satisfy these standards.

   a. Every foreign life insurer authorized to issue variable contracts must make the same determinations (or if the insurer has not paid dividends during each of the past five years) on a semiannual basis.

4. No insurer may issue any contract on a variable basis until it is licensed to sell life insurance and annuities and it has sold these products for a period of at least two years.

   a. In order to sell variable products a person must first be licensed to sell life insurance (or hold a license to act as a solicitor). The license (and examination) fee is $25 for variable products.

   b. Variable product renewal licenses shall be issued biennially and will expire April 30th of each odd numbered year (i.e., 2007, 2009, etc.).

   c. No written exam is required of: a renewal applicant; an applicant whose previous license has been suspended or revoked; a New Jersey citizen who is a veteran and who was a holder at any time of a (New Jersey) license to solicit variable contracts; anyone who has passed an exam administered by the NASD; or a applicant whose agent license has expired less than three years prior to the date of (variable) application.

5. Variable contracts are characterized by a separate account. The funds paid into a variable contract are segregated from other insurance accounts. These funds are invested into various types of securities (i.e., common stock) portfolios, thus the opportunity for future growth.

6. The value of the separate account will be determined by the net asset value of the common stock. Generally this value shall be deemed to be the market value of the account. The Commissioner has sole authority to regulate the issuance of separate account (variable) contracts.

F. LIMITED DEATH BENEFIT FORMS [11:4-21.1 THROUGH 21.4] The purpose of New Jersey regulations regarding these forms is to establish a guideline for the filing and review of limited death benefit policy forms which will: make life insurance available to people who are otherwise uninsurable; assure that limited death policies are not sold by agents in preference to full death benefit policies and that the applicant understands that he may qualify for a full death benefit policy; reduce through disclosure the likelihood of misunderstanding arising where the sales presentation emphasizes the underwriting feature while minimizing or ignoring the limitation on death benefits at early durations; and set standards for advertising of limited death benefit policy forms so as to eliminate unfair, misleading, or deceptive advertising practices.

1. These regulations shall apply to all life insurance policy forms delivered or issued for delivery after the operative date hereof that limit death benefits during a period following the inception of the policy as an alternative to underwriting.

2. A full death benefit policy means any individual life insurance policy, group life policy, group life certificate, or fraternal benefit society certificate issued in this state which provides the full face amount as the death benefit at all times following the inception date of the policy.

3. A limited death benefit policy means any individual life insurance policy, group policy, group life certificate, or fraternal benefit society certificate issued in this state which limits death benefits during a period following the inception date of the policy as an alternative to underwriting.

4. No limited death benefit policy shall be issued in this state unless the insurer has, at the time of application, obtained from the applicant a signed and dated statement attesting that the applicant understands that he may qualify for a full death benefit policy which provides full benefits from inception. A copy of this statement must be submitted to the Department of Banking and Insurance for review prior to its use.

5. All advertising of limited death benefit policies (and any revisions) must be submitted to the Department of Banking and Insurance for approval. All advertising shall prominently explain the nature of the limited death benefit policy and state the duration of the limited death benefit period.

6. When these policies are sold by agents, the commission may not be greater on the sale of limited death benefit policies than on the sale of full death benefit policies.

7. The limited death benefit shall not be less than the amount of premiums paid with interest at the rate used to determine nonforfeiture values under the policy.

8. The period during which a limited death benefit applies *shall not exceed 25%* of life expectancy at the issue age, as determined by the mortality table used for nonforfeiture values under the policy, or two years, whichever is shorter.

9. The face or ultimate amount of insurance shall not exceed $15,000. The issue age shall not be less than 45. The policy shall include a provision allowing for the return of the policy for a full refund of premiums within 30 days after delivery (free look).

G. **STUDENT LIFE INSURANCE [11:4-12.1]** The purpose of this regulation is to avoid any link or implication of association between a school or university and an insurance company soliciting life insurance unless specific endorsement by the school has been made.

1. Student life insurance is life insurance offered to a person because he is enrolled in an institution offering a post high school education.

2. Certain requirements governing solicitation materials are as follows:

- ■ all material must be clearly identified as coming from an agent, broker, or company;

- ■ names and addresses of the soliciting agent, broker, or company must appear at the top of the first page of the letter or brochure; and

- ■ no connection between the school and the insurance company, agent, or broker is to be implied unless the school has specifically endorsed the policy.

3. Records required to be maintained include:

   a. Complete sample mailings must be on file at the home office of the insurer for a period of five years subsequent to the date of mailing.

   b. The soliciting New Jersey agent or broker must keep the same records on file as the insurer. These files shall include the description of the target groups solicited; a specimen copy of the mailing; and the date of the mailing and number of pieces mailed.

H. PROTECTION OF BENEFICIARIES FROM CREDITORS

If a policy of insurance is effected by any person on his own life, or on another life, in favor of a person other than himself, then the lawful beneficiary, assignee, or payee of the policy shall be entitled to its proceeds and avails against the creditors and representatives of the insured and of the person effecting the same, whether or not the right to change the beneficiary is reserved or permitted, or the policy is made payable to the person whose life is insured or to the executors or administrators of the person if the beneficiary shall predecease the person. This statute will protect the beneficiary of a life insurance contract except in cases of transfer with intent to defraud creditors. If the death benefits are paid directly to the estate of the deceased insured, creditors may attach the funds.

1. These proceeds and avails shall be exempt from any liability for any debt of the beneficiary existing at the time the proceeds and avails become available for his use; provided that, subject to the statute of limitations, the amount of any premiums for the insurance paid with intent to defraud creditors shall inure to their benefit from the proceeds of the policy.

2. A policy shall also be deemed to be payable to a person other than the insured if and to the extent that a facility of payment clause or similar clause in the policy permits the insurer to discharge its obligation after the death of the individual insured by paying the death benefits to a person as permitted by this clause.

   a. Generally, a facility-of-payment clause provides that payment may be made to any relative by blood or by marriage or to any person who appears to the insurer to be equitably entitled to the proceeds of the policy because of having incurred expenses for burial of the insured. Many policies will allow a beneficiary to be named but the contract will retain the facility of payment clause. In addition, the insurer will reserve the right to disapprove a beneficiary if that individual has no apparent insurable interest. Some common examples of when such a clause will be activated involve if a beneficiary is a minor or is not competent, the beneficiary has predeceased the insured, or if a beneficiary fails to file a claim within a reasonable period of time after the insured's death.

I. **FRATERNAL BENEFIT SOCIETIES** Fraternal benefit societies were originally formed to provide life insurance coverage for members in order to cover burial expenses. These types of organizations were usually not incorporated as insurers under state insurance law but were established under special forms of legislation.

1. **Licensing of agents [17:448-32]** The term **insurance agent** as used in the fraternal benefit society context means any authorized or acknowledged agent of such a society who acts as such in the solicitation, negotiation, or procurement or making of a life insurance, accident and health insurance or annuity contract. In this context however, the term *insurance agent* shall not include:

   ■ any regular salaried officer or employee of a licensed society who devotes substantially all of his services to activities other than the solicitation of fraternal insurance contracts from the public, and who receives for the solicitation of these contracts no commission or other compensation directly dependent upon the amount of business obtained; or

   ■ any agent or representative of a society who devotes, or intends to devote, less than 50% of his time to the solicitation and procurement of insurance contracts for the society.

2. No person shall act in the state of New Jersey as an insurance agent, as defined in this section of New Jersey law without having authority to do so by virtue of a license issued and in force.

3. No society doing business in this state shall pay any commission or other compensation to any person for any services in obtaining in this state any new contract of life, accident or health insurance, or any new annuity contract, except to a licensed insurance agent of the society. In other words, a fraternal benefit society may not pay commissions to any other individual who is not licensed with such a society.

IV. **NEW JERSEY LAWS, RULES, AND REGULATIONS PERTINENT TO ACCIDENT AND HEALTH INSURANCE ONLY**

A. **MARKETING METHODS AND PRACTICES [17B:30-1 THROUGH 22)]**

1. **Health insurance solicitation regulation [11:4-17.1 through 17.9]** The purpose of this regulation is to eliminate unfair and deceptive practices in the promotion, solicitation, and sale of individual health insurance.

   a. State regulations apply to all individual health insurance policies delivered or issued in this state except that they shall not apply to conversion policies issued pursuant to a contractual conversion privilege or to credit health insurance.

   b. **Duplicate coverage** This means a transaction where health insurance is purchased and the insured already has existing coverage. This can cause total claim payments to be greater than the amount of the loss.

c. **Unfair acts** No person shall engage in any unfair or deceptive acts with regard to the solicitation of health insurance. Some examples of unfair acts include but are not limited to:

- inducing an applicant to purchase duplicate coverage;

- encouraging an applicant to omit pertinent underwriting information from an application for health insurance;

- inducing a prospective insured to sign a blank or incomplete application or form;

- failing to disclose upon initial contact with a prospective applicant the licensee's affiliation with an insurance company;

- making false statements regarding the length of time an insurance offering may or may not be available;

- selling any policy that is not approved by the state of New Jersey;

- selling Medicare supplement insurance to any person not eligible for Medicare;

- selling Medicare supplement insurance to any person on Medicaid;

- failing to deliver a Buyer's Guide and Outline of Coverage to the insured; and

- failing to remit, within seven business days, the amount of premium collected from an applicant that is due the company.

d. **Replacement** When replacement occurs in the sale of individual health insurance, the licensee must obtain a signed statement from the applicant stating that he knows that a replacement is occurring. Even direct response companies (e.g., direct mail) must find out if the new insurance to be issued is intended to replace insurance currently in force.

1.) A Notice to the Applicant Regarding Replacement must be provided by the licensee to the prospective insured when a replacement occurs. This notice informs the applicant that health conditions which presently exist may not be covered under the new policy or they may not be covered until a probationary or waiting period has elapsed.

2.) The applicant should be informed that he should talk with the present insurer.

e. **Complaint records** Complaint records shall be kept on a calendar-year basis and the number of complaints by line of insurance, function, reason, disposition and state of origin shall be compiled at least annually. Records must be maintained for at least five years or until the Department's next examination, whichever is later.

1.) A complaint is a written communication expressing a grievance.

2.) Complaints are to be classified according to the line of insurance involved. The records shall also note the disposition of the complaint.

3.) The date received and the date closed must be recorded.

4.) Whether the complaint was originated from the Department of Banking and Insurance should be recorded.

5.) Complaint records should also note the state from which the complaint originated (usually it is the state of residence of the complainant).

f. Penalties Any person in violation of this regulation may be fined an amount not exceeding $2,000 for each violation. The Commissioner may also revoke or suspend the license or certificate of authority of any agent, broker, solicitor, or insurer. Insurers are liable for violations committed by their agents.

2. **Advertising regulation [11:2-11.1 through 11.22]** Advertisements include: printed and published material; newspaper, television, and radio material; billboards; and any similar type of display which involves descriptive literature of a company used to attempt solicitations. New Jersey regulations regarding advertising of accident and health policies protect the public against deceptive and misleading advertising.

   a. Prepared sales talks, and any other materials used by agents, brokers, and solicitors are considered advertisements.

   b. Advertisements shall be truthful and not misleading in fact or in implication. An advertisement relating to any policy benefit payable, loss covered, or premium payable shall be sufficiently complete and clear as to avoid deception.

   c. Whenever an advertisement describes benefits and coverages provided by a policy, it must also disclose any exceptions, reductions, or limitations affecting the basic provisions of the policy.

   d. Policy provisions relating to the policy's renewability, cancelability, and termination must be disclosed in any advertisements.

   e. Testimonials must be genuine and represent the current opinion of the author, be applicable to the policy advertised, and be accurately reproduced.

   f. Statistics relating to dollar amounts of claims paid, the number of persons insured, or similar statistical information relating to an insurer or policy may not be used in an advertisement unless it is accurate and relevant.

   g. Any free look offers contained in a policy will not be a cure for misleading or deceptive information.

   h. No advertisements may contain disparaging comparisons and statements which are unfair or incomplete with regard to the policies of competitors.

   i. Advertisements of direct mail insurers shall indicate the specific states that an insurer is licensed in or is not licensed in.

   j. The identity of an insurer shall be made clear in all of its advertisements. Advertisements may not use a trade name, service mark, slogan, symbol, or other device which may be misleading.

k. No advertisements may imply that a prospective insured will be part of a special group enjoying special rates, benefits, or underwriting.

l. Advertisements may not refer to initial or special offers unless that is the case (e.g., policy being offered for the first time). No third-party endorsements may be claimed unless that is the case.

m. Advertisements may not contain false information regarding an insurer's assets, corporate structure, financial standing, age, or relative position in the insurance business.

n. All advertisements, regardless of who writes them (e.g., agents, brokers, etc.), shall be the responsibility of the insurer. The insurer must maintain at its home or principal office a copy of all advertisements used or disseminated. These advertisements must be kept in the insurer's file for five years from their last use. All insurers are required to file an annual statement verifying that all advertisements used were in accordance with state law.

o. Penalties Failure to comply with New Jersey law will subject the offender to any penalties provided by law.

3. Discrimination based on genetic characteristics [17:48-6.18; 17:48A-6.11; 17:48E-15.2; 17B26-3.3; 17B:27-36.2] Every individual or group medical service corporation contract providing hospital or medical expense benefits that is issued in the state of New Jersey, shall not exclude any person or eligible dependent and shall not establish any rates or policy terms based on an actual or expected health condition or on the basis of any genetic characteristic.

B. POLICY CLAUSES AND PROVISIONS

1. Minimum standards [11:4-16.1 through 16.11; 17B-26-45 through 47] The purpose of minimum standard regulations for accident and health insurance is to provide reasonable standardization and simplification of language, terms, and coverages to facilitate understanding and comparisons. These standards also help to eliminate misleading and confusing provisions in connection with the purchasing of insurance and the settlement of claims. They also help to eliminate unfair renewal practices which are contrary to the health care needs and economic well being of the public.

a. These regulations apply to all accident and health policies issued or delivered in this state.

b. A policy classified as "nonrenewable for stated reasons only" includes policies that limit an insurer's right of nonrenewal to reasons stated in the policy such as:

- fraud in applying for the policy;
- fraud in the submission of claims;
- duplication of benefits or overinsurance in accordance with the insurer's standards;
- attainment of a specified age;

- discontinuance of all policies issued on the same form in this state; and

- change of an insured's occupation to one classified as more hazardous.

c. **Preexisting conditions [17B:27A-22, 55]** Health insurance policies cannot exclude coverage for a preexisting condition; however, an exclusion may apply to a late enrollee or to any group of two to five persons if it does not exclude coverage for more than 180 days after the effective date of coverage and relates only to conditions appearing during the six months immediately preceding the enrollment date. However, if 10 or more late enrollees request enrollment during any 30-day enrollment period, then no preexisting condition exclusion will apply to them.

  1.) Prohibited exclusions No health insurer may exclude coverage for any of the following as a preexisting condition:

  - A newborn child who, as of the end of the 30 days following birth, is covered by creditable coverage

  - A child who is adopted or placed for adoption before age 18 and who, as of the end of the 30 days following the date of adoption or placement for adoption, is covered by creditable coverage

  - Pregnancy

  2.) Permitted exclusions A health insurer may impose a preexisting condition exclusion in a group health plan if:

  - the exclusion relates to a physical or mental condition for which medical advice, diagnosis, care, or treatment was recommended or received within six months before the enrollment date of the member or beneficiary;

  - the exclusion lasts for no more than 12 months, or 18 months for a late enrollee, after the enrollment date of the member or beneficiary; and

  - the period of the preexisting condition exclusion is reduced by the total period of creditable coverage that the member or beneficiary has by the enrollment date.

d. **Proof of loss [17B:26-10]** An insured is required to give written proof of loss to an insurer within 90 days after the date of a loss. With respect to policies that provide periodic payment contingent upon a continuing loss, the insured must give written proof of loss to the insurer within 90 days after the end of the period for which the insurer is liable. Failure to give this proof within the time required does not affect the claim if it was not reasonably possible for the insured to give proof within that time and the insured gives proof as soon as reasonably possible. Unless the insured is legally incapable of giving this proof (by reason of mental illness, for instance), the proof cannot be submitted more than one year after it is required.

e. **Payment to health care providers [17B:27-45]** Health insurance policies that indemnify for loss of life pay benefits to the insured's beneficiaries. Benefits may also be paid directly to a hospital or medical services provider with the insured's prior authorization. Such authorization does not require the consent of beneficiaries, if any.

f. Limitations on legal actions [17B:27-46] As noted before, no one can sue to recover on a policy until at least 60 days have passed after proof of loss has been filed in accordance with the terms of the policy. Furthermore, no one can bring suit when three or more years have passed after proof of loss was required.

g. Required coverages Group accident and health insurance policies sold or offered for sale in New Jersey are required to cover the following:

1.) Reconstructive breast surgery [17B:27-46.1a] A group health insurance policy must cover reconstructive breast surgery, corrective surgery, prostheses, and outpatient chemotherapy following surgery for cancer patients.

2.) Maternity benefits [17B:27-46.1b] A group health insurance policy covering two or more lives must cover maternity care without regard to marital status for expenses incurred in pregnancy and childbirth.

3.) Home treatment of hemophilia [17B:27-46.1c] A group health insurance policy must cover medical expenses incurred in the treatment of bleeding associated with hemophilia.

4.) Treatment of Wilm's tumor [17B:27-46.1e] A group health insurance policy must cover hospital or medical expenses incurred in the treatment of Wilm's tumor, including autologous bone marrow transplants when standard chemotherapy is unsuccessful.

5.) Mammograms [17B:27-46.1f] A group health insurance policy is required to cover one baseline mammogram examination for women who are at least 35 but less than 40 years old, a mammogram every year for women who are at least 40 years old, and a mammogram as often as deemed medically necessary by a woman's health care provider if the woman is under 40 years of age and has a family history of breast cancer or other breast cancer risk factors.

6.) Maternity care [17B:27-46.1k] A group health insurance policy must provide benefits for at least 48 hours of inpatient care following a vaginal delivery and at least 96 hours of inpatient care after a cesarean section for a mother and newborn child in a licensed health care facility. Nevertheless, an insurer need not provide these hours of coverage unless the attending physician determines that this inpatient care is medically necessary or the mother requests it. This determination is made at the time of birth, not upon the mother's admission to the facility.

7.) Other coverages required [17B:27-46.1(l-z)] Group health insurance plans must also cover lead poisoning screenings and child immunizations, treatment of diabetes, pap smears, diagnostic screenings, inpatient treatment of mastectomies, medical foods and low protein modified food products, audiology and speech pathology, anesthesiology and hospitalization for dental services, treatment of biologically-based mental illness, hemophilia, infertility treatments, colorectal cancer treatment, and nonstandard infant formulas.

h. Coordination of benefits provision [11:4-28.3, 5, 6] A group health insurance contract can use a coordination of benefits (COB) provision and may designate itself as the primary coverage. A group plan that uses a COB provision cannot take into account the benefits of another plan in determining its benefits. Group coverage that supplements basic benefits can stipulate that the supplementary coverage is in excess to any other parts of a plan provided by the same contract holder.

1.) Prohibited reduction of benefits A group health insurance policy cannot reduce benefits for any of the following reasons.

- Another plan exists.
- A person is or could have been covered by another plan, except with respect to Medicare Part B.
- A person has chosen an option under another plan that provides a lower level of benefits than another option that could have been elected.

2.) Rules for coordinating benefits The following is the order in which benefits are paid when the insured is covered by more than one policy.

a.) The primary plan pays benefits as if the secondary plan did not exist.

b.) A secondary plan takes the benefits of another plan into account only when it is secondary to that plan.

c.) A plan that covers the person other than as a dependent will pay benefits before any other plan that covers the person as a dependent.

d.) Rules for determining benefits for a dependent child when the parents are not separated or divorced:

- The benefits of the plan of the parent whose birthday is earlier in the year will be determined before the plan of the parent whose birthday is later.
- If both parents have the same birthday, the benefits of the plan that covered the parent longer will be determined before those of the plan that covered the parent for a shorter time.

e.) Rules for determining benefits for a dependent child when the parents are separated or divorced:

- The benefits of the plan of the parent who has custody of the child will be determined first.
- The benefits of the plan of the spouse of the parent (or step-parent) with custody of the child will be determined next.
- The benefits of the plan of the noncustodial parent will be determined last.
- If a court orders a parent to be responsible for the health care expenses of the child, and if that parent's plan is secondary and is given notice of the court order, its benefits will be determined first.

f.) Other rules for determining benefits:

- Benefits of a plan that covers a person as an employee (who is not laid off, retired, or a dependent of that person) are determined before those of a plan that covers the person as a laid-off or retired employee or a dependent of that person.

- If a person has continuing coverage under federal or state law (i.e., through COBRA) and is also covered by another plan, the plan covering the person as an employee, retiree, or dependent of that person is primary. The continuation coverage is secondary.

i. Prompt payment of claims [17B:26-9.1] A health insurer is obligated to pay a claim if the following conditions have been met.

- The claim is eligible for health care service from an eligible health care provider.

- The claim has no material defect or deficiency (such as lacking proper documentation).

- The payor has no reason to believe that the claim is fraudulent.

- The claim does not require special treatment that would prevent a timely payment.

An insurer that delays payment even though these conditions have been met is liable to the claimant for the sum plus simple interest at 10% per year.

1.) Timely payment of claims In general, a health insurer must pay all legitimate claims under the following time frames:

- Within 30 calendar days of having received a claim filed electronically
- Within 40 days of having received a claim filed by nonelectronic means

2.) Disputed claims [11:22-1.5] If a claim is disputed or denied because of missing information or documentation, the insurer must pay the claim within 30 or 40 calendar days of receiving the missing information or documentation.

3.) Record of payment A health insurer is required to keep an auditable record of when payments were made to health care providers or insureds.

j. Prohibited policy provisions Some provisions that are prohibited from appearing in accident and health policies issued in this state include:

- coverage for specified diseases or procedures or treatments which are limited to specified diseases;

- no policy except a short term, nonrenewable trip policy shall provide coverage solely for specifically identified kinds of accidents; however, a policy may provide increased benefits for specifically identified accidents for any accident only coverage;

- no policy shall provide for the payment of a single premium for the entire term of the policy, except for nonrenewable policies issued for a term of one year or less (as in the case of individual health insurance purchased to cover a person after he leaves one group and before he joins another);

- no policy shall provide benefits which duplicate the benefits provided by Part A and B of Medicare;

- no policy or rider for additional coverage may be issued as a dividend unless an equivalent cash payment is offered to the policyholder as an alternative to the dividend policy or rider; no dividend policy or rider shall be issued for an initial term of less than six months;

- no policy shall include a provision which predicates payment of benefits on the insured being house or home confined;

- policies providing hospital confinement indemnity benefits shall not contain provisions excluding coverage because of confinement in a hospital operated by the federal government;

- no policy shall limit coverage except for preexisting conditions (not including newborns); mental or emotional disorders (including drug addiction); normal pregnancy and childbirth; illness and treatment arising out of war, suicide, aviation, or interscholastic sports (short-term nonrenewable policies only); cosmetic surgery (elective); foot care (flat feet, fallen arches, corns, etc.); treatment for structural imbalance; treatment provided eye glasses and hearing aids and examinations; or routine physical exams or rest care;

- no policy shall include a provision that gives the insurer an unconditional right of nonrenewal (cancellable policies are prohibited);

- no policy shall include a provision which reduces, limits or excludes benefits solely on the basis of the sex or marital status of an insured; and

- except where a condition is specifically excluded by the terms of a policy, no policy shall exclude coverage for a loss due to a preexisting condition for a period of greater than 24 months if an application is used that is designed to elicit the complete health history of the insured or 12 months if a "simplified" application is used.

k. Minimum benefit standards Policies issued in this state shall have certain minimum benefit standards including but not limited to the following.

1.) Policies that include a military service exclusion shall provide for a refund of premium when coverage is suspended.

2.) Policies covering pregnancy shall cover pregnancy expenses if conception occurs after the effective date of coverage or after a probationary period of not more than 30 days after the effective date of coverage.

3.) In a family policy covering both husband and wife, the age of the younger spouse shall be used as the basis for meeting the age and durational requirements of the definitions of *noncancelable* or *guaranteed renewable*.

4.) Policies providing convalescent or extended care benefits following hospitalization shall not condition the benefits upon admission to the convalescent or extended care facility within a period of less than 14 days after discharge from the hospital.

5.) In policies that include a second surgical opinion benefit, the benefits must include a definition of elective surgery which is sufficiently clear to permit the average insured to distinguish between elective and nonelective surgery.

6.) Benefits for recurrent disability may be provided by a policy provided that no provision shall specify that a recurrent disability be separated by a period greater than six months.

7.) If disability is a criterion for payment of benefits under a policy, the policy must include a definition of disability.

    a.) Own occupation Policies issued in New Jersey must use their own occupation definition of disability to trigger at least the first 12 months of benefits. Under this definition, an insured will be considered totally disabled if he is unable to work at his own occupation as a result of an accident or sickness.

8.) Accidental death and dismemberment benefits shall be payable if the loss occurs within 90 days from the date of the accident (when the coverage is part of a policy).

9.) Policies which reduce benefits at a specified age shall only be issued at ages which provide full coverage for at least five years.

10.) Termination of a policy shall be without prejudice to any claim for continuous loss which commenced while the policy was in force.

11.) Additional standards [17B:27A-4.5] Health insurers writing policies for individuals must offer the following coverages:

- 90 days of hospital room and board expenses
- Outpatient and ambulatory surgery; fees for operating room and special care unit
- Emergency room fees
- Physician's fees incurred with hospital care, outpatient, and ambulatory surgery
- Anesthesia, oxygen, radiation, and x-ray therapy
- Delivery room fees, medical expenses of newborns, and treatment for complications of pregnancy
- Intravenous solutions, blood, and plasma
- Inpatient physical therapy
- Outpatient physical therapy at 30 visits each year per covered person
- Dialysis
- Diagnostic tests and hospital laboratory fees
- Pharmaceuticals administered in a hospital
- Dressings and splints
- Treatment for biologically based mental illness

■ Treatment for alcoholism and substance abuse

■ Childhood immunizations

■ Physician visits for illness or injury

l. Major medical expense policies shall provide hospital, surgical, and medical expense coverage for each covered person to a <u>maximum of not less than $10,000</u>; co-payment by the covered person <u>not to exceed 25% of covered charges</u>; a deductible stated on a per person, per family, per illness, per benefit period, or per year basis (not to exceed 5% of the maximum limit under the policy). The policy shall also include:

■ daily room and board expenses for a period of not less than 31 days during one period of hospital confinement;

■ miscellaneous hospital services for a maximum of not less than $1,800 or 15 times the daily room and board rate (if specified in dollar amounts during one period of hospital confinement);

■ surgical services to a maximum of not less than $600 for the most severe operation;

■ anesthesia services for a maximum of not less than 15% of the covered surgical fees; and

■ prosthetic devices, casts, splints, convalescent nursing home care, out of hospital prescription drugs, and so forth.

m. Disability income policies providing benefits payable after age 62 and reduced solely on the basis of age must contain an elimination period no greater than 90 days in the case of coverage providing a benefit of one year or less; no greater than 180 days when benefits of more than one year but less than two are provided; and no greater than 365 days in all other cases (more than two years of benefits).

n. Accident and health insurance applications must be on forms approved by the Commissioner. They may contain no questions or provisions that pertain to race, creed, color, or national origin; change the terms of the policy; require the applicant to agree that an untrue or false answer material to the risk shall render the contract void; or state that the applicant has not withheld any information or concealed any facts.

o. All health policies shall include a renewal, continuation, or nonrenewal provision. Whatever provision is used shall be appropriately captioned and appear on the first page of the policy.

p. Where riders or endorsements which reduce or eliminate coverage are attached to the policy at issue, the policy shall contain a prominent warning (of the rider or endorsement) on the first page.

q. Where a separate additional premium is charged for benefits provided in connection with riders or endorsements, this premium charge shall be set forth in the policy.

r. If a policy contains any limitations with respect to preexisting conditions, these limitations must appear as a separate paragraph in the policy and shall be labeled as preexisting conditions limitation.

s. An accident-only policy shall contain a prominent statement on the first page of the policy that identifies it as an accident-only policy.

t. All individual health policies issued in this state must be accompanied by an outline of coverage.

u. All insurers must file with the Commissioner all forms of individual health insurance for approval.

v. Where policies are to be sold through vending machines, the insurer shall agree that: a record will remain in the vending machine; and that the insurer will canvass the machines after each and every accident and notify the applicable beneficiaries.

w. If the Commissioner finds that a person has violated the law with regard to minimum standards, a penalty, in addition to any other penalty, not exceeding $2,000 for each violation may be imposed. The Commissioner may, through the attorney general, institute an action in the Superior Court to enjoin and restrain any insurer who has entered into a policy which does not conform to the regulations of this state regarding minimum standards.

2. **Benefits for the treatment of alcoholism [17B:26-2.1; 17B: 27-46.1; 11:4-15.1 through 15.4]** No health policy providing hospital and medical benefits shall be issued unless it provides benefits to covered persons in connection with the treatment of alcoholism.

a. These polices shall include coverage for: inpatient and outpatient care in a hospital; treatment at a licensed detoxification facility; confinement at a certified treatment facility.

b. This regulation does not apply to: Medicare complement (supplement) policies; hospital income policies; student accident trip or accident only policies; PIP coverage; cancer or dread disease policies; surgical expense policies, or policies issued before June 2, 1977 where the premium is guaranteed at issue and the insurer cannot increase the premium.

c. Alcoholism treatment is covered like any other sickness, subject to the same deductibles and coinsurance amounts. This coverage must be provided in all group policies issued or renewed in this state. New Jersey residents insured under group plans issued in other states are not covered by this regulation.

d. Policy exclusions relating to workers' compensation, employer's liability laws, veteran's hospitals, military service, and so forth may also apply to benefits for alcoholism treatment.

1.) Benefits need not be payable if no charge is normally made for the service.

2.) Benefits may be limited to the reasonable and customary charges for care and treatment.

3.) Benefits may be limited to expenses for treatment provided at the appropriate level of care.

3. **Home health care coverage [11:4-14.1 through 14.5]** Regulations regarding this coverage apply to individual and group health insurance policies which provide coverage for the costs of daily room and board while confined in a hospital or skilled nursing facility. This regulation does not apply to hospital indemnity policies which provide additional income while the insured is hospitalized, nor to Medicare Complement (supplement) policies since Medicare provides home health care.

   a. Home health care includes nursing care, physical therapy, occupational therapy, medical social work, nutrition services, speech therapy, home health aide services, medical appliances and equipment, and any diagnostic and therapeutic service (including surgical services).

   b. The policy may require no more than three continuous days of hospitalization or skilled nursing facility care prior to the provision of home health care benefits.

   c. Home health care services must provide for at least 60 home health care visits in any calendar year or in any continuous period of 12 months.

   d. Any visit by a member of a home health care team on any day shall be considered as one home health care visit.

   e. If the policy contains a number of days during which home health care benefits must commence following hospital discharge, that number of days must not be less than three.

   f. The dollar amount of payment for all home health care visits on each of the first three days of home health care services need not exceed the daily hospital room and board benefit provided by the policy during the period of prior confinement.

   g. Charges for home health care services may be limited to the usual and customary charges for these services.

   h. Policy exclusions relating to workers' compensation, employer's liability laws, Medicare, mandatory no fault auto insurance, veteran's hospitals, military service, and so forth, applicable to hospital and skilled nursing facility confinement benefits may also apply to home health care benefits.

   i. Benefits need not be payable if no charge is normally made for a home health care service.

j.   Policy provisions relating to coordination of benefits may apply to home health care services to the same extent that they apply to other benefits provided by the policy.

k.   The policy may require that home health care services will be provided only to residents of New Jersey.

l.   The initial care plan may not be required from the physician for at least 14 days, though subsequent care plans may be requested at 30-day intervals.

4. Health insurance reform markets [17B:27A-1 to 16]   Persons who are eligible to participate in a group health benefits plan that provides coverage for hospital or medical expenses must not be covered by an individual health benefits plans that provides the same or similar coverage provided in the group plan. An employer or producer who causes a person to be covered by an individual health benefits plan when that person is eligible to participate in a group health benefits plan, or already participates in one, is subject to a fine. This fine will be at least twice the annual premium paid for the individual health plan, plus penalties.

a.   Coverage for domestic partners [17B:27A-7.9]   An individual health insurance policy that offers dependent coverage must offer this coverage to the insured's domestic partner. A domestic partner is defined as a person, with the insured, in a registered domestic partnership recognized by the state, who shares a common address with the insured, lives in a domestic relationship with the insured, and who has expressed the intent to be in such a domestic relationship with the insured.

b.   Coverage for dependent children [17B:27A-4.1]   A health insurance policy that covers hospital or medical expense benefits under which dependent coverage is available cannot deny coverage for a policyholder's child because the child:

- was born out of wedlock;
- is not claimed as a dependent on the policyholder's federal tax return; or
- does not live with the policyholder or in the insurer's service area, if the child complies with the terms and conditions of the policy with respect to using specified providers.

1.)   If a child is covered by the policy of a noncustodial parent, the insurer must:
- give information to the custodial parent as needed for the child to obtain benefits through the child's noncustodial parent's coverage;
- allow the custodial parent to submit claims for covered services without approval of the noncustodial parent; and
- pay claims directly to the custodial parent, the health care provider, or the Department of Human Services administering the state Medicaid program, as appropriate.

2.) If a parent who is the policyholder is eligible for dependent coverage and is under a court or administrative order to provide the child with health insurance coverage, the insurer must:

- allow the parent to enroll the child as a dependent, regardless of any enrollment season restrictions;

- allow the child's other parent, the Division of Medical Assistance and Health Services as the state Medicaid agency, or the Department of Human Services to enroll the child under the policy if the parent who is the policyholder fails to do so; and

- not terminate the child's coverage unless the parent who is the policyholder gives the insurer satisfactory written evidence that the court or administrative order is no longer in effect, or that the child is or will be enrolled in a comparable health benefits plan with coverage taking effect on the day the existing coverage ends.

c. **Maternity coverage [17B:7.1]** Health insurance policies issued in New Jersey must provide the following benefits for maternity care provided to a mother and her newborn child in a licensed health care facility:

- At least 48 hours of inpatient care following a vaginal delivery
- At least 96 hours of inpatient care following a cesarean section

However, an insurer is not required to provide this minimal coverage for inpatient care unless the attending physician orders such care as medically necessary or the mother requests it.

d. **Mastectomy coverage [17B:27A-7.2]** Individual health insurance policies that provide hospital or medical expense coverage must cover inpatient care for at least 72 hours following a modified radical mastectomy and at least 48 hours of inpatient care after a simple mastectomy. If a patient, after consulting with the physician, decides that a shorter stay is sufficient, the insurer does not need to provide coverage for a longer stay.

e. **Renewal of coverage [17B:27A-6]** An individual health insurance policy must guarantee coverage for an eligible person and his dependents on a community-rated basis.

1.) Termination of coverage While a health insurance policy is renewable with respect to an eligible person and his dependents at his option, an insurer may terminate coverage if:

- the policy holder fails to pay the premiums; or
- the policyholder has acted fraudulently or made a material misrepresentation of material fact.

2.) Nonrenewal of coverage A health insurer may not renew a health insurance plan only if:

- the individual is no longer eligible for coverage because he is no longer a resident of the state or becomes eligible for a group health plan, government plan, or church plan;

- the insurer is allowed to cancel or amend the individual health benefits plan;
- the insurer is allowed not to renew that type of health benefits plan; or
- the insurer is allowed to withdraw from doing business in the individual health benefits market.

5. **New Jersey Individual Health Coverage Program [17B:27A-10 to 16, et seq.]** All qualified insurers are required to participate in the state's Individual Health Coverage Program, which helps insurers offer individual health insurance to persons who might otherwise be unable to obtain coverage as substandard risks. These insurers pay annual assessments to cover losses and administrative expenses borne by all members of the program. The assessments are based on the proportion of their respective market share. Insurers who pay claims in amounts that exceed a percentage of their income are entitled to reimbursement from the program.

C. MEDICARE SUPPLEMENT PLANS [17:35C-1 THROUGH 9; 17B:26A-1 THROUGH 8; 11:4-23.1 THROUGH 23.22]

A Medicare supplement contract is a group or individual subscriber contract which is advertised, marketed, or designed primarily as a supplement to reimbursements provided under Medicare. This type of health insurance contract is also discussed in Unit 9. In addition, in the state of New Jersey, the Commissioner requires that a buyer's guide must be delivered to any individual purchasing Medicare supplement policies in this state.

1. The Commissioner shall issue standards for Medicare supplements to regulate the following: terms of renewability; probationary periods; elimination periods; replacement requirements; recurrent conditions; benefit limitations, reductions, and exceptions; and conditions of eligibility.

2. A Medicare supplement contract may not deny a claim for preexisting conditions for losses incurred more than six months from the effective date of coverage.

3. An outline of coverage must be provided along with any Medicare supplement policy issued or delivered in this state. The outline of coverage shall include:
   - a statement of the limitations, exceptions, or reductions of coverage;
   - a description of the principal benefits provided; and
   - a description of the renewal provision included.

4. A 30-day free look provision must be included and prominently displayed on the first page of the policy.

5. Permitted exclusions under these contracts include: the cost of foot care (i.e., corns, calluses, flat feet, etc.); mental or emotional disorders; alcoholism and drug addiction; treatment or illness arising out of war, suicide or aviation; cosmetic surgery (elective); dental care; eye and hearing exams (glasses and hearing aids); routine physical examinations, custodial care, rest cures, and so forth.

6. This type of policy may not provide for the termination of coverage of an eligible spouse because of the termination of coverage of the insured other than for nonpayment of premium. Termination is also not allowed solely on the grounds of age or deterioration of health.

7. If any replacement occurs, the replacing insurer or its agent must provide a *Notice Regarding Replacement* to the applicant informing him of the possible benefits or coverages that might be lost when replacing one policy with another. This Notice must be given to the applicant before or at the same time the application is taken.

8. The buyer's guide shall contain an outline of Medicare coverage and include advice and other information regarding the purchase of Medicare supplement policies, including a reference to the right of the purchaser to cancel a policy during the first 30 days (30-day free-look) after it is delivered.

9. Individual Medicare Supplement policies must maintain a minimum loss ratio of 65% (65 cents of every premium dollar earned must be paid out as benefits to policyholders); group policies must maintain a minimum loss ratio of 75%.

10. **Open enrollment** A company may not deny coverage because of health status, claims experience, receipt of health care, or medical condition if the applicant submits the application during the six-month period beginning with the first month in which the individual, who is age 65 or older, first enrolled for Medicare Part B. A Medicare Supplement policy may not deny a claim for losses incurred more than six months from the effective date of coverage for a preexisting condition.

11. A policyholder who has applied for and has been determined entitled to Medicaid benefits may request a suspension of their Medicare Supplement policy for up to 24 months; upon notice to the carrier, the policy will be fully reinstated without any waiting period for preexisting conditions.

12. Termination of the Medicare Supplement policy shall be without prejudice to any continuous loss which commenced while the policy was in force.

13. No Medicare Supplement shall provide the same benefits (duplicate) that are provided by Parts A or B of Medicare.

14. All Medicare supplement policy advertisements must be submitted to the Insurance commissioner for approval.

15. **Compensation [11:4-23.14]** An insurer cannot pay a producer a first-year commission or compensation for the sale of a Medicare supplement policy that exceeds 200% of the commission to be paid by that insurer for selling or servicing the policy in the second or third year of the policy. The commission or compensation paid in subsequent renewal years must be, for at least five renewals, the same as the commission or compensation paid in the second year. When a policy is replaced, the insurer cannot pay compensation that exceeds the renewal commission that the insurer pays for renewal policies.

16. An agent must make a reasonable effort to determine the appropriateness of the recommended purchase or replacement of a Medicare supplement policy. Application forms should inform an applicant that he does not need to purchase more than one Medicare supplement policy. An applicant should also be told that if he is eligible for Medicaid, he may not need Medicare supplement insurance.

17. **Advertisements [11:4-23.17]** Insurers who sell Medicare supplement policies in New Jersey must file, with the Commissioner, a copy of all advertisements used to market these policies at least 30 days before using the advertisements in the state.

18. **Reporting multiple policies [11:4-23.20]** Each year by March 1, every insurer must report to the Commissioner the number of Medicare supplement policies it issued and the dates on which they were issued. The insurers must report individuals for whom it has more than one Medicare supplement policy or certificate in force.

D. **TEMPORARY DISABILITY LAW [43:21-27 THROUGH 36]** All covered individuals shall be entitled on and after January 1, 1949 to benefits provided under a private disability plan or a state plan.

1. **Covered individual** A covered individual is any person who is in employment for which he is entitled to remuneration from a covered employer, or who has been out of employment for less than two weeks. However, a covered individual who is employed by the state of New Jersey (including Rutgers, The State University, the College of Medicine and Dentistry of New Jersey, and the New Jersey Institute of Technology, or by any governmental entity) shall not be eligible to receive any benefits under the Temporary Disability Benefits Law until the individual exhausts all accumulated sick leave

2. **Compensable disability** Disability shall be compensable subject to the limitations of New Jersey law, where a covered individual suffers any accident or sickness not arising out of and in the course of the individuals employment or if so arising not compensable under the workers' compensation law, and resulting in the individual's total inability to perform the duties of employment.

3. **Nonduplication of benefits** No benefits shall be required or paid under New Jersey law for any period with respect to which benefits are paid or payable under any employment compensation or similar law. No benefits shall be payable (or required) for any period with respect to which benefits, other than benefits for permanent partial or permanent total disability previously incurred, are payable or paid on account of the disability of the covered individual under any workers' compensation law, occupational disease law, or similar type legislation:

   a. Disability benefits otherwise required hereunder shall be reduced by the amount paid concurrently under any benefit or allowance program to which his most recent employer contributed on his behalf.

4. **Excepted individuals** Any person who adheres to the faith or teachings of any church, sect, or denomination, and who in accordance with its creed, tenets, or principles depends for healing upon prayer or spiritual means, in the practice of religion, shall be exempt from the Temporary Disability Benefits Law Act, including any obligation to make contributions hereunder and any right to receive benefits hereunder.

5. **Private plans** Any employer may establish a private plan for the payment of disability benefits in lieu of the benefits of the state plan hereinafter established. Benefits under such a private plan may be provided by a contract of insurance issued by an insurer duly authorized and admitted to do business in this state, or by an agreement between the employer and a union or association representing his employees, or by a specific undertaking by the employer as a self insurer.

   a. All private plans must be submitted in detail to the Division of Employment Security. These plans may exclude a class of employees except based on age, sex, race, or by the wages paid to the employees. Covered individuals so excluded shall be covered by the state plan and subject to the employee contribution required by law to be paid into the state disability benefits fund.

   b. If employees are required to contribute toward the cost of benefits under a private plan, this plan shall not become effective unless prior to the effective date a majority of the employees in the class to be covered have agreed thereto by written election. A covered individual shall not be entitled to any benefits from the state disability benefits fund with respect to any period of disability commencing while he is covered under an approved private plan.

6. **Existing plan** If a private plan was already in existence when the Temporary Disability Law became effective, the plan shall be deemed to be an approved private plan. During the continuance of this private plan the employees covered shall not be entitled to any benefits under the state plan while covered under the private plan.

   a. No approved private plan may be terminated by an employer until at least 30 days after written notice of intention to do so has been given to the Division by the employer. The Division may rescind approval on any private plan where it is feared benefits will not be paid.

   b. No termination of a private plan shall affect the payment of benefits to disabled employees whose period of disability commenced prior to the date of termination.

7. **Additional benefits** Nothing in New Jersey law will prohibit an employer in establishing a supplementary plan to provide additional benefits (to the benefits provided by a private plan already in existence).

E. **HEALTH CARE QUALITY ACT [26:2J-1, 4]** All health maintenance organizations (HMOs) in New Jersey must meet the requirements to qualify for a certificate of authority as would any other insurer. They are to demonstrate financial soundness in the delivery of their health care services and the schedule of charges for these services.

   1. **Basic health care services [26:2J-2]** Basic health care services include emergency care, inpatient hospital and physician care, and outpatient medical services.

2. **Health care services required [26:2-4.1 to 17]** HMOs must provide coverage for the following services:

- Treatment of Wilm's tumor
- Basic health care services
- Mammograms
- Prescription drugs and pharmacological services
- Preventive medical examinations and tests, including annual consultations with a health care provider to encourage healthy lifestyles and habits
- Cancer treatment
- Maternity care
- Treatment for diabetes
- Pap smears
- Prostate cancer tests
- Mastectomies, related surgeries for reconstruction, and prostheses
- Treatment of inherited metabolic diseases (including medical and modified foods)

3. **Discrimination against victims of domestic violence prohibited [26:2J-18]** An HMO cannot deny health care services for treatment of injuries sustained as a result of domestic violence. Health care services are to be provided to the same extent as for any other treatment.

NEW JERSEY INSURANCE LAW PRACTICE FINAL

Student Instructions: Following your thorough study of New Jersey Life, Accident, and Health Insurance Law in Unit 12, take this 60-question sample examination. Grade your performance using the answer key provided. Review the information in the text concerning those questions answered incorrectly.

I. General Insurance

1. An agent who illegally induces an insured to lapse his or her current policy in order to purchase a new life insurance policy may be guilty of

    A. rebating
    B. larceny
    C. fraud
    D. twisting

2. When an agent offers an applicant something of value that is not specified in the insurance contract in order to persuade the applicant to purchase a policy, the agent is guilty of

    A. rebating
    B. twisting
    C. misrepresentation
    D. defamation

3. Illegally inducing an individual into lapsing his current plan of life insurance best describes

    A. rebating
    B. twisting
    C. false information
    D. false advertising

4. All of the following are considered to be transactions involving replacement EXCEPT

    A. a whole life policy is converted to reduced paid up insurance
    B. life insurance lapses due to nonpayment
    C. a modified life policy is reissued with a reduced cash value
    D. life insurance is continued as extended term insurance

5. Which of the following must be provided to all purchasers of life insurance?

    A. A policy summary
    B. A statement of paid commissions
    C. A designated beneficiary
    D. Nontaxable dividends

6. All of the following are considered to be forms of life insurance advertisements EXCEPT

    A. magazine advertisements
    B. prepared sales talks
    C. amortization tables
    D. material used for recruitment

7. Testimonials utilized in life insurance advertising must be

    A. purchased at the time of policy delivery
    B. disclosed at the time of application
    C. provided at the death of the insured
    D. genuine and represent the current opinion of the author

8. Insurers must maintain a file of all advertisements used in the solicitation of life insurance for a period of at least

    A. 5 years
    B. 3 years
    C. 2 years
    D. 1 year

9. How often must every domestic insurer that is authorized to issue variable contracts in New Jersey determine whether funds held in its variable accounts meet statutory requirements?

    A. Annually
    B. Semiannually
    C. Quarterly
    D. Monthly

10. A life insurance policy issued in this state which provides the entire face amount as a death benefit at all times best describes

   A. limited death benefit policy
   B. full death benefit policy
   C. modified benefit policy
   D. entire contract benefit policy

11. The ultimate amount of insurance available under a limited benefit life contract is

   A. $5,000
   B. $15,000
   C. $25,000
   D. $50,000

12. All of the following must be disclosed to a prospective purchaser of life insurance EXCEPT

   A. dividend information
   B. the type of policy being solicited
   C. the age when coverage decreases
   D. the compensation of an agent

13. How long must an insurer maintain records of all sample mailings regarding student life insurance after they are mailed?

   A. 2 years
   B. 3 years
   C. 4 years
   D. 5 years

II. Life, Accident, and Health Insurance

14. Under a credit life or credit accident and health insurance contract, the amount of coverage provided shall not exceed the

   A. premium paid
   B. agreement's consideration
   C. term of coverage
   D. amount of indebtedness

15. New Jersey regulations applying to group coverage discontinuance and replacement are applicable to all of the following EXCEPT

   A. temporary disability benefits
   B. term life insurance
   C. major medical coverage
   D. renewable term life

16. The term of credit life insurance cannot extend more than how many days beyond the scheduled maturity date of the indebtedness?

   A. 5
   B. 10
   C. 15
   D. 20

17. Group insurance replacement regulations apply to each of the following EXCEPT

   A. life insurance benefits
   B. temporary disability benefits
   C. major medical benefits
   D. long-term disability

18. Credit life, accident, and health insurance may be issued in all of the following forms EXCEPT

   A. individual policies of life insurance issued to debtors on a term plan
   B. group policies of life insurance issued to creditors providing insurance upon the lives of debtors on the term plan
   C. group health policies issued to debtors on a term plan
   D. individual health policies covering the lives of creditors on a term plan

19. The Commissioner of Insurance in the state of New Jersey is appointed by the

    A. Governor of New York
    B. New Jersey Senate
    C. Governor of New Jersey
    D. Attorney General of New Jersey

20. The Commissioner of Insurance has the power to

    A. prosecute insurance agents who break state insurance law
    B. subpoena witnesses
    C. withhold commissions of a broker in debt
    D. appoint brokers for various insurers

21. An insurer whose principal office is chartered in Canada but is authorized to solicit insurance in the state of New Jersey best describes a(n)

    A. domestic company
    B. alien company
    C. foreign company
    D. nonadmitted company

22. Which of the following involves a reinsurance company placing additional risks with another reinsurance company?

    A. Regression
    B. Controlled business
    C. Retrocession
    D. Extended rescission

23. A resident license may be issued by the Commissioner of Insurance to all of the following EXCEPT a(n)

    A. applicant who is 19 years of age
    B. applicant who has completed an approved course of education
    C. applicant who has passed the state insurance examination
    D. 22-year-old applicant who has spent the past 4 years in prison

24. The Commissioner of Insurance will assess which of the following penalties if an agent violates or ignores a cease and desist order?

    A. Up to $500 for each violation
    B. Up to $1,000 for each violation
    C. Up to $2,500 for each violation
    D. Up to $5,000 for each violation

25. In a reinsurance transaction, the originating insurer may also be referred to as the

    A. retroceding insurer
    B. ceding insurer
    C. assuming insurer
    D. obligatory insurer

26. A licensed producer acting as an agent in the state of New Jersey represents

    A. the insured
    B. the insurer
    C. the Commissioner
    D. a broker

27. Which of the following persons would be permitted to function as an insurance consultant?

    A. A former sales representative
    B. A certified public accountant
    C. An attorney-at-law
    D. A bank trust officer

28. An insurer which is chartered and formed under the laws of New Jersey may be referred to in this state as a(n)

    A. foreign company
    B. alien company
    C. unauthorized company
    D. domestic company

29. All of the following entities have the ability to secure a producer's license in the state of New Jersey EXCEPT a(n)

    A. individual
    B. partnership
    C. controlled business producer
    D. corporation

30. In most instances temporary licenses issued in the state of New Jersey shall not be valid for a period greater than

    A. 30 days
    B. 90 days
    C. 180 days
    D. 365 days

31. Which of the following best describes a person who secures an insurance license solely for the purpose of writing coverage to protect his own risks?

    A. Controlling stock
    B. Controlled interest
    C. Controlled business
    D. Aggregate business

32. The Commissioner of Insurance may take which of the following forms of action when it is determined that a producer has engaged in unfair methods of competition?

    A. Issue a cease and desist order
    B. Order payment of a $25,000 penalty for each unfair act
    C. Hold a public hearing
    D. Conduct an examination of the insurer involved

33. All of the following parties may receive commissions from an insurer EXCEPT a

    A. nonresident producer
    B. producer
    C. solicitor
    D. producer acting as a broker

34. A producer who has misappropriated funds belonging to policyholders or insurers may

    A. be fined $100,000
    B. have his license suspended
    C. only solicit controlled business
    D. secure a temporary license for his spouse or next of kin

35. The ability to transact insurance business in the state of New Jersey is granted to an insurer by the issuance of a(n)

    A. corporate charter
    B. certificate of authority
    C. insurance certificate
    D. formation contract

36. Which of the following statements best describes a mutual insurance company in the state of New Jersey?

    A. It is profit motivated.
    B. It is a company owned by its stockholders.
    C. It is a company which has its principal office in another country.
    D. It allows policyholders to share profits in the form of dividends.

37. Which of the following may be assessed for a person who violates a cease and desist order?

    A. A penalty not to exceed $5,000 for each violation
    B. Imprisonment not to exceed 5 years
    C. A fine of $10,000 and/or a year in jail
    D. A fine of up to $50,000 and or 6 months in jail

38. Which of the following would be considered as misrepresentation or false advertising under New Jersey law?

    A. A false statement regarding the dividends paid by a policy
    B. Statements regarding the financial condition of an insurer which are untrue
    C. A malicious and untrue statement about an insurer meant to injure that insurer
    D. All of the above

39. The party offering a rebate to an applicant for insurance is known as the

    A. assignee
    B. assignor
    C. offeree
    D. offeror

40. Violation of a cease and desist order may result in a monetary penalty not to exceed

    A. $1,000
    B. $2,500
    C. $5,000
    D. $10,000

41. An insurer which is owned by its policyholders and may allow sharing of profits in the form of dividends best describes a(n)

    A. mutual insurer
    B. stock insurer
    C. alien insurer
    D. nonadmitted insurer

42. Which of the following insurance court cases declared that an insurance policy was not an article of commerce and that it was actually a contract of indemnity?

    A. *McCarran v. Ferguson*
    B. *United States v. South-Eastern Underwriters*
    C. Sherman Anti-Trust decision
    D. *Paul v. Virginia*

43. Generally, the Insurance Commissioner of an individual state is appointed by which of the following parties?

    A. Attorney General
    B. Governor
    C. Commissioner of Labor
    D. Insurance Services office

44. Which of the following stipulated that federal antitrust laws would apply to insurance but only to the extent that state regulation was not effective?

    A. *Paul v. Virginia*
    B. McCarran Ferguson Act
    C. Sherman Anti-Trust Act
    D. National Securities Act

45. If a producer fails to complete the required number of continuing education hours the Commissioner will terminate his license

    A. for 3 months
    B. for 6 months
    C. for 2 years
    D. until the requirements are completed

46. An individual whose license is revoked for any reason must wait what period of time before the state of New Jersey permits reapplication?

    A. 1 year
    B. 2 years
    C. 3 years
    D. 5 years

47. All licensees must notify the Department of Banking and Insurance with any change of business or residence address within how may days of the change?

    A. 10
    B. 20
    C. 30
    D. 60

48. All of the following are considered legal disbursements from premium trust accounts EXCEPT

    A. involuntary deposits
    B. claim payments
    C. gross premiums due insurers

III. Accident and Health

49. Which of the following can cause total health claim payments to be greater than the amount of a loss?

    A. Coordination of benefits
    B. Duplicative coverage
    C. Regulatory practices
    D. Credit disability insurance

50. All of the following must be disclosed in any advertisement for accident and health insurance EXCEPT

    A. exceptions
    B. reductions
    C. earnings
    D. limitations

51. Which of the following statements regarding minimum benefit standards of accident and health policies issued in this state is TRUE?

    A. Policies covering pregnancy shall cover pregnancy expenses if conception occurs prior to the effective date of coverage.
    B. In a family policy covering both spouses, the age of the older spouse shall be used as the basis for meeting the contract's age requirements.
    C. Policies that include a military service exclusion shall provide for a refund of premium when coverage is suspended.
    D. Accidental death and dismemberment benefits must be paid within 180 days from the date of the accident.

52. Disability income policies providing benefits payable after age 62 and reduced solely on the basis of age must contain an elimination period no greater than how many days if written for a 1-year term?

    A. 30
    B. 60
    C. 90
    D. 120

53. An accident-only policy must contain a prominent statement of the limited coverage provided in which of the following areas?

    A. The exclusion section of the policy
    B. The copy of the original application attached to the entire contract
    C. The initial page of the policy
    D. The beneficiary designation section

54. All of the following are benefits provided by an accident and health policy's coverage for the treatment of alcoholism EXCEPT

    A. personal injury protection
    B. inpatient care
    C. treatment at a licensed detoxification facility
    D. outpatient treatment

55. New Jersey regulations regarding benefits for the treatment of alcoholism apply to

    A. Medicare complement policies
    B. student accident only policies
    C. medical expense policies
    D. dread disease policies

56. Medicare supplement policies may not deny a claim for preexisting conditions for losses incurred more than how long after the effective date of coverage?

    A. 1 month
    B. 3 months
    C. 5 months
    D. 6 month

57. Records of complaints must be kept by health insurers on which of the following bases?

    A. Pro rata basis
    B. Disposition basis
    C. Calendar year basis
    D. Renewable basis

58. All insurers are required by law to keep copies of their health insurance advertisements for a period of

    A. 2 years
    B. 3 years
    C. 5 years
    D. 7 years

59. Alcoholism treatment regulations apply to which of the following forms of health insurance?

    A. Dread disease policy
    B. Surgical expense policy
    C. Hospital income policy
    D. Major medical policy

60. According to New Jersey's Temporary Disability Law, a covered individual who is employed by the state shall not be eligible to receive temporary disability benefits until

    A. a 6-month waiting period is satisfied
    B. workers' compensation benefits cease
    C. all sick leave is exhausted
    D. residual disability begins

ANSWERS TO NEW JERSEY LAW PRACTICE FINAL

1. **D**	11. **B**	21. **B**	31. **C**	41. **A**	51. **C**
2. **A**	12. **D**	22. **C**	32. **A**	42. **D**	52. **C**
3. **B**	13. **D**	23. **D**	33. **C**	43. **B**	53. **C**
4. **B**	14. **D**	24. **D**	34. **B**	44. **B**	54. **A**
5. **A**	15. **A**	25. **B**	35. **B**	45. **D**	55. **C**
6. **C**	16. **C**	26. **B**	36. **D**	46. **D**	56. **D**
7. **D**	17. **B**	27. **A**	37. **A**	47. **C**	57. **C**
8. **A**	18. **D**	28. **D**	38. **D**	48. **A**	58. **C**
9. **B**	19. **C**	29. **C**	39. **D**	49. **B**	59. **D**
10. **B**	20. **B**	30. **C**	40. **C**	50. **C**	60. **C**

Glossary

A

Accidental Bodily Injury Bodily injury resulting from an accident.

Accidental Death and Dismemberment Insurance (AD&D) A form of insurance providing benefits in the event of accidental death, the accidental loss of sight, or the loss of a member(s), such as an arm or a leg.

Accidental Death Benefit A lump-sum payment for loss of life due to an accident that was the direct cause of death. The cause of the mishap must be accidental for a benefit to be payable under the policy.

Accidental Means An unforeseen, unexpected, unintended cause of an accident which results in an injury. The cause of the action and the result must not be intentional or there will be no coverage.

Accumulation Provision A percentage increase made in the benefits available under the policy. It is intended as a bonus to the insured for continuous renewals. (It is not usually included in policies issued currently.)

Adverse Selection The tendency of a disproportionate number of poor risks to purchase life insurance or maintain existing insurance in force (e.g., the selection against the insurer).

Agent An authorized representative of an insurance company who solicits, negotiates, or countersigns life insurance and/or annuity contracts (in many companies he also sells health insurance). An agent represents the company.

Aggregate Amount The maximum dollar amount that can be collected under any policy, for any disability or period of disability.

Annuity A contract providing periodic income payments for a fixed period of time or during the lifetime of an annuitant. It may be defined as the systematic liquidation of an estate.

Annuity, Cash Refund A life annuity contract that provides that upon the death of the annuitant, the beneficiary (or his estate) will receive a lump-sum payment which represents the difference between the amount the annuitant paid to the insurance company and the total income payments received by the annuitant.

Annuity, Certain Payable for a minimum specified period and continuing thereafter throughout the lifetime of the annuitant.

Annuity, Deferred Payments commence more than one year after the payment of the first (or single) premium to the insurance company, usually at a selected retirement age.

Annuity, Immediate The income commences 1, 3, 6, or 12 months after its purchase.

Annuity, Installment Refund Similar to a cash refund annuity, except that money is refunded in installment payments and the insurance company makes payments to the designated beneficiary until the total of the payments made to the annuitant and the beneficiary equals the consideration paid.

Annuity, Joint and Last Survivor An annuity issued on the lives of two or more persons, which is payable as long as one of them survives.

Assignee A person, firm, or corporation to whom the rights under a contract are assigned in their entirety or in part.

Assignment The legal transfer of the benefits or rights of a policy by the insured to another party.

Association Group Individual policies written to cover members of a trade or professional association (e.g., the American Medical Association or the Ohio Association of Hat Manufacturers).

Attained Age An age that a person or an insured has attained on a given date. For life insurance purposes, the age is based on either the nearest birthday or the last birthday, depending upon the practices of the insurance company involved.

Automatic Premium Loan (Automatic Premium Advance) A provision in a life insurance policy which states that if an insured fails to pay a premium by the end of the grace period, the amount of the premium due will be loaned to the insured automatically. However, the loan value of the policy must be sufficient to cover the loan plus interest. Generally, the insured must request that this clause be made a part of the policy at the time of application.

Average Earnings Clause (Relation of Earnings to Insurance) A provision in the policy which allows the insurance company to reduce the monthly income disability benefits payable if the insured's total income benefits exceed either his current monthly earnings or his average monthly earnings during the two-year period immediately preceding the disability.

Aviation Clause A clause that limits the liability of the insurance company if the death of an insured is caused by certain types of aviation accidents.

B

Beneficiary A person(s) designated to receive a specified payment(s) in the event of the insured's death.

Beneficiary, Contingent (Secondary) A person who is entitled to benefits only after the death of a primary beneficiary.

Beneficiary, Irrevocable The insured may not change the designated beneficiary without the beneficiary's consent.

Beneficiary, Primary A person who is entitled primarily to benefits upon the death of an insured.

Beneficiary, Revocable The designated beneficiary may be changed at the insured's request without the consent of the beneficiary.

Beneficiary, Tertiary The person who is entitled to policy benefits if the primary and contingent beneficiaries predecease the insured.

Binding Receipt Insurance becomes effective on the date of the receipt and continues for a specified period of time or until the company disapproves the application.

Blanket Accident Medical Expense Entitles the insured, who suffered a bodily injury, to collect up to a maximum established in the policy for all hospital and medical expense incurred, without any limitation on individual types of medical expenses.

Blanket Policy Coverage for a number of individuals who are exposed to the same hazards, such as members of an athletic team who are passengers on the same plane. The covered persons need not be identified individually.

Blue Cross An independent, nonprofit (for the most part) membership association providing protection against the costs of hospital care in a limited geographical area. Provides coverage for hospital costs.

Blue Shield An independent, nonprofit (for the most part) membership association providing protection against the costs of surgery and other items of medical care in a limited geographical area. Provides coverage for doctor's fees.

Broker An insurance solicitor, licensed by the state, who represents various insureds and who is permitted to place general insurance coverages with any insurance company authorized to transact business in the state in which he is licensed.

Business Insurance A policy whose principal purpose is to provide reimbursement to an employer for the time lost by a key-employee who is disabled.

C

Cancellable Policy A policy that may be terminated either by the insured or the insurance company by notification to the other party in accordance with the terms of the policy.

Capital Sum This is the amount payable under accidental dismemberment coverage. It may be the amount payable for accidental loss of two members or both eyes (or one of each). An indemnity for the loss of one member or the sight of one eye is usually a percentage of the capital sum.

Cash Surrender Value The amount stated in the policy that is available in cash upon the surrender of a policy for cancellation before or after the policy matures (as a death

claim or otherwise). This is one of three nonforfeiture options.

Catastrophe Insurance Health policies that provide substantial benefits for serious, prolonged, or expensive disabilities that cause enormous financial problems for the insurance. This is generally referred to as Major Medical Expense Insurance.

Coinsurance (Percentage Participation) A provision which specifies that the insurance company will pay only part of a loss and requires the policyholder to pay the balance himself. For example, in the case of Major Medical Expense Insurance, the insurance company may be obliged to pay 75% of an insured's expenses in excess of the deductible amount, if any, and the insured is required to pay the other 25% himself.

Common Disaster Clause This clause defines the method of the payment of the proceeds of the policy by the insurance company if the insured and the named beneficiary die simultaneously in a common disaster. It protects the contingent beneficiary since it would consider that the primary beneficiary predeceased the insured.

Comprehensive Major Medical Insurance A policy designed to give the protection offered by both a basic and a major medical policy. It is characterized by a low deductible amount, coinsurance clause, and high maximum benefits, usually $5,000 to $10,000. This policy is generally referred to by the shortened term of comprehensive insurance.

Compulsory Health Insurance A plan of insurance under the supervision of a state or the federal government that requires protection for medical, hospital, surgical, and disability benefits. Statutory Disability Benefit Laws are in effect in the states of New York, New Jersey, Rhode Island, California, Puerto Rico, and Hawaii (as of January, 1979). In the state of New York, the law requires the maintenance of an approved program of loss of time benefits (income benefits).

Concealment Failure by an applicant to disclose in his application for insurance a fact that is relevant to the acceptance or the rejection of his application.

Conditional Receipt A receipt given for the payment of the initial premium (accompanying the application) that makes coverage effective under the contract if the risk is approved as applied for, subject to the other conditions set forth in the receipt.

Consideration One of the elements of a valid contract. The premium and the statements made by the prospective insured in the application are construed as the insured's consideration. The insurance company's consideration is its promise to pay a valid claim.

Contributory Plan A term applied to employee benefit plans (such as group insurance or group annuities) under which both the employees and the employer contribute.

Conversion Privilege The right granted to the insured to change his coverage from a group policy to an individual policy. If a member of a group resigns therefrom, he is given an opportunity to secure an individual policy within a specified period thereafter regardless of whether or not he is in good health at that time. This term is also applied to the right of an insured to convert from a convertible term policy to a permanent form of insurance.

Credit Life Insurance Life insurance designed to pay the balance of a loan (usually repayable in installments) if the insured dies before the loan has been repaid in full. Generally, credit life insurance is handled by a bank, department store, or a finance company. Usually, this form of insurance is written on a group basis, but it may also be written on an individual basis.

D

Deductible The amount of loss or expense that must be incurred by the insured before benefits become payable. The insurance company pays benefits only for the loss in excess of the amount specified in the deductible provision. There are various types of deductible provisions.

Disability A physical condition that makes an insured incapable of performing one or more duties of his occupation, or, in the case of total disability, prevents him from performing any other type of work for remuneration. (This wording varies from one insurance company to another.)

Disability Benefit A feature added to some life insurance policies that provides for the waiver of premiums upon the furnishing of proof that an insured has become totally and permanently disabled and/or for the payment of monthly income benefits to the insured.

Dividend A refund of part of the premium under a participating policy or a share of policyholder surplus funds apportioned for distribution. They are derived from savings in mortality and expenses and interest earned in excess of the assumed rate used in the calculation of the premium in the policy reserves.

Dividend Options The insured is given the option to apply dividends as follows: he may receive the dividend in cash, apply the dividend toward the payment of any premium due on the policy, apply the dividend to the purchase of paid up additional insurance, or leave the dividend with the insurance company to accumulate an interest.

Double Indemnity A clause providing payment of twice the face amount of the policy if loss of life is due to an accident.

Duplicate Coverage A term usually applied to benefits (other than loss of time) where an insured is covered by several policies with one or more insurance companies providing the same type of benefits, and often resulting in overinsurance.

E

Elective Indemnity Fixed lump-sum payments that an insured may elect to receive instead of accepting the weekly or monthly indemnity provided for the policy. Usually, such payments are made for sprains, dislocations, fractures, or for the loss of fingers or toes.

Elimination Period A period of time after the inception of a disability, during which benefits are not payable. An elimination period must be satisfied for each separate disability that occurs. (*See* waiting period.)

Endorsement An attachment to the policy by which the scope of coverage is altered (e.g., restricted or increased). The terms of the endorsement, or rider take precedence over the printed portions of the policy which are in conflict with the endorsement.

Endowment Insurance A policy that, after a specified number of years, pays a stated amount to the insured. If the insured dies during the endowment period, the face amount of the policy is paid to the designated beneficiary. An endowment pays at the earlier of death or a specified period.

Evidence of Insurability Any statement or proof of a person's physical condition which may affect acceptance for insurance.

Exclusions Provisions in the policy that eliminate coverage for specified losses or causes of loss.

Experience Rating (Group Insurance) The premium is computed on the basis of past losses and expenses incurred by the insurance company in the settlement of claims and other expenses involving a particular group of risks.

Extended Term Insurance A nonforfeiture option, under which the face amount of the policy is continued in force for a specified additional period of time after default in the payment of a premium.

F

Face Amount The amount of insurance stated on the face of the policy that will be paid upon the death of the insured (or in some cases at the maturity of the policy). It does not include any amount that has been added through dividend additions or additional insurance payable in the event of accidental death, etc.

Facility of Payment Clause A provision in a policy that permits the insurance company to pay insurance proceeds to persons other than the insured, the designated beneficiary, or the estate of the insured.

Family Expense Policy A policy that insures both the policyholder and his immediate dependents, usually his spouse and children.

Family Income Benefits Under this form of life insurance, on the death of the insured, a monthly income is payable to the beneficiary(ies) to the end of the family income period stipulated in the policy in addition to the lump-sum payment (face amount). For example, it could run for a period of 10 years starting with the inception date of the policy, or it could run for 15 years, 20 years, or to age 65. Usually, it is a decreasing term insurance provision that is combined with whole life insurance. If the insured survives the family income period, the family income protection ceases. The policy reverts to the face amount (usually, payable in a lump sum upon the death of the insured).

Family Maintenance (Family Protection) Policy This type of policy combines ordinary life insurance and level term insurance. It affords the payment of a monthly income during a stated period of 10, 15, or 20 years or to age 65 as preselected by the insured. The monthly income is payable from the date of death to the end of the preselected period. The payment of the face amount of the policy is payable at the end of such preselected period.

Franchise Insurance An individual policy written to cover a group of persons that does not qualify for true group insurance. The benefits may vary slightly within the group.

Fraternal Insurance A cooperative type of insurance provided by a social organization for its members (e.g., life insurance offered by the Knights of Columbus).

G

Grace Period A specified period after a premium payment is due, during which the protection of the policy continues even though the payment for the renewal premium has not as yet been received.

Group Certificate Certificate given to employees participating in a group insurance plan that sets forth the protection to which they are entitled.

Group Insurance Policy A policy protecting a group of persons, usually employees of a firm. Generally called a master policy.

Guaranteed Renewable The option of renewal to a specified age, or for a lifetime, vested solely in the insured. However, the insurance company has the right to increase the premiums applicable to an entire class of policyholders.

H

Health Insurance A broad term covering the various forms of insurance relating to the health of persons. It includes such coverages as accident, sickness, disability, and hospital and medical expense. This term is used instead of *sickness and accident insurance.*

Hospital Benefits Benefits payable for charges incurred while the insured is confined to, or treated in, a hospital, as defined in the policy.

Hospital Expense Insurance Benefits subject to a specified daily maximum for a specified period of time while the insured is confined to a hospital, plus a limited

allowance up to a specified amount for miscellaneous hospital expenses such as operating rooms, anesthesia, laboratory fees, etc. Also known as hospitalization insurance.

I

Incontestable Clause A clause that makes the policy indisputable (except for nonpayment of premium and the operation of the war clause exclusion) regarding the statements made by the insured in the application after a specified period of time has elapsed (usually one, two, or three years).

Indemnity The payment of a benefit for a loss insured under a policy. The insured is indemnified for a specified loss, or part thereof.

Individual Insurance Policies that afford protection to the policyholder and/or his family (as distinct from group insurance). Sometimes it is referred to as personal insurance.

Industrial Policy A policy providing nominal indemnities for a short period of time, and characterized by premiums (collected in person by an agent) that are usually payable weekly or monthly.

Inspection Report A report that contains general information regarding the health, habits, finances, and reputation of an applicant made by a firm that specializes in rendering this type of service.

Insurable Interest Substantial economic interest of the beneficiary in the insured due to blood relationship, marriage, or economic dependence.

Insurance Protection in accordance with a written contract against the financial hazards (in whole or in part) of the happening of specified fortuitous events. May also be defined as the transfer of risk from one party to another.

Insuring Clause A clause that defines and describes the scope of the coverage afforded and the limits of indemnification.

J

Joint Life Insurance Insurance on the lives of two or more persons with the face amount payable in the event of death of either (or any one) of them.

Juvenile Insurance Life insurance policies written on the lives of children within specified age limits (e.g., a jumping juvenile policy).

K

Key-Employee Insurance An individual policy designed to reimburse an employer for the loss of a key-employee's service due to his death. Usually, the employer pays the premium and is the beneficiary.

L

Lapse Termination of a policy because of the policyholder's failure to pay the premium within the time required.

Legal Reserve Life Insurance Company An insurance company which operates under insurance laws that specify the minimum amount of reserves that the insurance company must maintain on its policies.

Level Premium A premium that remains unchanged throughout the life of a policy.

Level Term Insurance A term contract whose face amount remains level throughout the life of the contract but whose premiums increase according to the age of the insured.

Life Expectancy The average number of anticipated years of life remaining for individuals who are the same age (e.g., 35) in accordance with the mortality table indicated in the policy.

Life Insurance Insurance upon the lives of human beings that creates an immediate and guaranteed estate at the death of an insured.

Limited Pay Life Insurance A plan of permanent life insurance under which the premiums are payable for a specified number of years (e.g., 10, 15, 20, or 30 years, or to age 65) after which the policy can continue to remain in effect for life without it being necessary for the insured to make any additional payments.

Limited Policies Those that restrict benefits to specified accidents or diseases, such as travel policies, dread disease policies, ticket policies, accident only policies, and so forth.

Loading An amount that is added to net premiums in order to cover the insurance company's operating expenses and possible contingencies. The cost of acquiring new business, collection expenses, and general management expenses constitute loading.

Loan Value The amount specified in a policy that the insurance company will lend to an insured at the rate of interest that the insurance company may charge for such loans (as indicated in the policy).

Loss-of-Income (Time) Benefits Income benefits payable to the insured because he is unable to work due to an insured disability.

Loss-of-Income Insurance Policies that provide benefits to help replace an insured's earned income lost or curtailed as a result of an illness or an accident.

M

Major Medical Expense Insurance Policies especially designed to help offset the heavy medical expenses resulting from catastrophic or prolonged illnesses or injuries. Generally, they provide benefits payments of 75–80% of all types of medical expense above a certain amount first paid by the insured, and up to the maximum limit of liability provided by the policy, usually $5,000 or $10,000.

Maturity The date on which a policy becomes payable due to the death of the insured, or as a result of an insured's living to the end of an endowment period.

Medicaid A state medical assistance program for eligible needy or blind persons.

Medicare A program of health insurance and medical care for persons who are 65 years of age or over, operated under the provisions of the Social Security Act. It is comprised of two parts: Part A: Hospital Insurance and Part B: Supplementary Medical Insurance (this part is optional).

Miscellaneous Expenses Hospital charges other than room and board (e.g., xrays, drugs, laboratory fees, etc.). These are provided under hospital expense insurance.

Misrepresentation A false statement that the prospective insured makes in an application for a policy. An omission of a material fact can also be construed as a misrepresentation. A misrepresentation is material if the insurance company, having known the true facts, would have refused the policy as applied for by the prospective insured. Statements are considered representations, not warranties.

Moral Hazards Habits, morals, or financial practices of an insured which increases the possibility or extent of a loss.

Morbidity Table Shows the incidence and extent of disability which may be expected from a given large group of persons. This table is used in the computation of rates. It is comparable to a mortality table used in connection with life insurance.

Mortality Table A statistical table which indicates the probability of death and survival at each age.

Mutual Life Insurance Company A life insurance company owned and controlled by its policyholders. Mutual Life Insurance Companies issue participating policies.

N

Noncancellable A policy that an insurance company is not permitted to terminate or amend during its term (except for nonpayment of a premium). Usually, the renewal of the policy is guaranteed at the option of the insured to a specified age at a fixed premium. Also written as noncancellable and guaranteed renewable.

Noncontributory Plan A group employee benefit plan under which the employer pays for the full cost of the benefits for his employees.

Nonforfeiture Values (Options) Benefits required by law to be made available to the insured (or his beneficiary) in the event that he discontinues his premium payments. These provide that he does not forfeit or lose all that he has invested in the policy.

Nonmedical Life Insurance Insurance that is issued without requiring the applicant to submit to a medical examination. The insurance company relies on the applicant's answers to the questions regarding his physical condition, personal references, and inspection reports. However, the insurance company retains the right to require a medical examination, if an investigation indicates a need for one.

Nonparticipating Insurance Insurance that does not pay dividends to the policyholders.

O

Optional Renewal Policies Policies that are renewable at the option of the insurance company.

Ordinary Life Insurance Insurance policies of $1,000, or multiples thereof, that provide coverage for the entire life of the policyholder and for which the premiums are payable until death. It is also referred to as whole life insurance or straight life insurance, and is different from term insurance in that it includes a cash value build up.

Overinsurance An excessive amount of insurance carried by an insured which might tempt him to prolong his period of disability, remain in a hospital longer than necessary, etc.

P

Paid-Up Additions An additional amount of insurance purchased through dividends (single premium insurance) which increases the amount of protection afforded.

Paid-Up Insurance Life insurance on which future premium payments are not required. Frequently, the term is used to identify a 20-payment life insurance policy on which 20 annual premiums have been paid. Fractional paid-up insurance is the term applied to the policy that is issued under the nonforfeiture option (i.e., when the insured does not wish to pay further premiums on his policy and elects this option).

Partial Disability An illness or injury that prevents an insured from performing one or more of his occupational duties. Usually pays 50% of the total disability benefit.

Participating Insurance Insurance that entitles the policyholder to share in the divisible surplus of the insurance company through dividends.

Payor Clause A clause that provides for the waiver of premiums on a child's policy following the death or the total disability of the adult applicant for the child's policy.

Policy The printed document issued by the insurance company to the insured which is the insurance contract.

Policy Loan A loan made by an insurance company to an insured under his policy (not in excess of its cash value). Policy loans may be assessed a fixed interest rate or an adjustable rate.

Policy Term That period for which the premium is paid and coverage is provided.

Preexisting Condition Any injury occurring, sickness contracted, or physical condition which existed before the issuance of a health policy.

Premium The initial payment and the subsequent periodic payments required to keep a policy in force.

Presumptive Disability These are forms of disability involving loss of hearing, sight, speech or limbs.

Principal Sum The amount payable for loss of life due to accidental death.

Probationary Period A specified number of days after the date of issuance of the policy, during which coverage is not afforded for sickness. Sickness contracted during the probationary period is not covered regardless of the duration of such disability. This is a one-time event whereas an elimination period may occur upon each separate disability.

Proceeds The net amount of money which is payable by the insurance company at the death of an insured or when the policy matures.

Q

Qualified Plan A retirement or employee compensation plan established and maintained by an employer that meets specific guidelines set by the IRS and consequently receives favorable tax treatment.

Quarantine Indemnity A monthly benefit payable while the insured is involuntarily quarantined by a location health department because of exposure to a contagious disease.

R

Rating A method under which an insurance company can issue a policy for a subsequent risk by increasing the premium based on the increased risk involved.

Rebating Paying, offering, or giving anything of value (or any valuable consideration not specified in the policy) to any person as an inducement to purchase a policy of insurance. Rebating is illegal and both parties are guilty of it when it is done knowingly.

Recurrent Disability Clause A provision that specifies a period of time during which the recurrence of a condition is considered a continuation of a prior period of disability or hospital confinement.

Reduced Paid-Up Insurance A nonforfeiture value (option) in a policy that provides for the continuation of the insurance but at a reduced amount. (Sometimes called fractional paid-up insurance.)

Regular Medical Expense Insurance Policies that provide benefits for doctor's fees for nonsurgical care commonly rendered in a hospital, and visits at home or at physician's offices. Sometimes, these benefits are provided under hospital and surgical expense policies.

Reinstatement The resumption of coverage under a policy which lapsed.

Reinsurance The underwriting by one insurance company (called the reinsurer) of part or all of an individual risk written by another insurance company.

Renewable Term Insurance Insurance that may be renewed at the end of the term for another term(s) without evidence of insurability. The rates increase at the end of each term and are based on the attained age of the insured at that time.

Reserve A sum required by law set aside by an insurance company to assure the payment of future claims.

Rider A legal document amending a policy. Additional benefits or a reduction in benefits are often incorporated in policies by an endorsement (rider). A waiver for a health impairment may also be effected by a rider.

Risk (Impaired or Substandard) An applicant whose physical condition does not meet the normal minimum standards.

S

Schedule A list of specific maximum amounts payable, usually for surgical operations, dismemberments, and so forth.

Schedule Type Policy Includes a listing and a complete text of the provisions of each of several benefits, most of which are optional, and some of which may be omitted at the election of the applicant.

Service Benefits Those benefits which are received in the form of specified hospital or medical care rather than in terms of cash amounts.

Settlement Options Methods (other than immediate payment in lump sum) by which an insured (or beneficiary) may choose to have the proceeds of an insurance policy paid.

Single Premium The payment of one premium that is large enough to pay for the claims that may be made during a specified time or for life.

Special Class Risk An applicant who cannot qualify for a standard policy, but may secure one with an endorsement (rider) waiving the payment for a loss involving certain existing health impairments. He may be required to pay a higher premium, or to accept a policy of a type other than the one for which he had applied.

Standard Provisions Certain provisions that must be included in a life insurance policy.

Stock Life Insurance Company A life insurance company owned and controlled by its stockholders who share in its divisible surplus. Generally, stock insurance companies issue nonparticipating life insurance. However, some of them also issue participating life insurance.

Substandard Risk A risk that is less than the standard risk an insurer looks for.

Suicide Clause A provision specifying that in the event the insured commits suicide within two years from the date the policy was issued, the insurance company's liability is limited to the payment of a single sum equal to the premium(s) actually paid (less any indebtedness due the insurance company).

Supplementary Contract An agreement between an insurance company and an insured under which the insurance company retains the lump-sum payable (under a life insurance policy) and makes payments to the insured or the beneficiary in accordance with the settlement option selected by the insured.

Surgical Expense Insurance A policy that provides benefits to pay for the cost of operations.

Surgical Schedule A list of cash allowances which are payable for various types of surgery, with the respective maximum amounts payable based upon the severity of the operations.

Surplus The amount by which the assets exceed the liabilities.

Systematic Premium Plan (Check-O-Matic Plan) A plan under which the insured authorizes a bank to deduct the necessary funds from his account each month to pay a premium which is forwarded to his insurance company by the bank.

T

Term Insurance Insurance which is generally designed to afford coverage for a limited number of years. Usually, no provision is made for cash values. It can be described as pure protection.

Time Limit on Certain Defenses A required Uniform Provision that prohibits an insurance company from contesting the validity of the policy, or from denying a claim for disability commencing (or loss incurred) after two years (sometimes one or three years) from the date of issuance on the ground that the application had made misstatements (except fraudulent misstatements) in the application. This is the accident and health equivalent of life insurance's incontestability clause.

Total Disability An illness or injury that prevents an insured from continuously performing every duty pertaining to his occupation or from engaging in any other type of work for remuneration. (This wording varies from one insurance company to another.)

Travel Accident Insurance Provides benefits for accidental injury while traveling, usually a common carrier. A type of limited policy.

Twisting Inducing an insured to cancel his present insurance and replace it with insurance in the same or another insurance company by misrepresenting the facts or by presenting an incomplete comparison.

U

Unallocated Benefit Reimbursement up to a maximum amount for the cost of extra hospital services, but not specifying the exact amount to be paid for each charge. (This is often referred to as a blanket benefit.)

Underwriting The analysis of information pertaining to an applicant which was obtained from various sources and the determination of whether or not the insurance should be: issued as requested, offered at higher premium, or declined.

W

Waiting Period The duration of time between the beginning of insured's disability and the commencement of the period for which benefits are payable. (*See* Elimination Period.)

Waiver An agreement that waives the liability of the insurance company for certain disabilities or injuries ordinarily covered in the policy.

Waiver Endorsement An agreement that waives the liability of the insurance company for a loss which would normally be covered under the policy.

Waiver of Premium A provision included in many policies that waives the payment of premiums after an insured has been totally disabled for a specific period of time (usually six months).

War Clause A clause in a policy that limits an insurance company's liability if a loss is caused by war.

Warranties and Representations Most state laws specify that all statements by the applicant in the application (or to the medical examiner) are considered (in the absence of fraud) to be representations and not warranties. A warranty must be literally true. A breach of warranty may be sufficient to void the policy whether the warranty is material or not and whether or not such breach of warranty had contributed to the loss. A representation need only to be substantially true. Generally, a representation is considered to be fraudulent if it relates to a situation that would be material to the risk and which the applicant made with fraudulent intent.

Whole Life Insurance *See* Ordinary Life Insurance.

Wholesale Insurance Group insurance written for small groups of employees, usually less than 50. Each employee applies for and receives an individual policy. Usually, this type of insurance is written without a medical examination and the premiums are on a renewable term basis, but higher than on regular group insurance.

Appendix

This appendix contains a sample whole life participating life insurance policy and sample application, as well as a sample health insurance policy and application. These documents are representative of typical policies and applications issued by insurance companies in the United States and contain the standard language and provisions found in actual forms.

LONG LIFE INSURANCE
COMPANY OF AMERICA

WHOLE LIFE POLICY

• We pay the face amount on death of the insured

• Premiums payable as shown on page 3

• Nonparticipating (no annual dividends payable)

We agree to pay the face amount to the beneficiary when the insured dies. We must receive proof that the Insured died while the policy was in force.

Be sure to read this policy. It includes promises, rights, and benefits. These are subject to policy terms.

If you are not satisfied with this policy, return it within 10 days to us or to the representative or agent you bought it from. We will cancel it and return any premium paid.

This policy is a legal contract between you and us.

READ YOUR POLICY CAREFULLY!

Policy Number:	
Insured:	
Face Amount:	
Date of Issue:	
Policy Date:	
Age of Insured:	
Premium Class:	

DEFINITIONS

When we use the following words this is what we mean:

THE INSURED

The person whose life is insured under this policy as shown on page 3.

YOU, YOUR

The owner of this policy, as shown in the application, unless subsequently changed as provided for in this policy. The owner may be someone other than the insured.

WE, OUR, US

The Life Insurance Company

POLICY DATE

The effective date of coverage under this policy and the date from which policy anniversaries, policy years, policy months, and premium due dates are determined.

DATE OF ISSUE

The date the policy is issued and also the date used to determine the start of the suicide and incontestability periods.

POLICY ANNIVERSARY

The same day and month as your policy date for each succeeding year your policy remains in force.

WRITTEN REQUEST

A request in writing on a form acceptable to us signed by you. We also may require that your policy be sent in with your written request.

PROCEEDS

The amount we are obligated to pay under the terms of this policy when our policy is surrendered or matures or when the insured dies.

IN FORCE

The insured's life remains insured under the terms of this policy.

LAPSE

A premium is in default, and the insured's life is no longer insured except as may be provided for in the Policy Values section of this policy.

TERMINATE

The insured's life is no longer insured under any of the terms of this policy.

INDEBTEDNESS

Unpaid policy loans, unpaid policy loan interest, and unpaid premium.

AGE

The insured's age at the insured's nearest birthday.

BENEFICIARY

A beneficiary is any person named in our records to receive insurance proceeds after the Insured dies.

MODE

The manner of premium payment such as monthly, quarterly, semiannually, or annually.

GENERAL PROVISIONS

THE CONTRACT

This is your policy. We issued it in consideration of your application and your payment of premiums. This policy and the attached application make up the entire contract. We agree not to use any statements other than those made in the application in challenging a claim or attempting to avoid liability under this policy.

CHANGE OF PROVISIONS

No Representative or Agent or other person except our President, a Vice President, our Secretary, or an Assistant Secretary has authority to bind us, to extend the time in which you can pay your premiums or to agree to change this policy.

INCONTESTABILITY

This policy is incontestable, unless you do not pay the premium, after it has been in force during the lifetime of the Insured for two years from its Date of Issue, except for any rider which has a separate incontestability clause. This means that we cannot use any misstatement to challenge a claim or avoid liability after that time.

MISSTATEMENT OF AGE OR SEX

If the Insured's age or sex is misstated, we will adjust any proceeds payable to the amounts which the premiums paid would have purchased at the correct age and sex.

EXCLUSIONS

SUICIDE EXCLUSION

If the Insured commits suicide within two years from the Date of Issue, we will limit our payment to a refund of premiums paid, less any Indebtedness.

OWNERSHIP AND BENEFICIARY

OWNERSHIP

This policy belongs to you. The Owner is the Insured unless otherwise designated in the application or unless changed as provided under the Change of Ownership or Beneficiary provision. Unless you provide otherwise, you may exercise all rights and privileges granted by this policy during the Insured's lifetime.

BENEFICIARY

Unless you change the Beneficiary as provided under the Change of Ownership or Beneficiary provision, the Beneficiary will remain as designated on the application.

Any reference to a Beneficiary living or surviving means that the person must be living on the earlier of:

1. the day that we receive due proof of the Insured's death; or
2. the 15th day after the Insured's death.

The legal rights of a Beneficiary are subject to the legal rights of any person to whom the policy has been assigned.

ASSIGNMENT

You may assign this policy. We assume no responsibility for the validity of any assignment, and we will not be considered to have knowledge of it unless it is filed in writing at our Home Office. When it is filed, your rights and those of any Beneficiary will be subject to it.

CHANGE OF OWNERSHIP OR BENEFICIARY

You may change the Owner or Beneficiary of this policy during the lifetime of the Insured. Changes must be requested in writing on a form satisfactory to us and sent to our Home Office. Upon receipt, it is effective as of the date you signed the written request, subject to any payments made or other action taken by us before we received your written request. No change is valid until it is received by us in our Home Office.

You may also name an Owner's Designee in the same manner. The Owner's Designee is the person who will become the Owner if he or she is living and you are still the Owner at the time of your death. This designation may be changed or terminated in writing only.

Transfer to the new Owner is subject to any payment made or action taken by us before we are notified of the prior Owner's death. Notification must be received at our Home Office to be effective.

PREMIUMS

PREMIUMS

The Effective Date is the date from which premium due dates, policy years and policy anniversaries are determined. The first premium is due on the Effective Date. To keep this policy in force during the Insured's lifetime, you must pay each premium for as long as is shown on page 3. You may pay premiums under any mode of payment, subject to our approval. All premiums after the first must be paid by the due date to us at our Home Office.

GRACE PERIOD

All premiums should be paid by the due date. (You do have 31 days after the due date to pay each premium.) If you do not pay the premium within the Grace Period, your policy will lapse unless the premium is paid under the Automatic Premium Loan provision. Policy benefits may be continued under one of the options available if you stop paying premiums. If the insured dies during the grace period, we will deduct any premium due from the proceeds.

REINSTATEMENT

If our policy lapses because you did not pay a premium, we will reinstate it if you ask us to on four conditions:

1. your written request is received at our Home Office within five years of the due date of the first premium which you did not pay;
2. you show us that the Insured is still insurable according to our normal rules;
3. you pay all overdue premiums plus 6% compound interest on premiums; and
4. you repay, or agree to continue in effect, any loan made to you under this policy before it lapsed and also pay any interest on that loan.

CASH VALUE

You may surrender, or turn in this policy at any time, in return for its Cash Value less any Indebtedness. You may request instead, within 60 days after the date your premium was due, to have any one of the Paid-Up Insurance Options take effect instead of paying the premium due.

If you do not choose an option within 60 days after the date your premium was due, or if you die after the 31-day grace period without having chosen an option, the Extended Term Insurance option will automatically take effect if this policy is in the standard premium class. Otherwise, the Reduced Paid-Up Insurance option will automatically take effect.

If your insurance is continued under one of the Paid-Up Insurance Options, it will not include any benefits other than the Face Amount of this policy. No additional benefits in any riders attached to the policy are included in the Paid-Up Insurance Options.

CASH VALUE

The Cash values on policy anniversaries are shown in the Table of Values, assuming all premiums have been paid. The Cash Value at any other time will be determined by us with an allowance for the portion of the premiums paid and the time elapsed in the policy year. The basis for determining Cash Value is explained under Basis of Computation. We may delay the payment of the Cash Value for a period of no more than six months after you request payment.

If you do not pay a premium within 60 days of the date it is due, the Cash Value of the policy remains the same as it was on that date. After 60 days, the Cash Value will be used to purchase the appropriate paid-up benefits.

If the policy is being continued under one of the Paid-Up Options, you may surrender it for its Cash Value. That Cash Value may not be less than the Cash Value on the previous policy anniversary if the policy is surrendered within 31 days of that anniversary.

PAID-UP INSURANCE OPTIONS

EXTENDED TERM INSURANCE

This option is available only if this policy is in the standard premium class. This is shown on page 3. The amount of insurance continued in force will be in the Face Amount less any Indebtedness. The period of Extended Term Insurance will begin on the due date of the first premium which you did not pay. This period is calculated using the Cash Value less any Indebtedness as a net single premium for the Insured's sex and age. This period is shown in the Table of Values based on the assumption that there is no Indebtedness.

REDUCED PAID-UP INSURANCE

Instead of having Extended Term Insurance, you may continue this policy as Reduced Paid-Up Insurance. It is payable at the death of the Insured and is effective from the date to which you have paid premiums. The amount of the Reduced Paid-Up Insurance is shown in the Table of Values based on the assumption that there is no Indebtedness. It is calculated by using the Cash Value less any Indebtedness as a net single premium based on the Insured's sex and age. This option has Cash Value which may be used in the same manner as Cash Value while premiums are being paid.

POLICY LOANS

CASH LOANS

You may take a loan against this policy. You may borrow up to the amount of Cash Value available. The Cash Value available on a premium due date, or during a grace period, or on a policy anniversary date if the policy is on a Paid-Up Insurance Option, is the Cash Value of the policy less any Indebtedness. The Cash Value available at any other time is the amount that, together with loan interest, will equal the Cash Value available on the next premium due date or the next policy anniversary date if the policy is on a Paid-Up Insurance Option.

The annual rate of interest on your loan will be 8%, payable on each policy anniversary. If you do not pay the interest when due, the amount will be added to the loan.

You may repay all or any part of the loan at any time during the lifetime of the Insured. We will not terminate the policy if you do not repay the loan or loan interest unless the loan and the interest together are more than the Cash Value of the policy. In that case, we will terminate the policy 31 days after we mail a termination notice to the last known addresses of both you and any assignee of record.

We may delay making a loan for a period of no more than six months after you request the loan. However, we will not delay the making of loans to pay premiums for this policy.

INDEBTEDNESS

Indebtedness means that you owe money including any interest because of a loan on this policy. Any indebtedness at time of settlement will reduce the proceeds. Indebtedness may be repaid in whole or in part at any time before the policy matures. However, if you do not pay a premium within the grace period, any outstanding Indebtedness can be repaid only if the policy is reinstated. If at any time Indebtedness equals or exceeds the policy's value, the policy will terminate, and we will give any assignee 31 days notice. Notice will be mailed to your and any assignee's last known address.

AUTOMATIC PREMIUM LOAN

You may request on the application or by writing to us at our Home Office that the Automatic Premium Loan provision be used to pay premiums. If this provision is used and your policy has enough Cash Value available, any premium you have not paid by the end of the 31-day grace period will be paid by an Automatic Premium Loan.

When two consecutive premiums have been paid by Automatic premium Loans, the applicable Paid-Up Insurance Option will automatically take effect at the next premium due date.

BASIC OF COMPUTATION

The Commissioners 1958 Standard Ordinary Table of Mortality and compound interest at the rate of 4½% per annum for the first 20 policy years and 3½% per annum thereafter are used to calculate the reserves, cash values, net premiums, and reserve values for this policy; except that any such calculations for extended insurance are made using the Commissioners 1958 Extended Term Insurance table and compound interest at the rate of 4½% per annum for the first 20 policy years and 3½% per annum thereafter. In all such calculations death benefits are assumed payable at the end of the policy year of death. Cash values of the policy are shown in the Table of Values and are equal at each duration to the excess of the then present value per the face amount of future guaranteed benefits over the then present value of the non-forfeiture factors for the remainder of the premium paying period. Values for years not shown in the Table are available on request and will be calculated on the same basis as those shown. During any policy year the amount of cash value and paid-up insurance and the period of extended insurance will be calculated with the due allowance for the lapse of time and the payment of any fractional premiums. The cash value at any time of any paid-up or extended insurance will be the reserve at that time on such insurance, except that within 31 days after a policy anniversary it shall not be less than the cash value on that anniversary. All values are greater than or equal to those required by statute.

Any supplementary benefits which may be included in this policy shall in no way change the values of this policy, unless otherwise specified in those benefits.

CHANGE OF PLAN

You may exchange this policy for another policy on the same plan for a lesser amount. You may also exchange it for another on a different plan if we approve it and you meet all requirements and make all necessary payments.

SETTLEMENT OPTIONS

The policy proceeds payable at the death of the Insured will be paid in one sum or will be applied in whole or in part to any Settlement Option elected. You may select a Settlement Option while the Insured is alive. You may also select the use of more than one Settlement Option. Each election of a Settlement Option you make must include at least $2,500 of policy proceeds. The Settlement Options are described below.

If you have not made an election that is still in force when the proceeds become payable, the payee may elect any available option. Any election must be in writing in a form acceptable to us. Before the date the proceeds become payable, you may elect any valuable option or change a previous election by sending your written request to our Home Office on a form satisfactory to us. Your election or change will take effect as of the date you signed the written request, subject to any payments made or other action taken by us before receipt of the written request.

If no election has been made by the date of the death of the Insured, an election may be made by the Beneficiary within one year of the death of the Insured.

Payments under the following options may be made monthly, quarterly, semiannually, or annually, subject to our minimum payment requirement.

OPTION A—INTEREST PAYMENT

We will hold the proceeds as principal and pay interest at the current rate determined annually by us, but not less than 2½% compounded annually.

The proceeds may be withdrawn at any time by the payee in whole or in part (not less than $250 each time) upon written request.

OPTION B—INCOME OF SPECIFIED

We will pay an income of a specified amount until the principal and interest at not less than 2½% compounded annually are exhausted.

OPTION C—INCOME FOR SPECIFIED PERIOD

We will pay an income for a specified number of years in equal installments, as shown in the following table.

OPTION D—LIFE INCOME

We will pay equal monthly payments for a specified period certain and thereafter for life as shown in the following table.

OPTION E—JOINT AND SURVIVOR INCOME

We will pay an income, based on the age and sex of two payees, as long as either or both of the payees are alive. The following table shows sample minimum monthly installment payments under this option. Payments for different combinations of ages and sexes may be obtained upon request from our Home Office.

We will require proof of age and survival of the payee or payees under Options D and E.

OTHER SETTLEMENT OPTIONS

Provisions may also be made for payment of proceeds of this policy in any reasonable arrangement mutually agreed upon.

EXCESS IN INTEREST

We may pay interest in excess of the guaranteed rate on proceeds held under any option. Excess interest will be paid or credited in amounts and manner as we determine.

Settlement option benefits may not be assigned or subject to encumbrance and, as far as allowed by law, are not subject to claims of creditors or legal process.

We may defer the payment of any amount being withdrawn through the exercise of a withdrawal right for up to six months after it is requested.

AMOUNT OF EACH MONTHLY PAYMENT PER $1,000 OF PROCEEDS—OPTIONS C and D

OPTION C		OPTION D												
Period (Years)	Monthly Payments	Age of Payee		Period of Certain			Age of Payee		Period of Certain			Age of Payee		Period of Certain		
		Male	Female	10 Yrs	15 Yrs	20 Yrs	Male	Female	10 Yrs	15 Yrs	20 Yrs	Male	Female	10 Yrs	15 Yrs	20 Yrs
1	$84.28	11*	16*	$2.71	$2.70	$2.70	36	41	$3.48	$3.45	$3.41	61	66	$5.61	$5.21	$4.75
2	42.66	12	17	2.72	2.72	2.71	37	42	3.53	3.50	3.45	62	67	5.74	5.30	4.80
3	28.79	13	18	2.74	2.74	2.73	38	43	3.59	3.55	3.50	63	68	5.87	5.39	4.85
4	21.86	14	19	2.76	2.76	2.75	39	44	3.64	3.60	3.54	64	69	6.01	5.48	4.90
5	17.70	15	20	2.78	2.78	2.77	40	45	3.70	3.65	3.59	65	70	6.16	5.56	4.94
6	14.93	16	21	2.81	2.80	2.79	41	46	3.76	3.71	3.64	66	71	6.30	5.65	4.98
7	12.95	17	22	2.83	2.82	2.81	42	47	3.82	3.77	3.69	67	72	6.45	5.73	5.02
8	11.47	18	23	2.85	2.84	2.84	43	48	3.88	3.82	3.74	68	73	6.60	5.82	5.05
9	10.32	19	24	2.87	2.87	2.86	44	49	3.95	3.88	3.75	69	74	6.76	5.90	5.09
10	9.39	20	25	2.90	2.89	2.88	45	50	4.02	3.95	3.84	70	75	6.91	5.97	5.12
11	8.64	21	26	2.93	2.92	2.91	46	51	4.09	4.01	3.90	71	76	7.07	6.05	5.14
12	8.02	22	27	2.95	2.95	2.93	47	52	4.17	4.08	3.95	72	77	7.23	6.12	5.17
13	7.49	23	28	2.98	2.97	2.96	48	53	4.25	4.15	4.01	73	78	7.38	6.18	5.19
14	7.03	24	29	3.01	3.00	2.99	49	54	4.33	4.22	4.07	74	79	7.54	6.24	5.20
15	6.64	25	30	3.04	3.03	3.02	50	55	4.42	4.29	4.12	75	80	7.69	6.30	5.22
16	6.30	26	31	3.08	3.07	3.05	51	56	4.50	4.37	4.18	76	81	7.84	6.35	5.23
17	6.00	27	32	3.11	3.10	3.08	52	57	4.60	4.44	4.24	77	82	7.98	6.39	5.24
18	5.73	28	33	3.14	3.13	3.11	53	58	4.69	4.52	4.30	78	83	8.13	6.43	5.25
19	5.49	29	34	3.18	3.17	3.15	54	59	4.79	4.60	4.36	79	84	8.26	6.47	5.26
20	5.27	30	35	3.22	3.20	3.18	55	60	4.90	4.69	4.41	80	85	8.39	6.50	5.26
21	5.08	31	36	3.26	3.24	3.22	56	61	5.01	4.77	4.47	81	86	8.51	6.53	5.27
22	4.90	32	37	3.30	3.28	3.25	57	62	5.12	4.86	4.53	82	87	8.63	6.55	5.27
23	4.74	33	38	3.34	3.32	3.29	58	63	5.23	4.94	4.59	83	88	8.73	6.57	5.27
24	4.60	34	39	3.39	3.36	3.33	59	64	5.35	5.03	4.64	84	89	8.83	6.59	5.27
25	4.46	35	40	3.43	3.41	3.37	60	65	5.48	5.12	4.70	85†	90†	8.92	6.60	5.27
		*And under										† And over				

AMOUNT OF EACH MONTHLY PAYMENT PER $1,000 OF PROCEEDS—OPTION E
(Based on the payees' ages at their nearest birthdays on the date the proceeds are settled under the option)

Age	Amount	Age	Amount	Age	Amount
55	$3.92	62	$4.55	69	$5.46
56	3.99	63	4.66	70	5.63
57	4.07	64	4.77	71	5.80
58	4.16	65	4.90	72	5.98
59	4.25	66	5.03	73	6.18
60	4.34	67	5.16	74	6.38
61	4.44	68	5.31	75	6.60

Note: Values shown apply if the payees are a man and a woman of equal ages. Other values for ages 55–75 are available on request.

TABLE OF POLICY VALUES

The cash or loan values of the policy and amounts of paid-up insurance and nonforfeiture factors shown are for each $1,000 face amount. The periods of extended insurance shown are the same for any face amount. The values in the Table are applicable only at the ends of the policy years shown, provided no premium is in default. When an "Age" is shown in the "End of Policy Year" column, the values are those applicable at the policy anniversary nearest the birthday on which the Insured attains that age. The values are applicable to this policy, determined by the age nearest the birthday of the Insured on the policy date, assuming that there is no indebtedness.

End of Policy Year	Cash or Loan	Paid Up	†Extended Insurance Yrs	Days	Cash or Loan	Paid Up	†Extended Insurance Yrs	Days	Cash or Loan	Paid Up	†Extended Insurance Yrs	Days	Cash or Loan	Paid Up	†Extended Insurance Yrs	Days	Cash or Loan	Paid Up	†Extended Insurance Yrs	Days	End of Policy Years
	Issue Age M–24/F–30				Issue Age M–25/F–31				Issue Age M–26/F–32				Issue Age M–27/F–32				Issue Age M–28/F–34				
1	0.00	0	0	0	0.00	0	0	0	0.00	0	0	0	0.00	0	0	0	0.00	0	0	0	1
2	2.00	0	0	0	0.00	0	0	0	0.00	0	0	0	0.00	0	0	0	0.00	0	0	0	2
3	0.00	0	0	0	1.00	3	0	138	2.00	10	0	270	2.00	9	0	265	3.00	13	1	25	2
4	9.00	42	3	187	11.00	30	4	91	12.00	53	4	204	13.00	55	4	305	14.00	58	5	21	4
5	19.00	85	7	222	21.00	91	8	65	23.00	97	8	220	24.00	98	8	205	26.00	103	8	277	5
6	30.00	128	11	193	32.00	133	11	143	34.00	137	11	258	36.00	141	11	238	38.00	145	11	190	6
7	41.00	169	14	139	43.00	172	14	97	45.00	173	14	11	48.00	181	13	352	31.00	187	13	295	7
8	32.00	204	16	191	55.00	212	16	132	58.00	217	16	46	61.00	222	15	299	64.00	226	15	168	8
9	64.00	244	18	81	67.00	248	17	314	70.00	253	17	161	74.00	259	17	57	77.00	262	16	240	9
10	76.00	279	19	158	80.00	282	19	35	83.00	200	18	198	87.00	293	18	44	91.00	298	17	241	10
11	89.00	313	20	164	93.00	320	19	357	97.00	324	19	170	101.00	327	18	342	106.00	334	18	185	11
12	102.00	347	21	60	106.00	351	20	216	111.00	357	20	46	116.00	362	19	229	121.00	367	19	42	12
13	116.00	380	21	282	212.00	385	21	87	126.00	390	20	248	131.00	394	20	46	136.00	397	19	190	13
14	130.00	410	22	63	135.00	414	21	206	141.00	420	21	19	146.00	423	20	151	152.00	428	19	317	14
15	143.00	440	22	186	131.00	446	21	345	156.00	448	21	96	162.00	452	20	245	169.00	459	20	57	15
16	160.00	468	22	255	166.00	472	22	28	173.00	478	21	193	179.00	481	20	323	186.00	486	20	113	16
17	176.00	496	22	310	183.00	501	22	96	189.00	503	21	211	196.00	508	20	353	203.00	512	20	128	17
18	192.00	321	22	323	199.00	525	22	91	204.00	329	21	221	214.00	534	21	10	221.00	537	20	133	18
19	209.00	546	22	326	217.00	552	22	106	224.00	554	21	221	232.00	559	20	359	240.00	563	20	129	19
20	227.00	572	22	321	234.00	573	22	39	243.00	580	21	211	251.00	583	20	335	259.00	586	20	92	20
AGE																					AGE
M60	474.00	804	17	142	469.00	796	17	58	465.00	789	16	356	460.00	780	16	276	453.00	772	16	197	60-M
F-65	437.00	792	17	275	453.00	783	17	208	448.00	777	17	123	443.00	768	17	39	438.00	759	16	322	65-F
M65	333.00	849	13	101	530.00	844	13	55	546.00	838	14	359	542.00	832	14	302	538.00	826	14	246	65-M
F-66	474.00	804	17	142	469.00	796	17	58	465.00	769	16	356	460.00	780	16	276	435.00	772	16	197	66F

Years	Nonforfeiture Features	Years	Nonforfeiture Features	Years	Nonforfeiture Features	Years	Nonforfeiture Features	Years	Nonforfeiture Features
1–20	$11.08836	1–20	$11.43719	1–20	$11.80509	1–20	$12.19269	1–20	$12.60181
21–71	$9.62081	21–75	$9.97732	21–74	$10.35254	21–73	$10.74786	21–72	$11.16435

End of Policy Year	Issue Age M–24/F–30				Issue Age M–25/F–31				Issue Age M–26/F–32				Issue Age M–27/F–32				Issue Age M–28/F–34				End of Policy Years
	Cash or Loan	Paid Up	†Extended Insurance Yrs	Days	Cash or Loan	Paid Up	†Extended Insurance Yrs	Days	Cash or Loan	Paid Up	†Extended Insurance Yrs	Days	Cash or Loan	Paid Up	†Extended Insurance Yrs	Days	Cash or Loan	Paid Up	†Extended Insurance Yrs	Days	
1	0.00	0	0	0	0.00	0	0	0	0.00	0	0	0	0.00	0	0	0	0.00	0	0	0	1
2	0.00	0	0	0	0.00	0	0	0	0.00	0	0	0	0.00	0	0	0	0.00	0	0	0	2
3	4.00	17	1	148	5.00	21	1	262	6.00	24	2	2	7.00	27	2	87	8.00	30	2	150	2
4	14.00	64	5	200	17.00	66	5	218	19.00	72	5	316	20.00	73	5	278	22.00	78	5	317	4
5	28.00	108	8	310	30.00	112	8	214	32.00	116	8	282	34..00	120	8	234	36.00	123	8	172	5
6	40.00	148	11	117	43.00	154	11	104	45.00	157	10	357	48.00	163	10	302	50.00	164	10	167	6
7	53.00	189	13	141	56.00	194	13	47	59.00	198	12	300	62.00	202	12	177	65.00	206	12	47	7
8	67.00	230	15	25	70.00	233	14	233	73.00	236	14	71	77.00	242	14	319	80.00	244	13	144	8
9	81.00	267	16	105	83.00	272	15	325	88.00	274	15	122	92.00	278	14	329	96.00	282	14	165	9
10	95.00	302	17	66	99.00	306	16	250	104.00	312	16	106	108.00	315	15	379	112.00	318	15	84	10
11	110.00	337	17	344	115.00	342	17	172	119.00	344	16	323	124.00	349	16	142	129.00	353	15	324	11
12	126.00	371	18	212	131.00	375	18	14	136.00	379	17	175	141.00	382	16	335	146.00	385	16	126	12
13	142.00	403	19	10	147.00	406	18	152	153.00	411	17	326	158.00	413	17	100	144.00	417	16	267	13
14	158.00	433	19	112	164.00	437	18	268	170.00	441	18	57	176.00	444	17	207	182.00	447	16	356	14
15	175.00	462	19	197	181.00	465	18	335	188.00	470	16	133	194.00	472	17	268	201.00	476	17	62	15
16	192.00	489	19	237	199.00	493	19	22	206.00	497	18	168	213.00	500	17	314	220.00	503	17	93	16
17	210.00	315	19	264	218.00	521	19	59	225.00	524	18	191	233.00	528	17	346	240.00	530	17	113	17
18	229.00	542	19	280	237.00	546	19	59	244.00	548	18	180	252.00	552	17	323	260.00	535	17	100	18
19	248.00	566	19	262	256.00	569	19	29	264.00	572	18	160	273.00	577	17	312	261.00	579	17	79	19
20	268.00	590	19	235	276.00	593	18	356	285.00	597	18	132	294.00	600	17	273	303.00	604	17	50	20
AGE																					AGE
M60	449.00	762	16	101	444.00	753	16	22	438.00	743	15	295	432.00	733	15	205	425.00	721	13	100	60-M
F-65	433.00	751	16	243	427.00	740	16	147	421.00	730	16	32	414.00	718	15	309	407.00	706	15	203	65-F
M65	533.00	818	14	175	528.00	810	14	105	523.00	803	14	34	518.00	795	13	332	512.00	786	13	254	65-M
F-66	449.00	762	16	101	444.00	753	16	22	438.00	743	15	295	432.00	733	15	205	425.00	721	15	100	66F

Years	Nonforfeiture Features	Years	Nonforfeiture Features	Years	Nonforfeiture Features	Years	Nonforfeiture Features	Years	Nonforfeiture Features
1–20	$12.99747	1–20	$13.45368	1–20	$13.93581	1–20	$14.44525	1–20	$14.98462
21–71	$11.60317	21–70	$12.06613	21–69	$12.55471	21–68	$13.07110	21–67	$13.61718

End of Policy Year	Cash or Loan	Paid Up	†Extended Insurance Yrs	†Extended Insurance Days	Cash or Loan	Paid Up	†Extended Insurance Yrs	†Extended Insurance Days	Cash or Loan	Paid Up	†Extended Insurance Yrs	†Extended Insurance Days	Cash or Loan	Paid Up	†Extended Insurance Yrs	†Extended Insurance Days	Cash or Loan	Paid Up	†Extended Insurance Yrs	†Extended Insurance Days	End of Policy Years
	Issue Age M–24/F–30				Issue Age M–25/F–31				Issue Age M–26/F–32				Issue Age M–27/F–32				Issue Age M–28/F–34				
1	0.00	0	0	0	0.00	0	0	0	0.00	0	0	0	0.00	0	0	0	0.00	0	0	0	1
2	0.00	0	0	0	0.00	0	0	0	0.00	0	0	0	0.00	0	0	0	0.00	0	0	0	2
3	10.00	36	2	293	11.00	39	2	312	12.00	41	2	318	13.00	13	2	315	14.00	45	2	307	2
4	23.00	79	5	249	25.00	84	5	253	27.00	88	3	243	28.00	88	5	158	30.00	92	5	133	4
5	38.00	123	8	99	40.00	129	8	20	42.00	131	5	297	44.00	134	7	205	46.00	136	7	110	5
6	53.00	169	10	90	55.00	171	9	312	58.00	175	7	218	60.00	176	9	71	63.00	179	8	335	6
7	68.00	209	11	276	71.00	212	11	135	74.00	215	9	357	77.00	218	10	209	80.00	220	10	61	7
8	84.00	249	13	14	87.00	251	12	197	91.00	255	10	56	94.00	256	11	236	98.00	260	11	88	8
9	100.00	206	13	363	104.00	289	13	189	108.00	292	12	16	112.00	295	12	203	116.00	297	12	26	9
10	117.00	323	14	289	121.00	325	14	88	126.00	329	13	285	130.00	330	13	83	135.00	334	12	276	10
11	134.00	356	15	135	139.00	360	14	309	144.00	363	13	116	149.00	365	13	288	154.00	368	13	95	11
12	152.00	390	15	312	157.00	392	15	100	163.00	396	14	280	168.00	398	14	69	174.00	402	13	248	12
13	170.00	421	16	66	176.00	424	15	229	182.00	427	14	27	188.00	430	14	169	194.00	433	13	354	13
14	189.00	452	16	164	195.00	454	15	311	203.00	456	15	93	208.00	460	14	266	215.00	464	14	73	14
15	208.00	480	16	219	215.00	484	16	11	222.00	487	15	168	229.00	480	14	126	236.00	492	14	120	15
16	228.00	508	16	260	235.00	311	16	39	242.00	513	15	183	250.00	517	14	351	257.00	519	14	135	16
17	248.00	534	16	266	255.00	536	16	35	263.00	539	15	190	271.00	542	14	346	279.00	545	14	138	17
18	268.00	558	16	243	277.00	562	16	41	283.00	565	15	185	293.00	567	14	332	302.00	571	14	132	18
19	290.00	583	16	231	298.00	585	16	1	307.00	589	15	155	316.00	592	14	310	325.00	595	14	103	19
20	311.00	603	16	176	321.00	610	15	336	330.00	612	15	118	339.00	615	14	266	348.00	617	14	53	20
AGE																					AGE
M60	418.00	709	14	361	411.00	697	14	261	403.00	684	14	147	395.00	670	14	33	386.00	655	13	275	60-M
F-65	400.00	693	15	92	393.00	681	14	357	384.00	666	14	227	376.00	652	14	112	367.00	636	13	348	65-F
M65	506.00	777	13	176	500.00	767	13	97	493.00	757	13	6	486.00	746	12	286	479.00	735	12	201	65-M
F-66	418.00	709	14	361	411.00	697	14	261	403.00	684	14	147	393.00	670	14	33	386.00	655	13	273	66F

Years	Nonforfeiture Features	Years	Nonforfeiture Features	Years	Nonforfeiture Features	Years	Nonforfeiture Features	Years	Nonforfeiture Features
1–20	$15.55601	1–20	$16.16216	1–20	$16.80426	1–20	$17.48469	1–20	$18.20570
21–66	$14.19507	21–65	$14.80600	21–64	$15.45194	21–63	$16.13455	21–62	$16.85451

†Extended Insurance is not available if this policy is rated as a substandard class as shown on page 3.
Note: Not all age tables are shown.

LIFE INSURANCE APPLICATION
Long Life Insurance Company

PART I   The following questions relate to the person proposed for insurance

1. Proposed insured—First name, middle initial, last name ☐ Male ☐ Female	16. Beneficiary

16. Beneficiary

Class	Name(s) (please print clearly)	Relationship to insured

2. Date of birth month day year	3. Age nearest birthday	4. Place of birth	

5. Telephone numbers
Day: Night:

6. Address for premium notices (bills will be sent to owner at this address)

7. Residence of insured (if different)

If two or more beneficiaries are named, state the class: 1, 2, 3, etc. Surviving beneficiaries in the lowest class share equally. All decisions made by LL in good faith as to the identity of beneficiaries not designated by name shall be conclusive as to LL's liability, and any payment made in accordance therewith shall, to the extent thereof, discharge LL of its obligation for such payment.

8. Social Security number of the insured	9. Amount of existing LL Insurance $

17. Will coverage applied for replace or change any existing life insurance or annuity (other than LL)? If "Yes," submit form A-52.   ☐ Yes   ☐ No

10. Any other name now or previously known by (incl. maiden name, if applicable)

18.   If a group insurance conversion:
Group name: _____
Date group insurance
terminated: _____   ☐ Policy terminated
                                     ☐ Employment terminated

11. Within the last 12 months has the insured smoked: Cigarettes? ☐ Yes ☐ No
(a urine test may be required)   Cigars or a pipe? ☐ Yes ☐ No

Note: Part 2 on the reverse side should be completed only if Waiver of Premium is requested in question 12 or #5 in question 13.

12. Insurance amount and plan

Basic policy $ Plan

Insured rider $ Plan

Children rider $ Term to age 22 Insurance
                            (complete Child Rider questionnaire)
Waiver of Premium   ☐ Yes   ☐ No   (issue ages 15–55 only)

19. Conversion or exchange of existing LL insurance (other than group):
Total face amount: _____   Plan: _____

Policy numbers:

_____   _____   _____

_____   _____   _____

_____   _____   _____

13. Dividends (if selection is missing or not available, #4 will be effective)
1 ☐ Pay in cash
2 ☐ Reduce amount due—any excess dividend as ☐ #4   ☐ #3   ☐ #2
3 ☐ Purchase paid-up life additions (not available on term insurance)
4 ☐ Accumulate at interest
5 ☐ Purchase one-year term additions (not available on term insurance)

The above policies are hereby tendered (1) for endorsement, if a rider insurance conversion, or (2) for surrender, if basic policy conversion or exchange; in consideration for an effective as of the date of issue of the insurance herein applied for. If a surrender, pay any cash or dividend values to me. (The above policies must accompany this application).

If Term Conversion, Part 2 on the reverse side should be completed only if #5 is selected in question 13 or if Waiver of Premium is requested in question 2.

For Exchanges, Part 2 on the reverse side must be completed in all cases unless notified otherwise.

14. Premium payment frequency ☐ Annual ☐ Semiannual ☐ Quarterly	Automatic Premium Loan Provision to be effective on permanent insurance unless requested otherwise.

20.   Special requests

15. Owner (if no owner is shown, the applicant will be the owner.)

Class	Name (please print clearly)	Age	Relationship to insured
1.			
2.			
3.			

21.   How did you hear about LL?
☐ Family member has LL ☐ Newspaper ☐ Radio ☐ TV ☐ Mail insert
☐ Bank lobby sign ☐ Friend or relative ☐ Other:

22.   Changes made by LL

23.   Issuing bank:
No.   Name:

1. Under penalty of perjury, I certify that the Social Security number(s) is/are correct and that I am not subject to backup withholding.
2. I hereby certify that the statements above are correct and agree that LL, believing them to be correct, shall rely and act on them.
3. If LL makes a change in space 22, it will be approved by my acceptance of the policy.
4. I agree that the insurance applied for shall not take effect until the first full premium is paid and the policy delivered while each person to be insured is in good health. Once submitted, this application will remain the property of LL.

_____   X _____
Date   Signature of Insured (if age 15 or over)

X _____
Signature of First Owner in question 15, if any

X _____
Signature of Applicant (if other than Insured)
If Insured is under 15, check if: ☐ Mother ☐ Father ☐ Guardian

X _____
Signature of First Owner in question 15, if any

Action	Date	By	Agent No.	Agent Signature		
R/R			Agency	Source, if diff.	Initial Premium Rec'd $	Date Received

Name of Proposed Insured (print)

PART 2   To be completed by the LL agent if non-medical. (If this is to be a medical application, the examiner will complete this section.)

	Details of "YES" answers. Identify the question number. Include diagnosis, dates, duration, names and addresses of all attending physicians and medical facilities. Give reason for checkup, treatment, and medication.

1. (a) Employer's name and address

(b) Job title and exact duties

(c) Years so employed	(d) Change in occupation contemplated?	☐ Yes	☐ No
	Other occupations last two years?	☐ Yes	☐ No

2. (a) Do you intend to reside or travel outside the United States and Canada
        except for vacations?   ☐ Yes   ☐ No
    (b) Have you ever made claim for or received any pension or disability benefits?   ☐ Yes   ☐ No
    (c) Have you ever had an application for life or health insurance declined,
        postponed, modified or offered at other than regular premiums for your age?   ☐ Yes   ☐ No

3. (a) Do you participate in parachuting, motor racing, or any other
        hazardous avocations?   ☐ Yes   ☐ No
    (b) Do you own, operate or are you licensed to operate an airplane?   ☐ Yes   ☐ No
    (c) How many flights have you made in the past 12 months in other
        than commercial airlines/airplanes?   ☐ Yes   ☐ No

4. Have you ever consulted any doctor or practitioner for, or suffered from any illness or disease of:
    (a) The brain or nervous system?   ☐ Yes   ☐ No
    (b) The heart, blood vessels, or lungs?   ☐ Yes   ☐ No
    (c) The stomach or intestines?   ☐ Yes   ☐ No
    (d) The skin, glands, middle ear, hearing, eyes, or vision?   ☐ Yes   ☐ No

5. Have you ever had or been advised to have an electrocardiogram,
    Xray, or other diagnostic test?   ☐ Yes   ☐ No

6. Have you ever had or been treated for rheumatism, bone disease,
    cancer, syphilis, or other venereal disease, or any disorder of the
    muscle or bones, including the spine, back, or joints?   ☐ Yes   ☐ No

7. Have you ever had or been treated for: chest pain, dizziness, fainting,
    convulsions, allergies, asthma, shortness of breath, persistent cough,
    repeated headache, paralysis, stroke, or diabetes?   ☐ Yes   ☐ No

8. Have you even been treated for or had any known indication of:
    (a) Alcoholism?   ☐ Yes   ☐ No
    (b) Mental or nervous disorder?   ☐ Yes   ☐ No
    (c) Any deformity or congenital disorder?   ☐ Yes   ☐ No

9. Have you ever used or dealt in barbiturates, excitants or hallucinogens,
    narcotics, or other habit forming drugs?   ☐ Yes   ☐ No

10. Are you now being treated or taking medicine for any condition
    or disease?   ☐ Yes   ☐ No

11. Have you ever consulted a doctor or practitioner for, or had any known
    indication of, any illness, disease, or physical defect or disorder not
    included in the above question?   ☐ Yes   ☐ No

12. Other than above, within the past three years, have you had a checkup,
    consultation, illness, injury, surgery, or been a patient in a hospital,
    clinic, sanitarium, or other medical facility?   ☐ Yes   ☐ No

13. Females age 15 and over only:
    (a) Ever had any disorder of menstruation, pregnancy, or of
        the female organs or breasts?   ☐ Yes   ☐ No
    (b) Are you now pregnant?   ☐ Yes   ☐ No
    (c) Ever had a caesarean section?   ☐ Yes   ☐ No
    (d) Are uterine functions now irregular?   ☐ Yes   ☐ No
    (e) Number of children _____

14. Height (in shoes) _____ ft. _____ in. Weight (clothed) _____ lbs.
    Has weight changed in the past two years? ☐ Yes ☐ No
    If "Yes": Gain _____ lbs., Loss _____ lbs. How long at present weight? _____

15. Family History—Indicate below any diabetes, cancer, high blood pressure, heart or kidney disease, mental illness, or suicide.

Family Member	Age If Living	State	Age at Death
Father			
Mother			
Brothers & Sisters No. Living _____ No. Dead _____			

Date	X Signature of Examiner (Agent if non-medical)

I hereby certify that the above answers and statements are correct and I agree that LL, believing them to be correct, shall rely and act on them. I agree that they shall be a part of my application for insurance or policy change request. I acknowledge receipt of the attached Disclosure Notice and MIB Notification.

I HEREBY AUTHORIZE any licensed physician, medical practitioner, hospital, clinic, or other medical or medically related facility, insurance company, the Medical Information Bureau or other organization, institution or person, that has any records or knowledge of the Proposed Insured or his/her health to give to the Medical Director, Long Life Insurance, any such information.

A photographic copy of this authorization shall be as valid as the original.

Name of Proposed Insured (please print)	Date	X Signature of Proposed Insured (parent or guardian if insured under age 15)

2

PART 3   To be completed by an Examiner authorized by LL. Omit if non-medical.

16. Males only	17. Blood Pressure	18. Pulse	19. Urinalysis
Chest (inspiration) _____ in. Chest (expiration) _____ in. Waist _____ in.	Systolic Diastolic (All sound ceases) If over 138/88, repeat twice 3 minutes apart	Rate _____ Quality _____ Irregularities per minute _____	Albumin _____ Sugar _____

20. For question 14 answers Did you measure? ☐ Yes ☐ No Did you weigh? ☐ Yes ☐ No	21. Did you observe any indication of physical or mental impairment or abnormality not indicated in Part 2? ☐ Yes ☐ No If "Yes" explain:

I have personally seen the person whose name appears in Part 2. I am satisfied as to the identity of that person. I certify that the answers in Part 2 were correctly recorded by me.

Paramedic Stamp:

_____   X _____   _____
        Date   Examiner

ERIE HEALTH INSURANCE
COMPANY OF AMERICA

Erie Health agrees, in accordance with the provisions of this policy, to pay the benefits provided in this policy due to injury or sickness.

Twenty-Day Right to Examine Policy   You may return this policy by delivering it to the Home Office or to an agent of the Company within 20 days after receiving it. Immediately on such delivery, the policy will be void as of the date of issue and any premium paid will be refunded.

President

Secretary

Insured:	
Policy Number:	
Policy Date:	

1

DEFINITIONS

"You," "Your," and "Yours" means the insured named on the Policy Schedule. "Time," "Us," and "Ours" means the Company.

COVERED PERSON

Covered person means the insured and all eligible dependents shown on the policy schedule, or added by endorsement.

CUSTODIAL CARE

Means care given to a covered person if the person:

1. is mentally or physically disabled and such disability is expected to last for an indefinite time;

2. needs a protected, monitored, and/or controlled environment;

3. needs help to support the essentials of daily living; and

4. is not under active and specific medical, surgical and/or psychiatric treatment, which will reduce the disability to the extent necessary for the person to function outside a protected, monitored, and/or controlled environment.

DENTAL SERVICE

Means any medical or surgical procedure that involves the hard or soft tissue of the mouth that requires treatment as a result of a disease or condition of the teeth and gums. Treatment for neoplasms is not considered a dental service.

DISABLED DEPENDENTS

This section amends the Eligible Dependents section. An unmarried child who cannot support himself due to mental incapacity or physical handicap may continue to be insured. This child must be fully dependent upon you for support. The Company may inquire of you two months before attainment by a dependent of the limiting age set forth in this policy, or at any reasonable time thereafter, whether such dependent is in fact a disabled and dependent person. In the absence of proof submitted within 60 days of such inquiry that such dependent is a disabled and dependent person, the Company may terminate coverage of such person at or after attainment of the limiting age. In the absence of such inquiry, coverage of any disabled and dependent person shall continue through the term of such policy or any extension or renewal thereof.

EFFECTIVE DATE OF COVERAGE

A covered person's effective date of coverage is: (1) the policy date, if the covered person is listed on the application and the policy schedule; or (2) the date of policy endorsement, if the covered person is added.

ELIGIBLE DEPENDENTS

Eligible dependents are those dependents shown on the policy schedule or added by endorsement. This may include: (1) Your lawful spouse; and (2) Unmarried dependent children, including step-children and adopted children (or children who are in your custody pursuant to an interim court order of adoption),

if they are legally dependent on you for their support and under 21 years of age.

Your newborn children, born while the policy is in force, will be covered for 60 days after birth. For coverage beyond 60 days after birth, written application must be made to the Company within that 60-day period. An additional premium will be required retroactive to date of birth. Other eligible dependents may be added by you upon evidence of insurability satisfactory to the Company. Additional premium will be required.

ELIGIBLE FOR MEDICARE

Means that the covered person is either:

1. covered by both Part A and Part B of Medicare; or

2. not covered for both Part A and Part B of Medicare because of:

   a. a failure to enroll when required;

   b. a failure to pay any premium that may be required for full coverage of the person under Medicare; or

   c. a failure to file any written request, claim or document required for payment of Medicare benefits.

HOSPICE PROGRAM

Means a coordinated interdisciplinary program for meeting the special physical, psychological, spiritual, and social needs of dying covered persons and their immediate families. The covered person must be enrolled in the program by a physician.

HOSPITAL

Means a place other than a convalescent, nursing, or rest home, that:

■ provides facilities for medical, diagnostic, and acute care on an inpatient basis. If these services are not on its own premises, they must be available through a prearranged contract;

■ provides 24-hour nursing care supervised by registered nurses;

■ has x-ray and lab facilities either on its premises or available through a prearranged contract; and

■ charges for these services.

A special ward, floor, or other accommodation for convalescent, nursing, or rehabilitation purposes is not considered a hospital.

IMMEDIATE FAMILY

Means you, your spouse, and the children, brothers, sisters, and parents of either you or your spouse.

INJURY

Injury means accidental bodily injury sustained by a covered person while covered under this policy.

MEDICALLY NECESSARY CARE

Means confinement, treatment or service that is rendered to diagnose or treat a sickness or injury. Such care must be (1) prescribed by a physician; (2) considered to be necessary and appropriate for the diagnosis and treatment of the sickness or injury; and (3) commonly accepted as proper care or treatment of the condition by the US medical community. Medically necessary care does not include care considered to be: (1) experimental or investigative in nature by any appropriate technological assessment body established by any state or federal government; (2) provided only as a convenience to the covered person or provider; and (3) in excess (in scope, duration or intensity) of that level of care which is needed to provide safe, adequate and appropriate diagnosis and treatment. The fact that a physician may prescribe, order, recommend or approve a service or supply does not, of itself, make the service or supply medically necessary.

MEDICARE

Medicare means the Health Insurance for the Aged Act, Title XVIII of the Social Security Act as amended.

MENTAL ILLNESS

Mental illness means a mental or nervous disorder, including neuroses, psychoneurosis, psychopathy, psychosis and other emotional disorders. Affective disorders (including bipolar disorders and major depression), alcoholism, drug addiction and chemical dependency are also included in this definition.

OTHER HEALTH INSURANCE PLAN

This means any plan that provides insurance, reimbursement or service benefits for hospital, surgical or other medical expenses. This includes: (1) individual or group health insurance policies; (2) non-profit health service plans, including Blue Cross and Blue Shield; (3) health maintenance organization subscriber contracts; (4) self-insured group plans; (5) welfare plans; (6) medical coverage under homeowners or automobile insurance; and (7) service provided or payment received under laws of any national, state or local government. This does not include Medicaid.

If coverage is provided on a service basis, the amount of benefits under such coverage will be taken as the cost of the service in the absence of such coverage.

PART A

Means the Hospital Insurance Benefits for the Aged portion of Medicare.

PART B

Means the Supplementary Medical Insurance for the Aged portion of Medicare.

PHYSICAL MEDICINE

Means the diagnosis and treatment of physical conditions relating to bone, muscle or neuromuscular pathology.

PHYSICIAN

A person licensed by the state to treat the kind of injury or sickness for which a claim is made. The physician must be practicing within the limits of his or her license.

POLICY OWNER

The insured shown on the policy schedule unless someone else is designated the owner on the application.

PRE-EXISTING CONDITIONS

A pre-existing condition is a condition not fully disclosed on the application for insurance:

1. for which the covered person received medical treatment or advice from a physician within the six-month period immediately preceding that covered person's effective date of coverage; or

2. which produced signs or symptoms within the six-month period immediately preceding that covered person's effective date of coverage.

   The signs or symptoms must have been significant enough to establish manifestation or onset by one of the following tests:

   a. The signs or symptoms would have allowed one learned in medicine to make a diagnosis of the disorder; or

   b. The signs or symptoms should have caused an ordinarily prudent person to seek diagnosis or treatment.

Pre-existing conditions will be covered after the covered person has been insured for two years, if the condition is not specifically excluded from coverage.

REASONABLE AND CUSTOMARY CHARGE

Means the lesser of:

1. The actual charge;

2. What the provider would accept for the same service or supply in the absence of insurance; or

3. The reasonable charge as determined by the Company, based on factors such as:

   a. the most common charge for the same or comparable service or supply in a community similar to where the service or supply is furnished;

   b. the amount of resources expended to deliver the treatment and the complexity of the treatment rendered; and

   c. charging protocols and billing practices generally accepted by the medical community or specialty groups; or

   d. inflation trends by geographic region.

SICKNESS

Sickness means an illness, disease or condition of a covered person that manifests itself after the covered person's effective date of coverage. For sickness that manifests itself during the first 15 days following the effective date, coverage is provided only for covered expenses incurred after that 15-day period.

SKILLED NURSING FACILITY

Means a nursing home, licensed as a skilled nursing facility, operating in accordance with the laws of the state in which it is located and meeting the following requirements:

1. Is primarily engaged in providing room, board and skilled nursing care for persons recovering from sickness or injury;

2. Provides 24-hour-a-day skilled nursing service under the full-time supervision of a physician or graduate registered nurse;

3. Maintains daily clinical records;

4. Has transfer arrangements with a hospital;

5. Has a utilization review plan in effect;

6. Is not a place for rest, the aged, drug addicts, alcoholics or the mentally ill; and

7. May be a part of a hospital.

COVERAGE DESCRIPTION

DEDUCTIBLE AMOUNT

The deductible amount for each covered person during each calendar year is the larger of:

■ the basic deductible amount shown in the policy schedule; or

■ the amount of benefits paid for covered expenses by any other health insurance plan as defined in the policy.

The deductible amount must be:

■ incurred each calendar year; and

■ deducted from covered expenses.

A calendar year begins on January 1 and ends December 31.

MAXIMUM FAMILY DEDUCTIBLE AMOUNT

A maximum family deductible amount equal to three times the basic deductible amount will satisfy the deductible requirements for all covered persons in a family during a calendar year.

FAMILY CAP MAXIMUM

The maximum expense amount incurred per family for covered expense will not exceed the family cap maximum shown in the policy schedule for any calendar year.

CARRY-OVER DEDUCTIBLE

Any covered expense incurred and applied to a covered person's basic deductible amount during the last three months of a calendar year may also be used to reduce that person's basic deductible amount for the next calendar year.

The maximum family deductible and the carry-over deductible provisions will not apply if the benefits paid by other health insurance are used as the deductible.

RIGHT TO CHANGE DEDUCTIBLE AMOUNT

You may apply for an increase or decrease in the basic deductible amount within a 60-day period after a premium rate change, or during the first 30 days of a calendar year, provided that: (1) the new basic deductible amount is one that is available on this form, (2) a request for the change is made in writing to the Company, and (3) no claims have been incurred during that calendar year.

If you request a decrease in the deductible amount, the Company will require proof of continued insurability of all covered persons.

PAYMENT OF BENEFITS

Benefits for covered expense incurred will be paid in accordance with Sections A and B of the covered expense provision.

If benefits paid by other health insurance are used as the deductible amount, all covered expense will be paid at 100 percent, but payment will not exceed the amount that would have been paid in the absence of other health insurance.

Where applicable, the rate of payment starts again for each covered person each new calendar year after the deductible amount has been met. The Company will pay up to the lifetime maximum benefit shown in the policy schedule for each covered person.

If the payment by other health insurance is used as the deductible amount, the lifetime maximum benefit will be increased. The maximum benefit will be increased by $3 for each $1 paid by other coverage over the basic deductible.

PAYMENT OF BENEFITS WHEN ELIGIBLE FOR MEDICARE

When any covered person is eligible for Medicare, he or she will be deemed to have Part A and Part B Medicare coverage that is primary to the coverage under this policy. Services covered by Medicare will not be covered by this policy to the extent that benefits are payable by Medicare. If there is remaining covered expense after Medicare pays for assigned services, benefits will be paid at 100% up to the amount approved by Medicare; for unassigned services, benefits will be paid at 100% up to our reasonable and customary charge limit. Payment of benefits for services not covered by Medicare will be determined by the terms and limits of this policy.

COVERED EXPENSE

Covered expense means an expense that is (a) incurred for services, treatment or supplies prescribed by a physician and described in Section A below; (b) incurred by a covered person as the result of sickness or injury as defined; (c) incurred for medically necessary care; and (d) incurred while the covered person's coverage is in force. Covered expense does not include any charge in excess of the reasonable and customary charge.

A. The following items of covered expense are subject to the deductible and rate of payment as described in this policy and shown in the policy schedule.

1. Room, board and general nursing care while confined in a semi-private room, ward, coronary care or other intensive care unit in a hospital. For confinement in a private room, the covered expense is limited to the hospital's most common daily charge for a semi-private room.

2. Other hospital services including services performed in a hospital outpatient department or in a free-standing surgical facility.

3. Physician services and surgical services, including second surgical opinions by board-certified specialists. This does not include services rendered by members of your immediate family.

4. Reconstructive surgery to restore function for conditions resulting from accidental injury provided the injury occurred while the covered person was insured under this plan. Reconstructive surgery that is incidental to or follows covered surgery performed as the result of trauma, infection or other diseases of the involved part.

   Reconstructive surgery for congenital defects provided the covered person has been insured continuously under this plan since the time of birth.

5. Hospice programs when (a) the physician projects a life expectancy of six months or less; and (b) the physician enrolls a covered person in the program. Notification is to be made in writing to the Company within seven days of admission to a licensed hospice facility. Covered expense includes up to 30 days of inpatient treatment at a hospice facility. Hospice home care is covered in addition to benefits provided under item 6. Benefits for services that include inpatient hospice services, hospice home care and counselling under the authorized hospice program are limited to $15,000 during the covered person's lifetime.

6. Up to 40 home health care visits in any 12-month period. One visit consists of up to four hours of home health aide service within a 24-hour period by anyone providing services or evaluating the need for home health care.

For home health care to be a covered expense, the physician must certify that:

a. hospitalization or confinement in a skilled nursing facility would otherwise be required;

b. medically necessary care is not available from members of the covered person's immediate family or persons living with the covered person without causing undue hardship; and

c. the home health care will be provided by a state-licensed or Medicare-certified home health agency.

Home health care does not include:

a. services not included in the home health care plan established for the covered person by the physician;

b. services provided by the covered person's immediate family or anyone residing with the covered person;

c. homemaker services; or

d. custodial care.

7. Professional ambulance service to the nearest hospital that is able to handle the sickness or injury. One trip to a hospital for a covered person for each sickness or injury is covered.

8. X-ray, radioactive treatment, laboratory tests, and anesthesia services.

9. Outpatient physical medicine benefits to a maximum of $500 for each covered person per calendar year. Physical medicine benefits include but are not limited to: rehabilitative speech, physical, occupational and cognitive therapies; biofeedback; sports medicine; cardiac exercise programs; adjustments and manipulations. The limitation does not apply to the treatment of burns, fractures, complete dislocations; joint replacements or related conditions for which a covered person is hospitalized for surgery and physical medicine that immediately follows hospitalization.

10. Rental, up to the purchase price, or purchase, when approved in advance by the Company, of (a) a basic wheelchair, basic hospital bed or basic crutches; (b) the initial permanent basic artificial limb, eye or external breast prosthesis; and (c) oxygen and the equipment needed to administer oxygen.

    Casts, orthopedic braces, splints, dressings and sutures.

    Dental braces, dental appliances, corrective shoes, orthotics or repairs to or replacement of prosthetic devices are not covered expenses.

11. Drugs that require the written prescription of a licensed physician. However, if a prescription drug benefit rider is attached to this policy, covered drugs will be paid under that rider (to age 65 or prior Medicare eligibility) instead of under this policy.

12. Whole blood, blood plasma and blood products, if not replaced.

13. Dental service for an injury to a sound natural tooth when the expense is incurred within six months following the injury.

    "Sound" is defined as:

    a. organic and formed by nature;

    b. not extensively restored or endodontically treated; and

    c. not extensively decayed or involved in periodontal disease.

14. Treatment of mental illness. Expense incurred by a covered person while confined as an inpatient to a hospital or psychiatric hospital for mental illness as defined in the policy. Coverage is limited to a maximum benefit of $2,500 for a covered person during a calendar year. Outpatient treatment, drugs or medications are not covered.

15. Sterilization, if the covered person has been insured on this policy for at least two years.

16. Treatment of temporomandibular joint dysfunction except for: crowns that correct vertical dimension; splints, orthopedic repositioning appliances, biteplates and equilibration treatments (including splint equilibration and adjustments); bite functional or occlusal registration, with or without splints, and kinesiographic analysis; any orthodontic treatment, including extraction of teeth; study models, except for the complete model made necessary when surgical intervention is completed. Surgical charges for correction of orthognathic conditions are covered.

B. The following items 1, 2 and 3 of covered expense will not be subject to the basic deductible amount of the 80 percent rate of payment. Covered expense will be considered for payment under this section before it is considered under any other section of the policy. Covered expense for which a benefit is payable under this section will not be considered for payment under any other section of the policy.

1. Skilled nursing care: Medically necessary care in a skilled nursing facility for up to 30 days provided (a) the covered person enters the skilled nursing facility within 14 days after discharge from an authorized hospital confinement; (b) the skilled nursing facility confinement is for the same condition that required the hospital confinement; and (c) such care is authorized by the Company within seven days following admission to the skilled nursing facility. The daily benefit for confinement in a skilled nursing facility will not exceed one-half of the semi-private hospital room rate for the area.

2. Second and third opinions required by the Company's authorization service. Only an exam, x-ray and lab work, and a written report by the physician rendering the opinion are included. You will be supplied with a list of three recommended physicians from whom the second or third opinion may be sought. The service may allow another physician to be consulted if the physician is (a) a board-certified specialist in the field of the proposed treatment; (b) is not financially associated with the first physician; and (c) does not perform the treatment.

3. Pre-admission testing, x-rays, and lab work performed on an outpatient basis before an authorized hospital admission provided (a) the tests are related to a scheduled admission; (b) the charges for the tests would have been covered expense if the individual was confined as an inpatient in a hospital; and (c) the tests were not repeated in or by the hospital, or elsewhere.

HUMAN ORGAN/TISSUE TRANSPLANT OR REPLACEMENT

Covered expense incurred by a covered person for the following human organ or tissue transplants or replacements if the procedure is authorized as indicated below, to a maximum lifetime benefit of $250,000 for each covered person.

Human organ transplant. The following procedures are covered if the procedure is authorized in writing by the Company prior to the beginning of the donor search and selection:

a. Bone marrow transplant

b. Heart transplant

c. Liver transplant

No benefits will be paid if the procedure has not been authorized by the Company prior to the beginning of the donor search and selection. To begin the authorization process, the physician or the physician's assistant must contact the Company's authorization service.

Tissue transplant or replacement. The following procedures are covered if authorized according to the procedures outlined in the authorization provision:

a. Cornea transplant

b. Prosthetic tissue replacement, including joint replacement

c. Vein or artery graft

d. Heart valve replacement

e. Implantable prosthetic lens in connection with cataracts

Donor Expenses. Expense incurred for surgery, storage and/or transportation service related to donor organ acquisition is also covered, up to a maximum benefit of $10,000 per covered procedure.

If the transplanted organ is from a live donor, expense incurred by the donor that is not paid by any other plan of insurance will be covered as if the donor's expense were the expense of the covered person.

No benefits will be paid for any transplant not authorized in writing by the Company prior to the beginning of donor search and selection or any transplant or replacement procedure not specifically listed above.

Kidney Disease or End Stage Renal Disease. Expense incurred for dialysis, transplantation and donor-related services to a maximum of $30,000 for each covered person during a calendar year. The transplant must be authorized in writing by the Company prior to the beginning of the donor search and selection. No benefits will be paid if the procedure has not been authorized by the Company prior to the beginning of such search.

Together with expense for dialysis and/or transplantation, expense incurred for surgery, storage and/or transportation service related to donor organ acquisition is limited to the $30,000 annual maximum. If the transplanted organ is from a live donor, expense incurred by the donor that is not paid by any other plan of insurance will be covered as though the donor's expense were the expense of the covered person, and included in the $30,000 annual maximum.

The limits in this provision for kidney disease or end stage renal disease provide for coordination with the governmental coverage for end stage renal disease.

COVERED COMPLICATIONS OF PREGNANCY

You, your spouse or a dependent child are covered for complications of pregnancy as defined below. Benefits are provided on the same basis as any covered sickness. Covered complications of pregnancy are limited to:

1. Conditions (when pregnancy is not ended) whose diagnoses are distinct from pregnancy, but are caused or adversely affected by pregnancy. Some examples: acute nephritis, nephrosis and cardiac decompensation.
2. Non-elective caesarean section
3. Ectopic pregnancy that is terminated
4. Spontaneous termination of pregnancy (miscarriage) that occurs before the 26th week of gestation; or missed abortion

Covered complications of pregnancy do not include: high-risk pregnancy or delivery, false labor, premature labor, occasional spotting, physician prescribed rest, morning sickness, pre-eclampsia or placenta previa.

CONGENITAL ILLNESS OR DEFECT OF A NEWBORN CHILD

Congenital illness or defect of a child of the insured born while this policy is in force will not be considered a pre-existing condition. Benefits will be provided on the same basis as any other sickness.

AUTHORIZATION PROVISION

This plan requires pre-authorization of all hospital admissions, inpatient surgeries, outpatient surgeries and transplants. The payment of benefits for covered expense described under the "Coverage Description" section of this policy may be reduced if the authorization procedure described below is not followed.

AN AUTHORIZATION DOES NOT GUARANTEE THAT BENEFITS WILL BE PAID. PAYMENT OF BENEFITS WILL BE DETERMINED BY THE TERMS AND LIMITS OF THE POLICY.

ELECTIVE ADMISSION OR SURGERY

For non-emergency hospital confinement, inpatient surgery, outpatient surgery or day surgery performed in a hospital, you must have the physician ordering the confinement or surgery obtain authorization before the patient is admitted to the hospital or has surgery performed. The authorization is obtained by the physician or physician's assistant from the Company's authorization service. The service can be reached by telephone during normal business hours, each Monday through Friday. A toll-free number and the name of the Company's authorization service is provided on the ID card given to you by the Company. You must instruct the physician to obtain the authorization by using the authorization form provided by the Company.

The service may require a second opinion prior to granting authorization. In such cases, you will be supplied with a list of three recommended physicians from whom the second opinion may be sought. However, the service may allow another physician to be consulted who (a) is a board-certified specialist in the field of the proposed treatment or surgery; (b) is not financially affiliated with the first physician; and (c) does not perform the surgery or provide the treatment. If the second opinion confirms the need for admission, then the admission will be considered AUTHORIZED. If the second opinion does not confirm the need for surgery or treatment, the service may allow a third opinion to be sought from a physician meeting the qualifications described for second opinions.

The physician may proceed with treatment on the basis of verbal authorization from the service. This will be followed by a written authorization sent to you, the hospital and the physician. The authorization remains valid for 60 days from the date of the written authorization. For treatment beginning after the 60-day period, a new authorization must be obtained.

EMERGENCY ADMISSIONS

Emergency admissions are admissions for life-threatening conditions or for a condition for which the absence of immediate treatment would cause permanent disability. An emergency admission must also be authorized in the same manner as an elective admission or surgery, as soon as it is reasonably possible to give notice of such confinement. Otherwise that portion of an emergency confinement occurring beyond 48 hours after admission (excluding Saturdays, Sundays and legal holidays) is considered UNAUTHORIZED.

UNAUTHORIZED ADMISSION, CONFINEMENT, OR SURGERY

If authorization is obtained in accordance with the above procedures, the hospital admission or surgery will be considered authorized; otherwise, it will be considered UNAUTHORIZED. An admission, confinement or surgery for which authorization was obtained shall be considered UNAUTHORIZED if (a) the authorization is no longer valid when confinement begins or surgery is performed; or (b) the type of treatment, admitting physician or hospital differs from the authorized treatment, physician or hospital.

Also, that portion of a hospital confinement, whether non-emergency or emergency, that exceeds the number of authorized days will be considered UNAUTHORIZED, unless an extension is granted. To receive an extension, the physician must call the Company's authorization service at least 24 hours prior to the originally scheduled discharge date and request an extension. The authorization service may or may not authorize an extension. Unauthorized extensions will be considered on the same basis as an unauthorized admission.

REDUCTION OF PAYMENT

The first $500 of covered expense incurred for unauthorized hospital admissions, confinements (or the unauthorized portion thereof) or any surgery shall not be paid by the Company; nor will that $500, or any portion thereof, be applied to the basic deductible amount requirement or rate of payment determination. As described under the Coverage Description section, to be a covered expense, the services, treatment and supplies must be medically necessary and the resulting charges reasonable and customary.

EXCLUSIONS AND LIMITATIONS

EXPENSES NOT COVERED BY THIS POLICY

This policy does not provide benefits for the following:

1. pre-existing conditions during the first two years coverage is in force; except as provided by the policy;

2. expense incurred for a sickness during the first 15 days after a covered person's effective date of coverage;

3. intentionally self-inflicted injury, suicide or suicide attempt, whether sane or insane;

4. care, treatment or services while in a government hospital, unless the covered person is legally required to pay for such services in the absence of insurance;

5. injury or sickness to the extent that benefits are paid by Medicare or any other government law or program (except Medicaid); or any Motor Vehicle No-Fault Law;

6. injury or sickness covered by any Worker's Compensation Act or Occupational Disease Law;

7. war or any act of war; injury or sickness while in the military service of any country (any premium paid for a time not covered will be returned pro-rata);

8. treatment of Temporomandibular Joint Dysfunction except as provided in item 16 of the covered expense provision;

9. dental service including x-rays, care or treatment except as provided under item 13 of the covered expense provision;

10. treatment for infertility; confinement, treatment or services related to artificial insemination; restoration of fertility, reversal of sterilization or promotion of conception; or expense incurred for genetic counselling, testing or treatment.

11. eyeglasses, contact lenses, hearing aids, eye exams, eye refraction or eye surgery for correction of refraction error;

12. normal pregnancy or childbirth (except as may be provided by rider), routine well-baby care including hospital nursery charges at birth; abortion or caesarean section except as provided in the Covered Complications of Pregnancy provision;

13. expense incurred for weight reduction or weight-control programs, including surgery; treatment, medication or hormones to stimulate growth;

14. reconstructive or plastic surgery that is primarily a cosmetic procedure, including medical or surgical complications therefrom; except as provided in item 4 of the covered expense provision;

15. the first $500 of otherwise covered expense incurred during any unauthorized hospital confinement or the unauthorized portion of a confinement or unauthorized surgery (see Reduction of Payment Provision);

16. treatment, removal or repair of tonsils or adenoids during the first six months of coverage, except on an emergency basis;

17. expense incurred due to injury or sickness due to committing a felony or while under the influence of illegal narcotics;

18. sales tax or gross receipt tax;

19. custodial care.

CLAIMS

NOTICE OF CLAIM

If a covered person incurs covered expense, you must give the Company written notice of claim. The notice must be given within 60 days after the claim begins, or as soon as is reasonably possible. The notice must be given to the Company or its agent, and must include your name and policy number.

CLAIM FORMS

When notice of claim is received, the Company will send you claim forms. If you do not receive the forms within 15 days after the giving of such notice, you shall be deemed to have complied with the proof of loss requirements if: (1) you give the Company a written statement of the nature and the extent of the loss for which claim is made; and (2) such statement is given within the time limit stated in the Proofs of Loss provision.

PROOFS OF LOSS

You must give the Company written proof of loss within 90 days after the covered expense is incurred. If written proof is not given in the time required, this will not make the claim invalid as long as the proof is given as soon as reasonably possible. In no event, except in the absence of legal capacity, may proof be given later than one year from the time otherwise required.

PAYMENT OF CLAIMS

Benefits will be paid to you unless you have assigned them to a doctor, hospital or other provider. Any benefits unpaid and unassigned at your death will be paid to the designated beneficiary or your estate.

TIME OF PAYMENT OF CLAIMS

Benefits for covered expense will be paid promptly upon receipt of written proof of loss. If not paid within 30 days of receipt of proof of loss, interest at the rate of 8 percent per annum will be paid, in addition, after the 30th day.

PHYSICAL EXAMINATION

While a claim is pending, the Company has the right to have a covered person examined as often as reasonably necessary. This will be at the Company's expense.

CONTRACT

CONSIDERATION

This policy is issued on the basis of the statements and agreements in the application and payment of the required premium. Premium payment in advance on or before the policy date will keep this policy in force from the policy date until the first renewal date. The premium is set out in the policy schedule. Each renewal premium is due on its due date subject to the grace period. All periods of insurance will begin and end at 12:01 A.M., standard time, at your residence.

ENTIRE CONTRACT; CHANGES

This policy, your attached application and any endorsements constitute the entire contract. No change in this policy is valid unless approved by an executive office of the Company. The approval must be endorsed by the officer and attached to the policy. No agent can change this policy or waive any of its provisions.

TIME LIMIT ON CERTAIN DEFENSES

After two years from the effective date of coverage, no misstatement made in the application (unless fraudulent) will be used to void the policy or deny any claim beginning after the two year period.

No claim for expense incurred by a covered person that begins more than two years from that person's effective date of coverage will be reduced or denied on the grounds that a disease or physical condition (not excluded from coverage by name or specific description) had existed prior to the covered person's effective date.

GRACE PERIOD

There is a grace period of 31 days for the payment of each premium due after the first premium. The policy will stay in force during this grace period. If the premium is not paid by the end of the grace period, this policy will lapse. No coverage will be provided during the grace period if the covered person has similar coverage available through another carrier and does not pay premium to the Company.

NONRENEWAL

The grace period does not apply if the Company has given you written notice that it will not renew the policy. This notice must be sent to you at least 30 days before the premium is due. Notice will be mailed to your last known address in the Company's records. Coverage will continue for any period for which premium has been accepted.

The Company can only decline to renew the policy on the renewal date occurring on, or after and nearest, each anniversary. The anniversary will be based on the policy date or last reinstatement date. This does not apply if premiums are not paid. Nonrenewal will not prejudice any expense incurred while the policy was in force.

LEGAL ACTION

You cannot bring legal action to recover on this policy before at least 60 days have passed from the time written proof has been given to the Company. No action can be brought after three years from the time written proof has been given to the Company. The time limit is five years in Kansas; six years in South Carolina.

TERMINATION OF INSURED'S COVERAGE

Your coverage will end on the date the policy lapses or is nonrenewed.

TERMINATION OF DEPENDENT COVERAGE

Coverage will end for your dependent children on the date the policy lapses or is non-renewed, or on the premium due date following the earliest to occur of (a) the date of their marriage, (b) the date they reach age 21 (or age 25 if the dependent is enrolled in and actively pursuing a full-time course of study at an accredited institution of higher learning), or (c) the date they are no longer dependent on you. Coverage will end on your spouse: (a) on the date the policy lapses or is non-renewed; or (b) on the premium due date following the date of a divorce. Benefits will still be paid to the end of the time for which premiums were accepted.

CONVERSION

A spouse or a dependent child who is no longer eligible for coverage on this policy can obtain a similar policy. No proof of good health will be required, but written application must be made within 60 days after that person's coverage terminates.

MISSTATEMENT OF AGE OR SEX

If any age or sex has been misstated, an adjustment in the benefits payable will be made to recover any past premiums due.

REINSTATEMENT

If you do not pay a renewal premium within the time granted, your policy will lapse. It will be reinstated if the Company or its agent accepts the premium without requiring an application.

If the Company or its agent requires an application for reinstatement, and the application and one modal premium are received within six months of the lapse date, the policy will be reinstated when approved by the Company. The Company has 45 days to act on your application. Your policy will be reinstated unless the Company notifies you in writing of its disapproval.

You will be covered for an injury sustained on or after the reinstatement date. You will be covered for a sickness that begins more than ten days after the reinstatement date.

After the policy is reinstated, you and the Company will have the same rights as existed just before the due date. These rights are subject to any provisions endorsed or attached to the policy. Premium cannot be required for more than 60 days before the date.

CONFORMITY WITH STATE STATUTES

If this policy, on its effective date, is in conflict with any laws in your state of residence, it is changed to meet the minimum requirements of such laws.

EH Health Insurance Company of America
Major Medical Insurance Application

Name _____   Occupation _____   Sex _____
　　　Last　　　　　　　First　　　　　　Middle　　　　　　　　　　　　　　　　　　　　　　　　M/F

Billing Address _____   Height _____   Weight _____
　　　　　　Street　　　　　　　　City　　　State　　Zip Code　　　　　　Ft. In.　　　　　　Lbs.

Date of Birth _____   Place of Birth _____   Phone (_____)_____
　　　　　Mo./Day/Yr.　　　　　　　　　City/State　　　　　　　　　　　　Area Code　Number

Social Security # _____   Phone (_____)_____
　　　　　　　　　　　　　　　　　　　　　　　　　　　　　　Area Code　Number

1) I am a member actively at work at least 30 hours a week   ❏ Yes   ❏ No

YOUR CHOICE OF DEDUCTIBLE: ❏ PLAN A–$250   ❏ PLAN B–$500   ❏ PLAN C–$1,000

HOW WOULD YOU LIKE YOUR PREMIUM BILLED?   ❏ Monthly   ❏ Quarterly

WHICH PLAN ARE YOU APPLYING FOR?   ❏ Comprehensive   ❏ Basic

If you wish to include your spouse and/or eligible dependent children, complete this section

NAME (First, Middle, Last)	SEX	DATE OF BIRTH	HEIGHT	WEIGHT
Your Spouse				
Your Children				

THE FOLLOWING QUESTIONS ARE TO BE ANSWERED FOR EACH PERSON APPLYING FOR COVERAGE. ANY MISSTATEMENTS MAY AFFECT YOUR COVERAGE—GIVE FULL DETAILS TO ALL "YES" ANSWERS IN THE SPACE PROVIDED.

In the last 10 years, has any person proposed for insurance been diagnosed, treated by or consulted a licensed physician or practitioner for any of the following?

	Yes	No			Yes	No
a. Abnormal blood pressure, chest pain, stroke, heart attack or murmur or any other heart, blood or circulatory disorder	❏	❏	f. Ulcers, colitis, rectal disorder or any disorder of the digestive system, liver or gallbladder		❏	❏
b. Cancer, tumor, growth, enlarged lymph nodes, skin disorder or discolored areas or lesions of the skin or mouth	❏	❏	g. Diabetes, thyroid disorder, speech impairment or disorder of the eyes, ears, nose or throat		❏	❏
c. Emphysema, lung or respiratory disorder	❏	❏	h. Seizures or neurological disorder, mental, nervous or emotional disorder, psychiatric or psychological counseling or treatment		❏	❏
d. Arthritis, or any disorder of the back or neck, muscles, bones or joints	❏	❏				
e. Kidney or urinary system disorder, disorder of the prostate or reproductive system, or breast disorder	❏	❏	i. Alcoholism, drug or chemical dependency or substance abuse		❏	❏
			J. Acquired Immune Deficiency Syndrome or AIDS Related Complex (ARC)		❏	❏

For Office Use Only	Eff. _____	Ren. Date _____	Paid _____
	CC _____	Cert. No. _____	

NOTICE OF INSURANCE INFORMATION PRACTICES

TO PROPERLY UNDERWRITE AND ADMINISTER YOUR INSURANCE COVERAGE A CERTAIN AMOUNT OF INFORMATION MUST BE COLLECTED. THE APPLICATION FOR INSURANCE CONTAINS INFORMATION OBTAINED FROM YOU NECESSARY FOR THIS PURPOSE. IN ADDITION, AS PART OF OUR REGULAR UNDERWRITING PROCEDURE, OTHER INFORMATION MAY BE COLLECTED FROM OTHER SOURCES ABOUT YOU OR YOUR ELIGIBLE DEPENDENTS WHO MAY BE PROPOSED FOR INSURANCE.

GENERALLY, DISCLOSURE OF PERSONAL INFORMATION WILL NOT BE MADE TO THIRD PARTIES. HOWEVER, IN SOME CIRCUMSTANCES, THE INSURANCE COMPANY OR YOUR AGENT WILL MAKE DISCLOSURE OF PERSONAL INFORMATION WITHOUT YOUR AUTHORIZATION TO THIRD PARTIES. THIS MIGHT INCLUDE THE DISCLOSURE OF PERSONAL INFORMATION TO PERSONS OR ORGANIZATIONS WHO MAY WISH TO MARKET PRODUCTS OR SERVICES, INCLUDING AFFILIATES OF THE INSURANCE COMPANY, BUT ONLY IF YOU HAVE NOT INDICATED TO US IN WRITING THAT YOU OBJECT TO OUR DOING SO.

YOU HAVE THE RIGHT TO OBTAIN ACCESS TO PERSONAL INFORMATION ABOUT YOU OR YOUR ELIGIBLE DEPENDENTS, IF PROPOSED FOR INSURANCE, COLLECTED BY THE COMPANY OR YOUR AGENT, EXCEPT INFORMATION RELATING TO A CLAIM, CIVIL OR CRIMINAL PROCEEDING. MEDICAL INFORMATION WILL ONLY BE RELEASED THROUGH A DOCTOR, PRACTITIONER, OR OTHER MEDICAL PROFESSIONAL SELECTED BY YOU WHO IS LICENSED TO PROVIDE PROFESSIONAL CARE RELEVANT TO THE NATURE OF THE INFORMATION. YOU ALSO HAVE THE RIGHT TO SEEK CORRECTION OF INFORMATION YOU BELIEVE TO BE INACCURATE.

	Yes	No
2) Are you or any of your dependents currently pregnant? **If yes, list name and due date.**	☐	☐
3) In the last 2 years, has any person proposed for insurance taken prescription medication for more than 30 days? **If yes, state condition, name of medication, dosage and frequency in space provided below.**	☐	☐
4) In the last 5 years, have you or any of your dependents to be insured had any physical disorder, illness, injury, surgery, or check-up, or consultation other than admitted above?	☐	☐

Complete the following for each "YES" answer to questions 1 through 4:

Ques. No.	Name of Person	Date of Treatment From	To	Reason for Checkup, Diagnosis, Illness or Condition Frequency of Attacks	Treatment or Findings, Medication, Recommendations, Hospitalization and/or Surgery Degree of Recovery	Name and Address of Each Physician, Practitioner and Medical Facility

If additional space is needed, use a separate sheet. Sign, date and return it with this form.

	Yes	No
5) Has any person proposed for insurance had health insurance declined, postponed, ridered, rated, cancelled or had reinstatement or renewal refused? **If yes, state the name of the company, action, reason and date in the space below.**	☐	☐
6) Does any person proposed for insurance now carry health insurance or have an application pending with another company? **If yes, state name of applicant, company, type and amount of coverage in the space provided below.**	☐	☐
7) Will the coverage you are applying for replace any coverage listed above? **If yes, give details below.**	☐	☐

I understand and agree that the statements and answers in this application are complete and true to the best of my knowledge and belief and shall form a part of the contract of insurance. I also understand and agree that the insurance applied for, if issued, shall be subject to such statements and answers and will take effect on the effective date stated on the schedule provided the applicable first premium has been paid.

I AUTHORIZE any physician, medical practitioner, hospital, clinic, other medical or medically related facility, insurance or reinsuring company, Medical Information Bureau, consumer reporting agency, employer, or the Veterans Administration, having information available as to advice, diagnosis, treatment, or care of any physical or mental condition concerning me, my spouse, or my minor children, including information about drugs, alcoholism, or mental illness, and any other non-medical information concerning me, my spouse, or my minor children to give to the Company, its affiliates, its legal representative, or its reinsurers any and all such information.

I UNDERSTAND the information obtained by use of the Authorization will be used by the Company or its affiliates to determine eligibility for insurance.

I KNOW that I may request to receive a copy of this Authorization.

I ACKNOWLEDGE having received and read the Notice Regarding Medical Information Bureau and the Notice of Insurance Information Practices (where applicable).

I AGREE that a copy of this Authorization shall be as valid as the original.

I AGREE that this Authorization shall remain valid for two years from the date shown below.

DATE	SIGNATURE OF PROPOSED INSURED	SIGNATURE OF SPOUSE (IF APPLYING)

Notes

Notes

Notes

Notes

Notes

Notes

Notes

Notes

Notes

Notes

Notes